The Napoleon
of New York

NONFICTION BOOKS BY H. PAUL JEFFERS

*Measuring Up: The Life, Times and Testing
of Theodore Roosevelt, Jr.*

Diamond Jim Brady: Prince of the Gilded Age

*With an Axe: 16 Horrific Accounts
of Real-Life Axe Murders*

Sal Mineo: His Life, Murder and Mystery

*An Honest President:
The Life and Presidencies of Grover Cleveland*

Legends of Santa Claus

"21": Every Day Was New Year's Eve
(with H. Peter Kriendler)

*The Bully Pulpit:
The Teddy Roosevelt Quotation Book*

The Perfect Pipe

High Spirits

The Good Cigar

Colonel Roosevelt

Gentleman Gerald

Commissioner Roosevelt

A Spy in Canaan (with Howard Schack)

Hollywood Mother of the Year (with Sheila MacRae)

Bloody Business: An Anecdotal History of Scotland Yard

Who Killed Precious?

Murder Along the Way (with Kenneth Gribetz)

Wanted by the FBI

See Parris and Die

The Napoleon of New York

Mayor Fiorello La Guardia

H. PAUL JEFFERS

John Wiley & Sons, Inc.

ISBN 0-471-02465-1

Printed in the United States of America

10 9 8 7 6 5 4 3 2 1

*In memory of my uncle, Walter Tinney,
who was proud to have served under
Mayor La Guardia as a member
of the New York Police Department.*

In this administration, I am the majority.

—Mayor Fiorello H. La Guardia

Contents

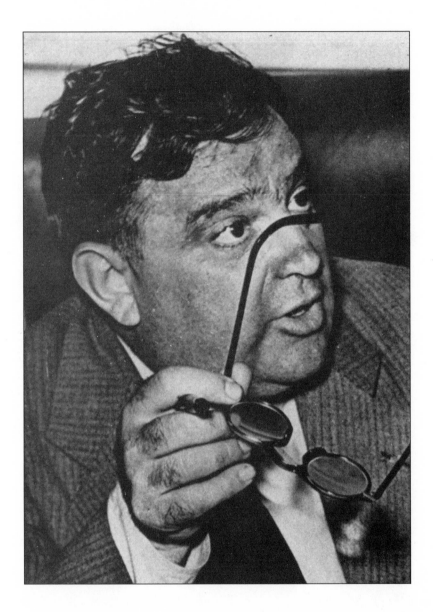

Introduction

Hizzoner

It had been a brutal day in which the entrenched powers had used every dirty trick in their formidable arsenal to try to steal the 1933 mayoral election. The scum and lowlife of the city had been rounded up to assist, from strong-arm thugs on the payroll of gangster Dutch Schultz to the lowliest thief who owed or sought a favor from Tammany Hall bosses and their lackies in the Police Department. Alerted to these bullying tactics, the mayoral candidate on a "Fusion" ticket, Fiorello H. La Guardia, stormed into one of the polling places, ripped the red Tammany badge from one of the illegal poll watchers, and in a high-pitched voice screamed, "You're all thugs! Get out of here and keep moving!" But it was La Guardia who found himself ejected, pushed out the door by cops who laughed at this pipsqueak who ludicrously vowed that a second after he was sworn in as mayor he'd boot them all off the force.

Fourteen years later, as a hearse carried the body of the ninety-ninth mayor of New York from the Cathedral of St. John the Divine in Manhattan to Woodlawn Cemetery in Queens, crowds lining traffic-halted streets were so respectfully quiet that a reporter assigned to cover the funeral of a man who had been called many things in his lifetime, including the affectionate nicknames "Little Flower" and "Hizzoner," could hear the clicks of the traffic lights as they changed.

New Yorkers had never experienced a mayor like him before. All his successors in City Hall have been measured against him. None has ever equaled him in accomplishments and esteem.

The enduring image is that of an endearing, cigar-puffing, short, roly-poly figure with a squeaky voice, bearing a strong resemblance to the movie comedian Lou Costello, a character in fireman's helmet at all the big blazes, and sporting other hats of all kinds; the crime-buster swinging a sledgehammer to smash slot machines; nemesis of "tinhorns and chiselers"; reader of the funny papers over the radio to the "kiddies" during a newspaper strike; the recipient of the baton from maestro Arturo Toscanini to conduct the New York Philharmonic; and an all-around charmer preaching that the way to deal with any problem was through "patience and fortitude."

Yet those who had known him best and who worked for him witnessed his other side—a driven, headstrong, personally insecure figure. In this La Guardia, Robert Moses, the city's master urban planner and leveler of the old to clear the way for La Guardia's vision of utopia, detected "omniscience and megalomania."

Significantly, La Guardia kept a bust of Napoleon on his desk.

When not engaging in "amusing antics," wrote another observer, the mayor could be a tyrant, vindictive, and snarly as a Brooklyn junkyard dog. "When he was happy under the wide brim of a black Stetson hat," noted another City Hall journalist, "he looked like a baggy-pants vaudeville comedian, but when he wasn't he could be as scary as any of the gangsters in the Lucky Luciano mob."

Providing a fresh perspective of Fiorello La Guardia's life and mayoralty, this informal biography contrasts the public's image that has lasted through eight decades with a complex and paradoxical man and cunning politician who was as tough and unforgiving as the metropolis his despairing predecessors and successors often described as "ungovernable."

As he took office on January 1, 1934, he found a city mired in the depths of the Great Depression and that felt betrayed by corruption in government. When he retired at the end of 1945 he left a New York that was revitalized and optimistic. He had restored public faith in City Hall by filling municipal jobs without obedience to party bosses, saved the city's credit, unified the city transit system, reorganized the sanitation and police departments, claimed victories in battles with mobsters, cleared slums, built low-cost public housing projects that would be emulated in other places. He fashioned "the welfare city" in which compassion for the underprivileged was as much a part of government's duty as police protection, service to citizens, cleaning streets, and hauling away garbage.

"If there is anything I hate," he told his staff, "it is indifference."

The first words out of his mouth after being sworn in were, "To the victor belongs the responsibility of good government."

Good quotes that expressed his personal nature and that of his administration never stopped flowing. Of himself: "They didn't elect me for my good looks." And "When I make a mistake, it's a beaut."

In a letter to commissioners: "The Mayor decides the policy of this City."

On honest government: "Running a city resembles running a house. If the servants are honest then the house can be managed and economically run."

Appointing a new fire commissioner: "The new commissioner will be a fire fighting commissioner, not a swivel chair commissioner."

Regarding his budget director's plan to take a vacation: "You may stay away permanently if you do."

After a commissioner arrived late for a meeting, La Guardia sent him an article from a magazine about a Japanese official who had missed an appointment and been so ashamed that he committed suicide. A penciled mayoral note said, "That is class."

When another commissioner was hospitalized: "You can do your work from your bed."

To the president of the Civil Service Commission: "If you cannot agree with my policy, you know the honorable thing to do."

When Commissioner Robert Moses repeatedly threatened to quit, La Guardia had a form printed: "I, Robert Moses, do hereby resign as _____ effective _____ ."

Upon receipt of a written report from Police Commissioner Lewis J. Valentine: "I am too busy to read such stupid writings, but I am not too busy to go over to headquarters and take hold of the department if that is necessary."

To Commissioner Newbold Morris: "You're so stupid it's an art."

To an employee at one of the city's jobless assistance offices: "Take your hat off when you talk to a citizen."

To his tax commissioner: "There is something wrong in the tax department. I don't know what it is. Find out."

On the pitfalls of graft: "Beware the nickel cigar."

On being indispensable: "There is no one who cannot be replaced. That includes everyone from the mayor on down."

For twelve years voters of New York City felt otherwise. Had he chosen to seek a fourth term, they would have welcomed the announcement. When he died fewer than two years after doffing his many hats, an editorial in the *New York Times* declared, "He did not find us brick and leave us marble, but he rescued our public credit, put non-partisan experts in charge of city departments, expanded parks and playgrounds, developed clinics, public markets, housing projects, and airports. He did much of this in a continual uproar of controversy but he did it."

The La Guardia years are those of a shrewd politician who knew what he wanted to do and how to go about it in a city renowned for skepticism. In examining the carefully cultivated, amusing personality that he chose to present to an adoring public and the tough administrator seen by the City Hall insiders, this biography of La Guardia also explores the early experiences that shaped the character of the man and the motivations that put the son of an agnostic Italian immigrant and Jewish mother from Austria on a path to the pinnacle of power in the largest city in America in a job that his predecessor, James J. "Jimmy" Walker, called the most difficult in the world, except that of president of the United States.

Always acutely conscious of his mixed heritage, La Guardia called himself "American," but he could not shake off feeling alien. With swarthy looks, black hair, and a name with a lot of vowels in it, he knew the sting of being called a "dago." Having once served as an Ellis Island immigration officer, he sympathized with the plight of everyone who had come to the United States with a dream of becoming "American" but found it hard to achieve because of prejudice. When he was in a position to make their lives easier, he acted with an untiring and unswerving passion. In becoming mayor of New York he wanted, above all, that New Yorkers be happy, live with a sense of ease and security, and dwell in decent homes.

He came into office with the intention of making New York City the symbol of what could be done and what might be. As the 1939–1940 World's Fair was rising from the muck of a former garbage dump in Queens he declared, "While other nations of the world are wondering what the spring will bring, we will be dedicating a fair to the hope of the people of the world. The contrast must be striking to everyone. While other countries are in the twilight of an unhappy age, we are approaching the dawn of a new day."

When he died, Robert Moses wrote, "The Mayor seemed to have a vision, not of the Statue of Liberty, calm, static, dignified, lifting her lamp beside the Golden Door, but of the little Fleur-de-Lis himself, his torch a flaming sword, riding the whirlwind of reform and directing the storm of progress straight into the millennium."

Part I

A Little Flower Blooms

We are fighting against a cruel, vicious political system.

—Fiorello La Guardia, 1933

1

"What if . . . ?"

The question arises again and again in the pages of the history of mankind and in the biographies of those who shape it.

What if Christopher Columbus's three little ships had been sunk in a hurricane?

What if George Washington had surrendered to Lord Cornwallis?

If there had been rain in Dallas, Texas, on November 22, 1963, and the bulletproof top had not been removed from President Kennedy's car. . .

If President Nixon had burned his secret White House tapes. . . .

If in November 2000 Al Gore had won the Florida recount. . . .

And if Achille La Guardia had not put a tack on his teacher's chair in school in Foggia, Italy, would Fiorello La Guardia have been mayor of New York?

For Achille's boyish prank the punishment imposed was to lie on the floor and trace a cross with his tongue. Humiliated and furious, Achille raced home to tell his father what had happened. A veteran "red shirt" in the army of Giuseppe Garibaldi in a war with the Papal States, Don Rafael Enrico La Guardia was a Protestant and a minor municipal official in Foggia. Instead of receiving consolation and sympathy, Achille found his father taking sides with the teacher of the religious school. Determined to have nothing more to do with Father, school, and religion, the boy fled Foggia, never to return.

A gifted musician and talented cornetist, Achille at first played for food, but soon earned a modest living with his horn. He traveled through northern Italy and Switzerland and as far as the East Indies, and then as a musician on ships of the Hamburg Line. In 1878 he was accompanist and arranger for famed diva Adelina Patti. Traveling with her to America at twenty-nine years of age, he became enchanted with the United States and went back to Europe with dreams of one day returning and settling in New York.

When he did so in 1880, he was married to twenty-one-year-old Irene Luzzato-Coen. He had met her at a dance. Born in Fiume in 1859, Irene was Jewish. One of her grandparents had been a refugee from the Spanish Inquisition. The eldest of five children of Isacco Coen and Fiorina Luzzato, Irene noted on the marriage papers that her religion was "Israelite." Achille scribbled "*nessuno*," Italian for "nothing."

Soon after the wedding, the couple sailed for Achille's dream city. But unlike thousands of Italian immigrants, they chose not to find a home in the tenements of New York's Mulberry Street, known derisively as Little Italy. The address Achille preferred was an apartment on Varick Place between Sullivan and Bleecker Streets in the "American Ward." Known later as Greenwich Village, it was a neighborhood of artists, musicians, "Bohemians," and others with whom Achille formed a bond of worldliness and sophistication. Having gained a fluency in several languages as a result of his travels, he had an urbanity that was unexpected in an Italian settler at that time. Determined to be an "American," he spoke only English in his day-to-day life and made up his mind that it would be the sole language of his children. His first was a girl, Gemma, born on April 24, 1881. Nineteen months later, Irene gave him a son.

Delivered at home on December 11, 1882, he was named Fiorello ("Little Flower," after Irene's mother, Fiorina) and Rafael Enrico (for Achille's father). Rafael would later be dropped, and Enrico Americanized to Henry.

To be an Italian or a Jew in America at that time, wrote biographer Jay Franklin in 1937, the fourth year of La Guardia's first term as mayor, "was to be something between an economic helot and a third-class citizen." In New York City in 1882 "kikes" were deemed worthy of being no more than push-cart peddlers, rag dealers, and pawnbrokers. They were all gyps and shysters, and unless they were kept in line, potential revolutionaries who would turn America "Socialist." The "dago" and "wop" were fit for digging ditches, dock-walloping, and any other physical labors that were required to foster the fortunes of the country's premier city in an age that the white Anglo-Saxon ruling class was already calling "gilded."

The United States was also, in their view, endowed with a "Manifest Destiny" to fill up the continent, conquer its vast expanses west of the Mississippi River, and take its rightful place in the world as a nation not to be trifled with. To attain this goal railroads were being built all across the country to convey a restless population to build cities, plow the prairies, and subdue frontier territories lying between Canada and Mexico.

Leading the way into this rough and rugged wilderness with orders to tame it and make it safe for white settlers was the U.S. Army. In the decade before Fiorello La Guardia was born, the white population of the Dakota Territory surpassed 20,000. A "Texas boom" that began in 1870 would account for an increase in the number of farms in the state from 61,125 to more than 174,000 by 1880. Lone Star ranchers had blazed northbound trails to drive millions of heads of cattle to the railroad towns of Kansas named Abilene, Ellsworth, Caldwell, and Dodge City. Gold, silver, and copper had turned camps into towns and then into burgeoning cities in Montana, Wyoming, and Nevada and created overnight millionaires who helped put the gilt in the Gilded Age, along with industrial tycoons named Carnegie and Morgan. To fence in the land, Joseph F. Glidden had invented barbed wire. In a campaign to assure Manifest Destiny, soldiers waged war against Indians to clear the route for settlers. Despite the destruction of cavalrymen led by a dashing officer named George

Armstrong Custer at the Little Big Horn, the Indian chiefs who had led the Sioux in that battle, Sitting Bull and Crazy Horse, were soon defeated. In the year of Fiorello's birth only the Apache warrior Geronimo remained at bay to terrorize white people in raids across the Mexican border.

No written record exists to explain why Achille La Guardia decided in 1885 to join the army that had conquered the West. He probably did so because he found himself unemployed as a horn player. Knowing only music, and unfit and unwilling to become just another ditch-digging dago, he enlisted in the rank of warrant officer and was appointed chief musician of the Eleventh Infantry Regiment, posted at Fort Sully, South Dakota.

When the family headed west, Fiorello was three years old. Understandably, he would say to a reporter with an interest in writing a biographical sketch of Mayor La Guardia in 1937, "I was too young when we left New York to remember anything about the city at that time."

His most distinct childhood memory, he said, was a "long trip to Arizona in 1891 when I was nine years old. It seemed as if we would never get there."

In the later parlance of children with a parent serving in the army, he was "an army brat" who went wherever his father's regiment was assigned. Achille's posting at Fort Sully with the Eleventh Regiment lasted until August 9, 1887, when the unit received orders transferring it to Sackets Harbor, New York, near Watertown. Shortly before the move, Irene gave birth to a boy, Richard Dodge, named after the fort's commanding officer.

Fiorello could tell City Hall reporters little about Fort Sully. But he had bits of memory of "trips to Watertown with the band." He did not dispute the recall of others who knew the five-year-old as a charming lad, but reckless, who pulled girls' hair, stood up to bullies, and had a vocabulary of curse words worthy of an army sergeant. One of his teachers spoke of him as "a quick, keen little fellow" who once corrected another teacher on the pronunciation of his given name. "It is not 'Fie-o-rello,'" he pointed out. "It is 'FEE-or-ELLO.'"

Another teacher noted, "He was not only stubborn in having his way, but he also knew what he was talking about."

This was a verity that would be discerned by all of Mayor La Guardia's commissioners and department heads in New York City government.

Sister Gemma observed that her brother at play would always be the leader.

In 1889 Achille's regiment again headed west, this time to Fort Huachuca, Arizona, on the journey that Fiorello remembered as seemingly endless. The fort was a place of sunlight glaring from the whitewashed adobe walls of low, flat-topped buildings. Days were hot, dusty, and dull. Starry nights were cold and still. But a few months later, the family pulled up stakes again to move to Whipple Barracks. Near Prescott, the post afforded the spectacular scenery of foothills covered with pine trees and more distant mountains veined with lush valleys and lofty rock peaks. The soldiers who had been there for a time spoke of the excitement of fighting Indians and looking for outlaws who'd robbed stagecoaches or rustled cattle.

"It was all a little fabulous, incredible, zestful and bracing," wrote one historian. There were tales of sweating horses, the "U.S." brand on their hairy flanks, the rattle of carbines, the bugles crying clear and far in the thin western air, and the comfortable regularity of army rations and army pay against a backdrop of self-reliant privations. Only a few years before Fiorello's arrival, the Earp brothers had finally settled a festering feud with the Clantons in a brief, brisk gun battle at the O.K. Corral in not-so-far-away Tombstone. Just two years earlier, in Tonto Basin south of town, the troops had to ride in to quell a range war between cattlemen and sheep ranchers. And who in America hadn't heard of General George Crook's orders to his troops in their long hunt for the rampaging Chief Geronimo and his Apache raiders to shoot any "savage" who was found where he shouldn't be?

"Prescott was really my hometown. It was there that I grew up," Mayor La Guardia told reporter and biographer

Fiorello with his cornet,
Prescott, Arizona, 1895.

Lowell Limpus in 1937. "My sister and I went to school there, and as soon as Richard was old enough, he came, too. It was during those days at Prescott that I became seriously interested in music. That was quite normal. Father lived for music and began teaching Gemma and me as soon as we could distinguish one note from another."

Fiorello's instrument would be the cornet, Gemma's the violin, and Richard's the piano.

Envisioning Fiorello becoming an accomplished musician and a bandmaster who would be "a second John Philip Sousa," Achille was a demanding teacher. But his outbursts in demand of perfectionism were accepted by Fiorello with patience and fortitude and the frequent retort "Keep on screaming, Papa. In this way I'll learn."

His words contained both truth and sarcasm. They also reflected an outward toughness in the face of criticism of his deeds, coupled with a resentment he felt deeply, but masked. While Achille was teaching his son music, he was also giving him lessons in the use of a sharp tongue and that the way to exercise authority was to make it clear who was the boss. The lasting result was that his son would be known to associates, allies, and enemies in politics and government as prickly, caustic, combative, critical, insensitive to others' feelings, and downright rude. Growing up as a westerner and an army brat, he also picked up a salty lingo from the cowboys and soldiers that could lace his language, if that's what a situation required.

In the school at Prescott he was no longer among students who were also children of the army. Most of his classmates were sons and daughters of civilians. Two of his friends were Tom Campbell and Ben Pope. Remembering a fight the boys had in a barn, Fiorello said, "It was epic! It lasted from the time school was dismissed until well after dark—and then it ended in a draw! I recall how I danced around them and egged them on and I was very much disappointed the next day when they made up and failed to renew the fight according to agreement."

A mayor who would have ringside seats for championship boxing bouts featuring Joe Louis would declare, "I still think that it was one of the best fights I ever saw."

Standing fast and battling for what he believed in would also be an enduring La Guardia trait. Having an Italian name, being short, and speaking with a high-pitched voice that lowered very little during adolescence, he often found himself in a stance of self-defense. The status of his opponent meant nothing to him. He fought with the sons of officers as readily as those of the enlisted ranks. "I would just as soon fight with an officer's kid," he boasted years later, "as I would with anyone else."

If he lost one day, he was back the next. One of his classmates recalled, "I licked him every day, but Fiorello kept coming back for more."

In one memorable skirmish in which he was on the losing end because of his height, he dashed into the school, returned with a chair to stand on, and resumed slugging.

Discerning in his diminutive stature the possibility of becoming a jockey, he tested himself by riding untamed burros and an occasional wild mustang.

"Obstacles never seemed to faze him," said one of his teachers. "He was always ready to get into anything."

While his father was a hard taskmaster in teaching him music, his mother provided him a different kind of instruction. Among his chores was assisting her with housework. She also saw to it that he learned how to cook. His specialty became—and remained—spaghetti with a sauce that garnered high praise from the toughest politicians in the city he would dominate politically for twelve of the hardest years in New York history.

Except for the music of great composers, spaghetti was the only vestige of his parents' heritage that Achille countenanced in his "American" home. Fiorello would not learn to speak Italian until he was twenty.

The family's connection to New York continued in the form of the once-a-week arrival of the newspaper *New York World*. Reading it after his father was finished, Fiorello found stories about the bastion of the city's Democratic Party, Tammany Hall. The editorials denounced its corruption and bossism in every edition. Fiorello would remember them.

Also following the La Guardias to Arizona was the ethnic bigotry of the East they'd left behind, which labeled Italians dagos and wops. The words were as familiar to Fiorello's ears in Prescott as they'd been to Achille on the streets of New York.

The American-born boy who became the city's first Italian-named mayor recalled a day of play in Prescott when an Italian organ-grinder and his red-hatted monkey came to town. "A dago with a monkey," shouted one of Fiorello's playmates.

A second boy yelled, "Hey, Fiorello, you're a dago, too. Where's *your* monkey?"

"It hurt," recalled the mayor as he reminisced bitterly.

He asked, "What difference was there between me and the Prescott boys? Some of their families hadn't been in the country any longer than mine."

Although Achille had no use for organized religion, he sent his three children to the local Episcopalian church. He also acknowledged Irene's religion by letting them learn their mother's Jewish prayers. When mayor, Fiorello was asked about his Jewish heritage; he replied that there was hardly enough for him to boast about. Few New York Jews who voted for him knew that his mother was Jewish, and many of the Italians who cast their ballots for him assumed that because he had an Italian name, he must be a Roman Catholic.

Although Fiorello La Guardia would be enshrined during three terms as the quintessential New Yorker, he considered himself a product of the frontier where, as one of his biographers wrote, "integrity was unambiguous, the air pure, and justice unhampered." It was in Arizona that he observed "tinhorns and sharpies" in the town's gaming rooms who enticed hardworking men and women to gamble away their wages and slight savings. He observed and came to detest the political lobbying he saw in the form of money paid to congressmen to back the granting of army commissions. When his father was solicited for a month's pay and an extra fifty dollars to bribe a congressman to "improve" the status of army bandleaders, Fiorello called the appeal "a fake" and persuaded Achille not to participate.

Growing up in Arizona he also observed corrupt agents of the federal Indian Affairs Department and the brutal treatment given to immigrant Italians, Chinese, and migrant Mexicans working on the railroads. He nurtured the outrage he felt about the powerful trampling upon the helpless by "politicians" throughout his life.

Although Achille La Guardia had abandoned school in Italy, he insisted that his children be as well educated as possible. This meant sending them to the public schools of Prescott, however limited they were in facilities and teaching staff. Attending the town's high school would be the limit of Fiorello's formal scholastic education. Abandoning thoughts of possibly becoming a jockey or even a prizefighter, he pondered his knack for language and considered a career as a journalist. Persuading the editor of the Prescott newspaper that he could be a good reporter, he wrote a column of news of Fort Whipple. He used the names "Arizona Pete" and "Alkalai Ike."

To hone his skills and compare them with professional newspapermen, he continued to read the New York newspapers that became available at Prescott's general store.

Among stories and editorials of the *New York World* about the abuses of power by the sachems of Tammany Hall and efforts by a "reform" government in City Hall to clean out civic corruption, which fourteen-year-old Fiorello read by the light of an oil lamp in the La Guardias' comfortable house at Whipple Barracks in 1897, were accounts of maltreatment of the people of Cuba by their Spanish rulers. It seemed that every week there was a new outrage to be reported, followed by demands from leading figures in commerce, industry, the clergy, and a vociferous group of politicians, mostly Republicans, that President William McKinley send the navy and the army to join forces with Cuban rebels and kick out the Spaniards.

The loudest of these voices was that of McKinley's brash assistant secretary of the navy. After two colorful years rooting out corrupt cops as the head of New York City's Board of Police Commissioners, Theodore Roosevelt arrived in Washington, D.C., as a vigorous proponent of an American military intervention in Cuba. In reading about Roosevelt, Fiorello came to admire him not only for his positions on Cuba and other national issues but also because he knew that in his youth Roosevelt had also "gone west," in his case to the Dakotas.

But on behalf of a war to attain Cuban liberation, nothing said by Roosevelt surpassed the passion of the feisty, civic reformer mayor of Prescott, Arizona. Chain-smoking, rawboned, and with prematurely grizzled hair and leathery face, Bucky O'Neill had earned a reputation for his toughness as a sheriff tracking down road agents, gunmen, and renegade

Apaches. He had been a friend of Colonel Leonard Wood, a surgeon by training who had joined the army and earned the Congressional Medal of Honor for his exploits in the capture of Geronimo. Now Wood was the personal physician to President McKinley, newfound friend of Theodore Roosevelt, and ardent supporter of the cause of *Cuba Libre*.

The son of a hero of Meagher's Brigade during the Civil War, Bucky O'Neill would be described in Roosevelt's book *The Rough Riders* as "born soldier, a born leader of men," but also a "wild, reckless fellow, soft spoken, and of dauntless courage and boundless ambition."

Born in 1860, William O. O'Neill had a law degree and the distinction of having been a pistol-packing frontier sheriff who never killed a man in a gunfight. At age twenty-one, before he strapped on a six-gun and pinned a badge to his shirt, he edited the *Phoenix Herald.* Moving to Prescott, he published a stock growers' paper, *Hoofs and Horns,* and wrote short stories of the wild and woolly West for eastern magazines.

The best story young Fiorello La Guardia heard about O'Neill before he came to Prescott involved O'Neill being deputized by the marshal of Phoenix, Henry Garfias, to help cool off a gang of troublemaking Texans who had been shooting up several saloons and otherwise vexing the citizenry. The showdown resulted in Garfias killing two of the hooligans and O'Neill simply "winging" another pair.

When O'Neill was not editing or gunslinging in Phoenix, he was most likely to be found in a gambling house playing faro. This popular pastime was known as "bucking the tiger," hence O'Neill's nickname "Bucky." Elected sheriff of Yavapai County in 1889, he held the post for a year and spent much of that time tracking a quartet of desperadoes who'd held up the Atlantic and Pacific Express near Flagstaff on March 20, 1889. Bucky chased them for six hundred miles and corraled them after a brief, nonfatal shootout.

Elected mayor of Prescott in 1897, he was in the wide, admiring eyes of fifteen-year-old Fiorello La Guardia the most famous and colorful figure in town. Consequently, in February 1898, when Mayor O'Neill addressed a huge, outraged crowd in Prescott a few days after the U.S. battleship *Maine* was blown up in the harbor of Havana, Cuba, supposedly by Spaniards, Fiorello was there. He heard Bucky declare that the United States had a "moral obligation" to rid the Western Hemisphere of Spain's "autocratic influence."

Presently, when Leonard Wood and Theodore Roosevelt announced that they would be "raising a regiment" to help in that endeavor, Bucky was one of the first to volunteer. The press immediately christened the combined force of cowboys, lawmen, other westerners, and eastern gentlemen who rode horses to play polo "Roosevelt's Rough Riders." Bucky would soon ask Roosevelt on the eve of battle in Cuba, "Who would not risk his life for a star?"

With the United States officially at war with Spain, the Eleventh Regiment received orders to pull up stakes and move to Jefferson Barracks in St. Louis and onward for subsequent training at Mobile, Alabama, while the wives and children of the troops remained in St. Louis.

Eager to follow his father to war, Fiorello begged his mother for permission to enlist. But Irene would have none of it. Strong-willed and determined, he ignored her objections and went to a recruiting station. While admiring Fiorello's patriotism and courage, the officer in charge informed him that he was too young to be a soldier. Even if he were a couple of years older, he was told, at only five feet two in height he was much too short.

Bristling with anger and seething about this outrageous discrimination, Fiorello remained determined to go to war. If he could not do so as a combatant, he'd become a reporter. With that goal in mind he barged into the offices of the *St. Louis Post-Dispatch* and asked for a job as a war correspondent. As proof of his ability he presented clippings of his columns and pointed out that he was also a rather good amateur photographer. He also advised the editor that he would not leave the office without a press card and a travel allowance. He got both, but no salary.

Flushed with excitement, he left immediately for the Eleventh Regiment's training camp at Mobile. Reunited with his father, he accompanied him, the unit's band, and the troops to the army's mustering point at Tampa, Florida.

⊘

At age sixteen, the representative of the *Post-Dispatch* suddenly found himself amid the men of two armies. In camps surrounding the city were thousands of enthusiastic soldiers with rifles who would soon embark upon a liberating invasion of Cuba. Observing the troops as they trained was a horde of keen-eyed reporters eager to record American bravery in accounts that would ring with patriotism and brim with phrases about the romance and glories of men at war. As the youngest of more than two hundred correspondents, Fiorello La Guardia looked with awe at journalists with towering reputations.

Most famous of them was Stephen Crane, author of a bestselling novel about the Civil War, *The Red Badge of Courage.* He had been hired to cover the Spanish-American War by the *New York World* while he was in Greece reporting the Greco-Turkish War. Although Crane was a famous writer, the unchallenged standout in the ranks of the reporters was Richard Harding Davis. Along with illustrator Frederic Remington, he had actually been in Cuba for two years, reporting Spanish atrocities, both real and invented, on behalf of readers of William Randolph Hearst's *New York Journal.*

Now, seated in a rocking chair on the veranda of the hotel that was Army headquarters for visiting encampments, Davis was a flamboyant figure in a white pith helmet with a white sash and clad for action in a khaki suit tailored by Brooks Brothers of New York. He claimed that he was not a "reporter" but a "descriptive writer."

Less flamboyant, but barely, was Edward Marshall, also a Hearst man.

As reporters covering police headquarters in New York City in 1895, Davis and Marshall had become friends and journalistic allies of the man who had been charged with cleaning out the corruption in the department and who was now second in command of a cavalry regiment that proudly bore his name. Just arrived from their training camp near San Antonio, Texas, "Teddy" Roosevelt's Rough Riders were by every measure in the minds of Davis, Marshall, Crane, and most correspondents the most interesting story leading up to embarkation from Tampa Bay, nine miles away. But for the correspondent of the *Post-Dispatch,* the primary attraction was the Eleventh Regiment.

"Everybody in fine spirits," wrote Fiorello in his first report.

The story was in the form of a letter and was headlined "The *Post-Dispatch's* Youthful Correspondent Heard From." The byline got his name wrong, crediting the account to "F. LaGuardi." Printed with the report was one of the author's earlier photographs of himself, holding his cornet. The caption explained that the correspondent in Florida was "bright" and "an exceptional cornetist." It also noted that when a fire broke out in Jefferson Barracks at Tampa, he had dashed into the burning building to grab his horn and sound the alarm.

Several decades later, for twelve years starting in 1934, photographs of Mayor Fiorello La Guardia rushing to the scenes of fires would be a staple of New York newspapers.

"A nice lot of spirited boys," Fiorello's account from Tampa continued, "[they are] the right sort of men to defend their country, ready and anxious for orders to go to Cuba."

Although the activities of the men of the Eleventh were the main concern of the sixteen-year-old *Post-Dispatch* correspondent, the former columnist for the Prescott newspaper could not forget that also in Tampa was the ex-mayor of the town he considered home. Visiting the camp of Roosevelt's Rough Riders, he found Bucky O'Neill wearing the twin bars of captain. The Rough Riders were a mixture of American types. John Greenway was from Arkansas, but he had been both a star footballer and an ace catcher in baseball for Yale. John McIlhenny could have been an officer in a Louisiana regiment, but the former planter, big-game hunter, and avid book reader chose to ride with Roosevelt. Among these remarkable individualists in the camp were men from other countries. One was a tall Australian who had been an officer in the New South Wales Mounted Rifles. Another was an Englishman by way of South Africa.

Of considerable interest to a cornetist were the trumpeters. The first was American, but the second was an Italian who had been a soldier of fortune in Egypt and with the French army in southern China.

At some point in wandering from one camp to another or investigating the officers who stayed at the luxurious hotel, the son whom Achille La Guardia envisioned becoming a second John Philip Sousa would have seen that lean, ramrod-straight leader of the Marine Corps band accepting congratulations for his rousing and wildly popular new march, "The Stars and Stripes Forever." But even more frequently played by the regimental bands in and around Tampa was "There'll Be a Hot Time in the Old Town Tonight." The troops who sang along with the bands altered the lyrics to "There'll be a hot time in *Santiago* tonight," meaning the then capital of Cuba.

Everywhere Fiorello went on the pine-covered sand flats of Tampa he found officers and their staffs in crisp uniforms; troops in the blues that had become so familiar in Arizona; foreign observers in a variety of outfits and speaking German, French, Russian, and even Japanese; officers' wives in pretty dresses; and rumpled-looking newspapermen, with the exception of Richard Harding Davis, of course.

Overheard conversations among the troops dealt with the excitement of going into battle, bragging predictions of a swift victory, and longing and often lewd descriptions of what they'd be doing when they were home again. And, in keeping with the timeless tradition of soldiers, they griped about everything. "Why was it always a matter of 'hurry up and wait'?" "Where does the army find so many stupid officers?" "I'd like to find one tent in this here man's army that won't leak." "If the ships we're sailing on are waiting at Tampa Bay, why are we in camps that are nine miles away?"

Most of all they complained about the quality of the food, especially cans of meat. Known as "embalmed beef," it was notorious for making anyone who ate it violently sick. The reason for this, it was universally believed, was that the meat was already bad when it was canned, then heavily spiced to hide the rancid smell and putrid taste. Theodore Roosevelt would later say that the contractors who sold the army "rotten food and shoddy materials" were on equal footing with white slavers in infamy.

To Fiorello La Guardia's dismay and alarm, one of those who fell victim to embalmed beef was his father. Instead of sailing to Cuba with the regimental band to provide inspiring music and entertainment for the troops, Achille became dangerously ill. The army diagnosis was "diseases of the stomach and bowels, catarrh of the head and throat, and malarial poisoning." He was declared unfit for duty, honorably discharged with a monthly pension of eight dollars, and put on a train, accompanied by his distraught son, for St. Louis.

❧

Not since joining the army in 1885 had Achille La Guardia been unemployed. Being in uniform had meant not only a comfortable life for him and his family, but also being a bandmaster had kept him employed in music, the only work he knew and wanted to do. Suddenly homeless and almost penniless, he packed up Irene, Gemma, Richard, and Fiorello and returned to the city of Fiorello's birth. Unable to find a job befitting a man of his age (fifty) and temperament, and giving up on America, he looked again to the native land he had disowned as a youth. Returning to Italy, he elected to take the family to Irene's former home in Trieste and settled down with her mother, Fiorina Coen. It was the first time that Fiorello met the grandmother for whom he had been named. With the little money he had, Achille leased a seaside hotel at Capodistria and built it into a thriving enterprise.

Having no desire to work in a hotel but needing a job, eighteen-year-old Fiorello turned to a friend of his father,

Raymond Willey, for assistance. Willey told him about a clerical post with the American consulate in Budapest, Hungary. Discerning an opportunity to "learn useful things and gain valuable experience," Fiorello applied for the position and was hired by the U.S. consul general, Frank Dyer Chester.

Fiorello would later describe Chester with the highest accolade in his vocabulary as "not a politician." At no time in his life in politics would Fiorello La Guardia countenance the label being appended to his name. When he reviewed a proposed entry for him, citing his present occupation, in the 1941 *International Who's Who,* he sent a letter to its editor. "I do not want the word 'politician' used," he wrote. "Its connotation is such that I don't think it ought to be used except for politicians—and there are many of them around. I do not happen to be one of them."

He suggested "municipal officer."

While Frank Dyer Chester was not a politician in his new clerk's estimation, Dyer was a man who was well connected politically. He'd received his consular appointment at the request of one of the most influential figures in American politics and government, U.S. senator Henry Cabot Lodge. The chief political mentor of Theodore Roosevelt, Lodge had predicted that TR would one day "inherit a higher kingdom." Lodge was talking about the presidency. That Teddy, as everyone but TR's friends and family called him, would get there certainly seemed to be in the cards. Following his leading of the Rough Riders and other troops in a charge up Kettle Hill in the San Juan Heights overlooking Santiago, Cuba, Colonel Roosevelt had returned to New York a hero. The most famous man in America, he was promptly elected governor of New York

When Fiorello La Guardia was taking on the consular clerkship in Budapest, Roosevelt was being boosted by Republicans as vice-presidential running mate with President McKinley. As a graduate of TR's alma mater (Harvard), Frank Dyer Chester counted himself a Roosevelt supporter. Having observed Roosevelt inspiring the Rough Riders at Tampa, and knowing that Roosevelt had been honed by the rigors of the

La Guardia (standing) as consular official in Budapest, Hungary, 1903.

West, Fiorello had no difficulty in seeing Teddy ascend to the White House. Nor was Theodore Roosevelt, as far as Fiorello could tell from the reports about him in the newspapers and magazines, deserving of being assigned to the dubious category of "politician" by the La Guardia definition.

Getting a hold on what made Theodore Roosevelt tick was one thing. Grasping the nature of Frank Dyer Chester was quite another. On the surface the consul general was exactly the sort of man Fiorello had expected. He was twelve years older. Fiorello noted he was a "scholarly gentleman who had won honors at Harvard." He enjoyed the benefits of a superb formal education, he belonged to a respected family, he had influential friends, and he was in all respects a member in good standing of the ruling class of America. Yet he'd given a job to a five-foot-two, coal-black-hair-parted-down-the-middle, impatient, restless son of a Jewish mother and an Italian bandleader whose only claim to an education was classes in a high school in a dusty frontier town that was halfway between nowhere and no place on the way to California.

Unfortunately, without a Harvard degree, Chester informed Fiorello, he would "never get any higher than the menial position of clerk in the foreign service." But that did not mean that he should not be the best possible clerk. If Fiorello wanted to flourish, Chester advised, he should study the languages of the people who would come into his office—German, the tongues of the Slavs, Serbo-Croatian, and, yes, Italian. He must also keep on top of world events and the happenings in the United States. Taking the advice, Fiorello began studying languages and by reading, as he would recall, "every newspaper and magazine I could lay my hands on."

He soon found himself described in Chester's periodic reports to the State Department in Washington as Chester's "amanuensis." It was a word that Fiorello had to look up. When he read its definition, he felt pleased and proud.

Not all of Chester's terminology was as glowing. He faulted Fiorello's handwriting for being illegible and "a flagrant affront" to anyone who had to try to decipher its scrawl. But the most annoying of La Guardia's traits was a roving eye for girls. When Chester observed Fiorello flirting with a bleached blond whom Chester recognized as a notorious blackmailer, he warned his amanuensis that if he ever found La Guardia in the woman's company, he would be left with no choice but to dismiss him.

Rather than obeying the edict, Fiorello invited her to a night on the town. This did not go unnoticed by Chester. Fiorello learned that his boss was a man of his word. He was fired. Only a plea from the vice consul got him reinstated.

In fact, Chester had no use for any woman. When Fiorello inquired into Chester's misogyny, Fiorello took out a revolver that any prudent man carried in a city known for brigands, placed it on Chester's desk, and asked, "What do you have to live for?"

During his employment in Budapest, Fiorello exhibited a considerable ambition to move up in the foreign service. When he learned of an opening as consular agent in Fiume, he applied and was accepted. The job paid eight hundred dollars a year, a princely sum for a single man of twenty-one. Some of it went to help support his father, mother, sister, and brother. Much of the remainder financed dinners and evenings at concerts in the company of attractive women, lounging in beer gardens, membership in the Austrian Soccer Club, sunny resorts on the Adriatic Sea coast, and anything else that struck a bachelor's fancy.

Among his duties was handling a growing number of emigrants whose destination was Ellis Island in New York. This required dealing with the main steamship company in Fiume, the Cunard Line. He quickly learned that many of the people who sailed for America found themselves turned away from entering the United States because they were rejected by the health inspectors at Ellis Island. Most were sent back because they had diseases, such as trachoma, that could have been detected before they'd departed Italy. Under Italian and American regulations, no passenger ship could sail without a signed certification of health. The official whose signature they needed was Fiorello La Guardia.

One day, feeling irate at the prospect of immigrants crossing the Atlantic only to be sent back, he marched aboard a Cunard liner that was scheduled to depart that day and informed the captain that the ship wasn't going anywhere until all immigrants were examined. Furthermore, he declared, the costs of the health checks would be billed to Cunard and the price of tickets for those who were not allowed to sail must be returned.

Infuriated Cunard officials lodged an objection with Chester, who relayed word of what had happened to Washington. The State Department replied that La Guardia had been within his rights as consular agent. Many years later, Mayor La Guardia chortled with glee as he recalled a State Department official referring to him in those days in Fiume as "the worst headache in the history of the State Department."

No record exists of the sentiment expressed on another occasion by the archduchess of Austria, Her Highness Maria Josefa, after La Guardia refused to allow her to be amused with a "presentation of immigrants" when she visited Fiume.

"Tell the archduchess that she may boss her own immigrants," Fiorello declared, "but she can't boss the American consul."

Presently, understanding that promotion in the foreign service was highly unlikely, and bored with his post, he decided to book passage on one of the ships and return to the city of his birth. "I wanted more action," he recalled. "I didn't see any future for myself in diplomacy."

2

When Fiorello La Guardia arrived in New York in 1907, he was fatherless. Achille had died in 1904. The cause was attributed to a heart attack, but Irene believed his death resulted from the illness that befell him in Florida. Blaming the U.S. Army, she applied for a widow's allowance. After two years of correspondence with the government in Washington, D.C., she was granted a settlement of $12.80.

The first bill to be introduced in the House of Representatives by freshman congressman Fiorello H. La Guardia of New York would impose the death penalty on anyone who sold tainted supplies to troops in time of war.

With two hundred dollars in his pocket, almost twenty-four years old, looking as rumpled as an immigrant, but with an American passport in hand, he reentered the United States without having to go through the ordeal of a health examination. He saw New York City as a "seething, sparkling, darkling" place of opportunity. His timing in looking for employment could not have been worse. The American economy was in the midst of one of its cyclical downturns. This one would be remembered as the Panic of 1907.

Hoping for any kind of job, Fiorello discovered that no one had any place for a young, multilingual, former consular official with a talent for cutting red tape and offending European royalty. Help came again in the figure of his late father's friend Raymond Willey. But the job he found for Fiorello was with Haberson and Walker Company, a fireproof brick manufacturer. The job was in Portsmouth, Ohio. He took it, but quickly despaired of life in the Buckeye State, quit, and hurried back to New York and into a string of other dead-end employments.

In the first, with the Society for the Prevention of Cruelty to Children, he was paid ten dollars a week to translate a section of the French Penal Code. When that task was done, he was again unemployed. On the basis of his consular experiences in dealing with the Cunard Line and other shipping firms, he landed a post with a steamship company at a salary of fifteen dollars a week. While working there, he expended half a week's pay to take a course in stenography at the Pratt School. His shorthand skills garnered him a clerkship with the renowned sporting goods firm of Abercrombie and Fitch at twenty dollars a week.

"I had a definite plan worked out in my mind for my future," said Mayor La Guardia as he looked back to a period in which he seemed to be adrift. The goal he had set, he continued, was to complete his education (by getting the high school diploma that had been put off when the family moved to St. Louis at the outbreak of the Spanish-American War), study law, and be admitted to the New York bar.

In setting this course he appeared to be at odds with his opinion of attorneys. They were, he often said, "semicolon boys" who could always find a way to employ language and punctuation to disguise legal chicanery, usually to dupe poor people. He also felt that "too many lawyers were being turned out like so many sausages every year."

But his ultimate goal was not lawyering. After earning his degree he would "enter public service." A man to whom "politicians" were anathema did not say he would "go into politics."

To earn the scholastic diploma and a law license would mean working days and going to classes at night. By now his employment was as an interpreter in Serbo-Croatian at the immigration center on Ellis Island. Winning the post had required taking a competitive examination. Scoring the highest among dozens of applicants, he had been appointed on November 7, 1907. The work put him in the shoes of the Ellis

Island officials he had scorned when he was on the departure side of the torrent of hopeful immigrants flowing toward New York. Often called to be on duty seven days a week, he was now on the receiving side. Many years later he recalled the plight of a young girl who had come from the mountains of northern Italy and spoke a dialect that was unknown to the little ex-consular official and master of several languages. Questioned endlessly, she answered as well as she could, and found herself queried and examined physically again and again.

After two weeks, La Guardia remembered bitterly, she was "a raving maniac." Still sad in retrospect, he said, "I suffered a great deal because I could not help these people."

This was not exactly true. Some of them he was able to assist. If he encountered a young woman whose purpose in coming to America was to reunite with a young man who'd preceded her and be wed, he accompanied her across the bay to City Hall, where her fiancé was waiting. The ceremony would be performed by a city alderman, for an illegal gratuity.

The despicable practice would not be forgotten after Fiorello H. La Guardia was elected president of the Board of Aldermen. More than one of the men who had extracted such money learned to their dismay and embarrassment that La Guardia had a long memory.

Day-to-day observation of the plight of the immigrants left him frustrated and angry at a situation that long after his death would be termed a "Catch-22." Fiorello put it this way: "It is a puzzling fact that one provision of the immigration law excludes any immigrant who has no job and classifies him as likely to become a public charge, while another provision excludes an immigrant if he *has* a job."

During three frustrating years at Ellis Island, he studied law at night. One of his classmates, James I. Ellman, sat behind him and had many opportunities to observe him. "He made a very sharp impression upon me at the time because of his capacity and sure-footedness," Ellman told reporter Lowell Limpus in 1937. "Thin and wiry, he always seemed alert. He had the capacity for dealing intellectually with any question that came up. He was a very quiet and unassuming student, striving sincerely to learn the intricacies of the law. We all respected him."

When Fiorello began his final year at NYU Law School, an Immigration Department official, Anthony Tedesco, assigned him to act as interpreter for the Immigration Service in the city's night court. The change allowed Fiorello to attend day classes. A major portion of the matters handled by the night court involved deciding if immigrants with questionable moral and legal backgrounds should be sent back to their countries of origin. Some concerned a racket known as "white slavery," in which women were brought to the United States and required to repay their "sponsors" the cost of their passage by engaging in prostitution. Tedesco was in charge of the Immigration Service's white slave division. Other immigrants whose only means of earning a living was by prostitution had been arrested either for streetwalking or in raids on brothels that had not paid corrupt cops "protection" money. Fiorello immediately recognized the arrests and threats of deportation as just another racket to line the pockets of the police, lawyers, and judges, almost all of whom served political bosses of the same Tammany Hall he'd read about in newspapers in Prescott.

Anthony Tedesco was untainted by this corruption, but he understood the potential for temptation.

"You can get experience on this job," he told La Guardia, "or you can make a great deal of money. I don't think you'll take the money. But remember, the test is if you hesitate. Unless you say 'no' right off, the first time an offer comes your way, you're gone."

Thirty years in the future, Mayor La Guardia would tell those who worked in his administration, "Beware the nickel cigar."

However, he considered the honest money he was being paid for long hours seven days a week insufficient. Accordingly, he asked for a raise. In a letter to Immigration Service commissioner Robert Watchorn, he opined that he deserved the boost in salary because he was "the only interpreter you have who is a stenographer and the only stenographer who is a linguist."

He got the raise just as he was completing law school. After exhibiting patience and fortitude for three years, he resigned from the Immigration Service in 1910, and at age twenty-eight and with sixty-five dollars as capital, he hung out his shingle.

For fifteen dollars a month he rented space in the law offices of McIllhenny and Bennett at 15 William Street, a few blocks from City Hall and Municipal Court. More money went for the printing of letterheads and pieces of secondhand furniture.

His only extravagance in the way of decoration was a bust of another short, ambitious, smart man of Italian lineage. A likeness of Napoleon Bonaparte would adorn Fiorello H. La Guardia's several desks in several offices for the next thirty-five years.

3

※

"I never managed to become callous to the mental anguish, the disappointments and the despair I witnessed almost daily," said Fiorello H. La Guardia of the three years he'd worked in the shadow of the Statue of Liberty and her upraised torch "beside the golden door," beckoning the countries of the world, in the words of the poet Emma Lazarus, to send America "your tired, your poor, your huddled masses yearning to breathe free."

When the statue was dedicated by President Grover Cleveland in 1886, Fiorello had been a four-year-old in South Dakota. In the same year, another transplanted New Yorker, Theodore Roosevelt, was ranching at a place in the Dakotas called Little Missouri, while contemplating a return to the city of his birth and possibly running for mayor as a Republican, but a reformer.

In the years since returning to New York, and despite placing third in the mayoral race of 1886, Roosevelt had remained steadfast in opposition to the entrenched bosses of the Tammany Hall that young Fiorello La Guardia read about in far-off Arizona, and learned to despise. It was an animosity rooted in contemptible exploitation of the poor and disadvantaged, most of whom were immigrants. Observation of the power of Tammany Hall from the vantage point of Ellis Island and as a lawyer practicing in the courts served to deepen the La Guardia resentment.

In taking up the law he defended the very people who passed by the Statue of Liberty on their way to Ellis Island expecting to reap all her promises, only to become pawns in the games played by crafty politicians. With the courts as a lucrative chessboard, they represented the landlords, employers, and a corrupt city government against which tenants, workers, and small shopkeepers didn't stand a chance. In his own way, Fiorello H. La Guardia, their attorney-at-law, would be their champion; a "people's lawyer." Those who had ten dollars for his fee paid it. Anyone who didn't also got his help. Most who knocked on his door were immigrants facing deportation. They were given his address by his friends on Ellis Island.

Should a client have no case, or if he thought a lawyer wasn't needed, he told the client so, then tried his best to settle the matter out of court. He would also refuse to take a case unless he believed that the client's claim was justified. There would be no taking a case for the sake of money, or raising false hopes that he knew would be dashed in court. Remunerated or not, he worked hard in preparing for the cases he accepted, then dashed to the courts to argue them.

He performed so well in a case he lost that the judge complimented him.

Puzzled, attorney La Guardia retorted, "If I did so well, why didn't you decide in my favor?" The judge smiled down at him benignly. "Oh, young man," he answered, "I'll give you a break some other day."

Concealing his outrage, the "people's lawyer" left court muttering, "This is a hell of a way to dispense justice."

As mayor, and often taking to the bench to conduct trials as the city's chief magistrate, he would wage war against "the divine rights of judges."

"The more I got to know about lawyers and their ethics," he said of his years as a trial lawyer, "the less respect I had for them."

⧽⧾

Upon his return from Italy, Fiorello had chosen as his residence the same neighborhood that his father had favored. Living in a small apartment on Charles Street in the heart of Greenwich Village, he found himself among artists, sculptors, poets, writers, and educated professionals. His Italian friends included the flutist of the New York Philharmonic, Giovanni Fabrizio; a former Catholic priest, Antonio Calitiri, who wrote poetry; and Italian-language magazine publisher Onorio Rutolo. A political radical, he had a favorite observation: "Society will tolerate anything but genius."

Of this La Guardia "circle" biographer Thomas Kessner wrote, "With this group of friends, he shared dinners, stories, and the excitement of New York in its years of fantastic possibility." They were the happy times before "the Great War," when "the environment seemed soft and pliable, amenable to all sorts of plans for improvement and the rehabilitation of evil."

Three years earlier, Henry James had written on the occasion of his return to New York from "the Far West," of his "happily-excited and amused view of the great face" of the city. He wrote, "There is the beauty of light and air, the great scale of space, and, seen far away to the west, the open gates of the Hudson, majestic in their degree, even at a distance, and announcing still nobler things. But the real appeal, unmistakably, is in [a] note of vehemence in the local life . . . for it is the appeal of a particular type of dauntless power."

In 1905 O. Henry wrote that "the voice of the city" was "the composite vocal message of massed humanity" and the "voice of the agglomerated mankind."

If ever a place fit both descriptions, it was New York in the year that Fiorello La Guardia hung out his lawyer's shingle and became the people's advocate.

Two years before O. Henry took up his pen and while Fiorello was making a pain in the neck of himself as a U.S. government agent in Fiume, 857,000 immigrants arrived in New York. They settled in national and ethnic ghettoes: Jews north and east of the bend of Mulberry Street; Chinese in Chinatown encompassing Mott, Pell, and Dyer Streets; Germans around Tompkins Square downtown and Yorktown ("Germantown") on the Upper East Side around Eighty-sixth Street; the Irish in Brooklyn; and Italians around Thompson and

Sullivan Streets and also around Second Avenue and 100th Street, a section known as East Harlem.

Native immigrants also poured into the city, brought by trains from the west and south to Grand Central Terminal and a brand-new cathedral to railroading between Seventh and Eighth Avenues between Thirty-first and Thirty-third Streets, built by the Pennsylvania Railroad on a plan by the firm of McKim, Meade, and White. When novelist Theodore Dreiser arrived in New York, he found in its people a contrast of "the dull and the shrewd, the strong and the weak, the rich and the poor, the wise and the ignorant." But the number was so great that "the strong, or those who ultimately dominated, were so very strong, and the weak so very, very weak, and so very, very many."

Some of them, though never many, sought legal assistance from Fiorello La Guardia, and now and then one of his clients would say in halting English as he went out the door that it was too bad that a man like him wasn't mayor.

～

A member of the small circle of Italian intellectuals who came to have a spaghetti dinner prepared by Fiorello La Guardia thought that seeing "the Little Flower" in City Hall was not so far-fetched an idea. Fannie Hurst was a brilliant writer who had met Fiorello in St. Louis. She would remember the fledgling lawyer's "magnificent unrest coupled with a desire to be a leader on his own terms." Also vividly recalled was his outrage against the courts and a legal system that was for sale to the highest bidder. Born on October 18, 1889, in Hamilton, Ohio, Fannie grew up and attended schools in St. Louis. She graduated from Washington University in 1909 and came to New York City to continue her studies at Columbia University. With the aim of gathering material for her writing, she worked at various times as a waitress and nursemaid and in the garment business. A collection of short stories titled *Just Around the Corner* would be published as a book in 1914. She would go on to write more than forty novels and story collections and see some of her work become successful movies, including *Back Street*. Throughout her literary career and Fiorello's rise in the arenas of politics and social and political reform she remained his ally and trusted friend.

Having been employed in the garment industry and feeling outraged by abuses inflicted on the workers, Fannie took it upon herself during dinners at La Guardia's apartment to educate "the people's lawyer" on the plight of the laborers, most of them women, in the clothing trade. Over plates of spaghetti, Fiorello heard about sixty-hour workweeks, the abysmally low wages, crowded and unsafe "sweatshops," and the prevailing employers' attitude of "If you're not happy with five bucks a week pay, there are plenty of people out there to take your place."

In the 1910 Census the number of factories in the Greater New York area was put at about twenty-six thousand, employing roughly three-quarters of a million men, women, and children.

The vast majority of the workers in lofts and tenements that served as cutting and sewing rooms in the garment industry who shared Fiorello H. La Guardia's Italian and Jewish heritages frequently found themselves pitted against one another for jobs by shameless employers whose goal was to get as much work from them as they could. They labored at the lowest possible wages in airless spaces deservedly called sweatshops.

To find such a place, Fiorello could walk a few blocks to the Asch Building on the corner of Washington Place and Greene Street, just up the block from Washington Square. Occupying the top floors was the Triangle Shirtwaist Company. More than four hundred women and girls on the seventh, eighth, ninth, and tenth floors produced women's clothing in the fashionable style of the "Gibson Girl" from paper patterns. Cloth scraps that should have been collected from the waste bins daily were actually removed six times a year. On March 25, 1912, they had not been emptied for three months. At approximately twenty minutes to five in the afternoon on that day, probably because one of the workers dropped a lighted cigarette or match onto a littered floor, a fire broke out. Panicky workers scrambling to get out found doors bolted. There was one fire escape, but as several women climbed onto it, the rickety framework collapsed, sending them hurtling eight floors to their deaths.

Having an afternoon repast in a tearoom on nearby Waverly Place was Frances Perkins. A Chicago-born social reformer and now a lobbyist in Albany for the New York Consumers' League, she had recently testified at a session of the state senate's Committee on Labor and Industry on the subject of deplorable conditions in sweatshops. She had presented evidence in the form of photographs of the unhealthy, dangerously cramped quarters and pictures of weary, exhausted women and girls at the end of their workday. But she had been told by Assemblyman Alfred E. Smith, a sympathetic Democrat from Manhattan, that the reform measure she had gone to the capital to support had no chance of passage.

"You won't do any good staying around here," said Smith, "because it's not going to be taken up."

One of the witnesses before the committee had been the Manhattan fire chief, Edward Croker. Describing the conditions in sweatshops, he'd told the legislators, "A fire in the daytime would be accompanied by a terrible loss of life."

When Croker rushed to Washington Place, he found the horrible proof of his grim prediction. In a fifteen-minute period forty-seven bodies had slammed to the ground, some with a force so great that they shattered thick glass coverings of vaults beneath the sidewalks. On the day after the fire a New York newspaper's front page headline read: THUD . . . THUD . . . THUD.

The official count of the dead was 146. No one knew exactly how many people had been injured. Many of them had staggered away in shock.

On the evening of April 2, 1912, at a mass meeting in the Metropolitan Opera House to protest working conditions in the women's garment industry, a leader of the Shirtwaist Makers' Union, Rose Schneiderman, told the audience of 3,500,

"This is not the first time girls have been burned alive in this city. Every week I must learn of the untimely death of one of my sister workers. Every year thousands of us are maimed. The life of men and women is so cheap and property is so sacred! There are so many of us for one job, it matters little if 140-odd are burned to death. Public officials have only words of warning for us—warning that we must be intensely orderly and must be intensely peaceable, and they have the workhouse just back of all their warnings. The strong hand of the law beats us back when we rise—back into the conditions that make life unbearable."

In the following months Frances Perkins and other reformers trekked to Albany in the name of their cause and on behalf of an outraged public, only to find legislators who were willing to listen but, with the exceptions of Al Smith, Senator Robert F. Wagner, and a handful of others, either unprepared or unable to act. Reluctantly, the legislature authorized the New York State Factory Investigating Commission, with Wagner as chairman and Smith as vice chairman. It held its first public meeting in October. Perkins appeared before it on November 15. The subject was working conditions in bakeries located in basements of tenements.

A representative of real-estate interests, Stewart Browne, asked Perkins, "Have you ever been a baker?" Perkins said she had not. "Have you ever made a loaf of bread in your home?" "No, sir." Did she have a degree and a license to practice medicine? No. A license to practice engineering? "No, sir."

"Then by what right do you propose to testify here?"

Al Smith gruffly answered, "Because we've asked her to."

"She's a totally ignorant and incompetent person," Browne replied, "and a *girl,* and I protest her being allowed to testify."

Smith asked Perkins, "Have you ever been in a cellar bakery?"

"Yes, sir."

Smith certified her as an expert on the subject, winked, and said around the cigar he had in his mouth, "Give 'em the best you've got."

The hearings made Frances Perkins famous as a fighter for the rights of labor, and when Franklin Delano Roosevelt became president in 1933, the first woman member of a presidential cabinet. The commission's work also set the course of the political careers of Smith, who went on to become governor and Democratic candidate for president, and Wagner, who as a U.S. senator wrote the National Labor Relations Act. Signed into law by Roosevelt in 1935, it had the enthusiastic backing of Mayor La Guardia.

While the Smith-Wagner Commission's public hearings shone a spotlight on the plight of factory workers, whatever effect they might have in the shape of remedial legislation would be long in coming. The blunt reality was that on the day after Al Smith validated Frances Perkins as a legitimate voice for change, the men and the women who toiled in sweatshops went to their jobs as usual for the same length of time and for the same meager wages.

But one day in December, some sixty thousand laborers who were members of a union employed in factories producing men's garments refused to work. Among them was August Bellanca. The head of the Italian section of the union, he appealed for help from his friend Fiorello La Guardia. What the people's lawyer could do to help, said Bellanca, was handle legal problems that were certain to ensue.

Suddenly the scrappy little figure was not only working late at night and showing up in courtrooms the next day on behalf of union members who'd found themselves under arrest for picketing, but also on the picket lines himself. "During the day," he recalled proudly, "I appeared in court to fight cases against pickets and other cases. Night after night I spent my time with the union leaders."

He also addressed meetings of all sizes. In his numerous languages he cajoled, exhorted for solidarity, and denounced the chiselers in posh offices who begrudged giving a workingman and workingwoman a decent wage. A comic-looking figure wearing a black Stetson cowboy hat and a western string bow tie, he spoke Yiddish to Jews, German to Germans, Croatian to Croats, Hungarian to Hungarians, Italian to Italians (without an accent), and American English to anyone else who cared to listen.

Due in no small measure to his efforts, the strike ended in January 1913 with a contract giving the workers a fifty-three-hour workweek and a weekly raise in pay of a dollar.

Nine years later, he proudly wrote to one of the union leaders of "how we all worked joyfully" to put an end to "the racial hatreds among the workers, owing to the system of exploitation which had been practiced in shops for years."

An unexpected result of Fiorello's taking up the union cause was falling in love with a delicate-looking blond young woman named Thea Almerigotti. A native of Trieste, twelve years younger than he, and several inches taller, she was in the eyes of an observer of this incipient romance "porcelain-like, frail, and willowy," but also assertive if required. Otherwise, Thea had a charming European reserve. Talents as a dress designer had earned her a position in a Fifth Avenue clothing firm, a circumstance during the strike that brought her into the union cause and to the appreciative attention of the union's battling lawyer. That she was a devout Catholic did not appear to concern the grandson of a "redshirt" in Garibaldi's battles against the papacy.

A La Guardia friend, Louis Espresso, opined that Fiorello would marry Thea "as soon as he finds the time."

For a young man with ambitions to go into public service but who preferred not to be called a "politician," large portions of that precious commodity had to be devoted to a goal that had not been out of his thoughts since he'd returned to America in 1906.

⟡

Enlisting in the ranks of Tammany Hall was out of the question for a number of reasons. First, he had hated the corrupt political machine since reading about its corruptions in Arizona. Second, the leadership and the ranks of Tammany were overwhelmingly Irish. No one hung a sign on the door of its "Wigwam" on Fourteenth Street stating "No Wops Need

Apply," but it was understood by New Yorkers who knew that in the Democratic Party embodied by Tammany there could be no room for an ambitious Italian. Third, and much more importantly to a man ablaze with ideas of *reform,* Tammany Hall stood for everything that Fiorello La Guardia was vehemently against.

That left him the Republicans. Its bastion in La Guardia's neighborhood was the Madison Republican Club, whose membership the Democratic boss George Washington Plunkitt once derided as "dudes who part their names in the middle." People who voted Republican in the Fourteenth Congressional District (all the territory below Fourteenth Street) were white Anglo-Saxons who lived around Washington Square; independently minded West Side Irish; Italians who eschewed living in the uptown and downtown Little Italy; and Bohemians of Greenwich Village who liked to march to their own, different drummer.

The leader of the Madison Republicans had a middle-parted name, Frederick Chauncey Tanner. Son of a college president, he was a member of the Order of Mayflower Descendants and the Order of Cincinnati. The Republican county chairman was Samuel Koenig. A politician in every sense of Fiorello La Guardia's definition, Koenig was infamous for having said "We Republicans and Democrats fight only one day a year. The rest of the time we talk patronage."

In 1911, having served the party dutifully for five years, Fiorello found himself proposed for a post in the office of the state's Republican attorney general. The recommendation came in a letter to Koenig from Tanner. He wrote, "Mr. Fiorello La Guardia, who is a bright young lawyer, has done good service in my district."

Fiorello eagerly pursued his reward, but the job went to someone else. Disappointed, he bided his time and continued to build a reputation as a "promising comer" in the eyes of the party's leadership.

But much more to La Guardia's taste was Theodore Roosevelt. An implacable foe of the political "bossism" of the period and a stalwart proponent of honest government and civic reform, the ex-Rough Rider and friend of Bucky O'Neill had cut a swath through the old-style politics as governor of New York and for seven years as president of the United States. In 1912, when Roosevelt ran again, as the candidate of the Progressive Party, more popularly known as the "Bull Moose Party," he'd gotten enough votes to bring him in second to Democrat Woodrow Wilson and ahead of Republican president William Howard Taft. But as much as the people's lawyer admired Roosevelt and shared his ideals of "good government," Fiorello felt that as a young Republican with aspirations for advancement, he could not buck the party. He campaigned hard for Taft and exclaimed his pride in "being regular in every sense of the word."

In 1913, when Republican reformers joined a "fusion" committee to back John Purroy Mitchel, a Democrat, for mayor in the interests of nonpartisan city governance, La Guardia declined to join the insurgency. While working for others on the slate, he refused to do so for Mitchel. He disdained the Republicans who had backed him as "a few disgruntled" individuals "now classifying themselves as 'Progressives.'"

Exercising patience and fortitude, he waited, practiced law, courted Thea, and took up aviation. While flying had been a fascination of his for some time, his serious interest in it was the result of conversations on the subject with a member of the "La Guardia circle" of Italian friends. Giuseppi Bellanca was a designer of airplanes and owned a company that built them. He also ran a flying school. He invited Fiorello to act as the firm's attorney and serve on the board of directors. Presently, he was taking him to the airfield in Mineola, Long Island. He didn't need a great deal of persuading to entice Fiorello into the wild blue yonder.

Three decades later, Mayor La Guardia saw to it that airports were built to serve New York City, first at North Beach Field in Queens—later renamed "La Guardia Airport"—and one on marshland on the southern coast of the borough that would be named "Idlewild," and then renamed in the 1960s to honor the memory of an assassinated president, John F. Kennedy.

While Bellanca was giving instructions in flight, two other La Guardia friends were busily teaching him the ups and downs in the more dangerous atmosphere of politics. In that undertaking no one was better suited than Louis Espresso and Harry Andrews. Several decades before getting someone elected became the province of professional imagemakers, pollsters, and "spinmeisters" in "war rooms," they educated La Guardia in the peculiar politics of New York City in which winning was a matter of fighting with the gloves off. It was a gospel of bare-knuckled battling that Fiorello had known as a little dago who had grabbed a chair to put himself on the same footing as a taller opponent, except that the fists were words. It was fine to make a great speech to a large crowd, but the way to win an election was man-to-man. The way to win one man's vote was to come across not as just another politician, but as a friend whose interests were the well-being of the voter. More votes could be had by shaking a man's hand than in talking to the masses about "the people." Consequently, La Guardia found himself attending the weddings, funerals, christenings, and parties in all the ethnic neighborhoods south of Fourteenth Street and between the East and Hudson Rivers.

That Fiorello La Guardia was running was not in doubt. The only matter to be settled was "For which office?"

The answer presented itself one night in late summer 1914. By chance—Fiorello would later call it "serendipity"—he was in the Republican club room of the Twenty-fifth Assembly District.

The "boys" were filling in petitions for the party's nomination for Congress in the Fourteenth District. Because no Republican had ever been elected there, whoever ran was sure to lose, so the nomination meant nothing. Unable to think of anyone who might be willing to fill the role of sacrificial lamb, the "boys" sat and stared. Gazing across the smoke-filled room, one of them noticed a short black-haired figure waving his arms. Plucking a cigar from his mouth, he said, "What about La Guardia?"

Rushing toward them, Fiorello exclaimed, "I'll take it!"

With a shrug, the man with the petitions asked, "What's your first name?"

"Fiorello."

"Oh, hell. Let's get someone whose name we can spell."

"F-I-O-R-E-L-L-O."

The name that went on the petition was "Floullo."

4

In the 1913 mayoralty race in which Fiorello La Guardia had refused to go along with the Republican Party leadership in backing John Purroy Mitchel, everyone expected the victor to be incumbent mayor William Jay Gaynor. He had been elected in 1909 and would soon claim the distinction of being the most cantankerous top city official since one-legged Peter Stuyvesant took charge of New Amsterdam in 1647 and promised the Dutch settlers, "I shall govern you as a father his children."

Not for another 286 years would New Yorkers hear such a promise from a new mayor. And City Hall observers would quickly note, Stuyvesant's demands that things be done his way paled in comparison to the single-handedness with which Fiorello La Guardia thought he could run the city, and vigorously set out to prove it.

As Stuyvesant ruled with an iron fist, he'd overseen many "firsts" in the tiny settlement that would grow into the greatest city in America that would for a dozen years be La Guardia's domain (some saw it as his playground, others as his laboratory for social reform). Under "Peg Leg Pete" the seeds of the character of Fiorello's city were planted. In 1648 the first pier was built on the East River, portending a center of world commerce. In 1652 the first Latin School was opened, foreshadowing a huge and mostly unwieldy city educational system. That year the first law against speeding on city streets went onto the books. In 1653 the first prison was built, the first poorhouse opened, a night watch was created, and City Tavern was converted to the first City Hall. Three years later, the first brokerage went into business; the first market was opened; and the first population survey was conducted, showing that there were 120 houses and 1,000 inhabitants. In 1657 Jacques Courtelyou of Long Island claimed the dubious fame of becoming the first man to commute to work in Manhattan. In 1661 enough people were without jobs that unemployment relief was introduced.

By 1910 there had been ninety-three mayors of New York, almost none of whose names anyone could remember when William Jay Gaynor assumed office on January 1. As he took the oath, he was expected to be yet another tool of the bosses of Tammany Hall. But he proved to be more interested in doing things his way than by Tammany's. Looking on with dismay as Gaynor cut patronage jobs and killed off superfluous boards and bureaus, one disgusted denizen of the Wigwam griped, "That bastard Gaynor is doing more to break up the Democratic organization than any other man has in this city."

Seven months and eight days after Gaynor was sworn in, a man named James Gallagher, who'd lost his job in the City Docks Department and blamed it on the mayor, waited for Gaynor at a pier in Hoboken, New Jersey. The mayor was to board the German ocean liner *Kaiser Wilhelm der Grosse* for a European vacation. While Gaynor accepted wishes for a *bon voyage* from three city commissioners, the city's corporation counsel (chief lawyer), and others, Gallagher stepped forward with a gun in hand and shot Gaynor in the back of the neck. Gaynor survived and returned to his City Hall desk on October 3. But according to his predecessor as mayor, George B. McClellan, Gaynor was "never quite normal" after the shooting.

But crankiness, frequent bizarre behavior, and the displeasure of Tammany Hall did not prevent Gaynor from declaring his intention to seek reelection in 1913. In advance of the campaign he sailed away for another vacation. But New Yorkers learned that as his ship was a few miles off Liverpool, their blunt-talking, combative mayor had keeled over and died.

The *New York Sun,* which had excoriated Gaynor as mayor, now said, "First and foremost, he was, as no other Mayor ever was, the people's champion, the actual father of the city."

When Fiorello La Guardia died in 1947, the *Sun* and other newspapers would use similar language to sum up his dozen years as ninety-ninth mayor.

With Gaynor gone, Tammany reasserted itself by running a man it could control. But the voters of New York were suffering one of their periodic "reform" fevers and chose the "fusion" candidate whom La Guardia refused to back, the support of the Republicans notwithstanding. As president of the Board of Aldermen, John Purroy Mitchel had administered city affairs while Gaynor recuperated from his gunshot wound. Taking office in his own right on January 1, 1914, he was thirty-four years old, making him the youngest New York mayor to that time. Tall, longlegged, and sometimes as tactless as his late predecessor, Mitchel was brilliant, well educated, and honest. He gave the city, in the words of Theodore Roosevelt, "as nearly an ideal administration as I have seen in my lifetime." High praise, indeed.

Wrote New York historian Edward Robb Ellis in his 1966 book *The Epic City of New York,* John Purroy Mitchel "gave New York the best government it has ever known." But this laurel was preceded by the modifier "next to La Guardia."

On Friday, April 17, 1914, Mayor Mitchel left City Hall to have lunch with corporation counsel Frank Polk, Tax Commissioner George V. Mullan, and the police commissioner, Arthur Woods. As they reached the bottom of a flight of steps, an elderly man rushed up to Mitchel and shot him pointblank. The bullet grazed the mayor's ear and hit Polk in the face, puncturing a cheek and lodging under his tongue. Commissioner Woods and others wrestled the gunman to the ground and, accompanied by Mitchel, hustled him through City Hall Park to a police station. The assailant was Michael P. Mahoney. He'd acted out of an imagined grievance against the city administration. Judged insane, he was committed to a mental institution.

New Yorkers were shocked, sickened, and outraged that for the second time in less than a year, their mayor had been the target of an assassin. Two years earlier, a gunman had wounded the beloved Teddy Roosevelt as the candidate of the Bull Moose Party was about to enter an auditorium in Milwaukee, Wisconsin, to give a speech. They were not surprised that Teddy went ahead with his address.

But sixty-three days after the bullet nicked Mayor Mitchel's ear, the same New Yorkers shrugged off the big headlines in the June 28 editions of their daily papers. The one in the *New York Times* blared:

HEIR TO AUSTRIA'S THRONE IS SLAIN WITH HIS WIFE BY A
BOSNIAN YOUTH TO AVENGE SEIZURE OF HIS COUNTRY

In Sarajevo, capital of Serbia, that day someone had hurled a bomb at an auto carrying Archduke Franz Ferdinand, the heir to the Hapsburg Empire. The bomb bounced off the side of the royal vehicle and exploded against a following auto, injuring two officers. Continuing to City Hall, the archduke was greeted by Sarajevo's mayor. The archduke teasingly asked the red-faced, embarrassed city official, "So you welcome your guests with bombs?"

That evening as Ferdinand and his wife were driven through the city again, on their way to a reception at the governor's residence, nineteen-year-old Gavrilo Princip, a Bosnian Serb who had a role in the failed attempt at the earlier assassination by bombing, took advantage of the slowing of the car to step toward it with a pistol in hand. He fired two shots. One struck the archduke, who bled to death as he was being rushed to a hospital. The other killed his wife.

Over the next month the nations of Europe mobilized for war. Presently, Austrian troops attacked Belgrade. Germans marched into Luxembourg and demanded passage across Belgium. Britain demanded German observation of Belgian neutrality. When Kaiser Wilhelm paid no heed to the ultimatum, Britain and France declared war. As the conflict erupted, President Woodrow Wilson declared U.S. neutrality.

All this was welcome news to Thea Almerigotti. She discerned the possibility of liberation of her beloved, native Trieste from the Austro-Hungarian Empire. While she talked of this in excited tones to Fiorello, he listened politely, but he was more concerned with running for Congress as the Republican candidate in the Fourteenth District. Concerning marriage, they agreed that serious planning for a wedding should be put off while he campaigned. Thea dreamed that the ceremony would take place in a free Trieste.

In the meantime, she was content to stand aside while he sought votes in an electoral contest that everyone agreed would be an uphill fight. He would be taking on the most powerful political machine in America, whose traditional symbol was a tiger with fangs bared and claws unsheathed. Not since young, fresh-from-the-Dakota-wilds Teddy Roosevelt had run for mayor in 1886 had keepers of the Tammany tiger witnessed such unbridled enthusiasm in a lost cause. No one in the Wigwam could remember anyone like the stubby, rumpled-looking, black-hair-parted-in-the-middle, arm-waving, squeaky-voiced, comical figure storming through downtown wards like a tornado on two feet, or zipping around the streets in a Ford plastered with VOTE FOR LA GUARDIA signs, actually thinking that he could whip the tiger.

As for the Republicans, Mayor La Guardia recalled with a cackling laugh, "They didn't even know I was running!" He cited a meeting when all the candidates on the Republican ticket were introduced, except the one running for Congress. He was "right on the platform" with his speech "fairly bubbling to get out."

Sitting forward in his chair, always expecting that the next candidate to be introduced would be himself, he heard the meeting being adjourned. Grabbing the district leader by the sleeve, he demanded to know why he hadn't been called to speak.

"Why, Fiorello, you haven't a chance of winning," came the reply. "We've never elected a Republican to Congress from the Fourteenth C.D."

Candidate La Guardia expected his Tammany opponent to be incumbent congressman Jefferson M. Levy, but the sachems on Fourteenth Street surprised him by giving the nomination to an Irishman, Michael Farley. A well-known saloonkeeper and also president of the National Liquor Dealers' Association, he was picked on the basis of a Tammany tradition of counting on the votes of Irish patrons of drinking establishments. It was a cynical view of the Irish that was in step with the consensus of New York's non-Irish that the easiest way to find a son of Erin was to look into the nearest barroom.

La Guardia's strategy in dealing with Farley before a largely Irish audience was to claim that Farley was not sufficiently anti-British. He also asserted, with no evidence, that Farley was unable to read and write. The worst of Farley's sins, according to La Guardia, was that in Farley's saloon a thirsty Irish worker who found himself a day or two short of payday could not get even one drink on credit. Furthermore, did New York really want a *bartender* as their congressman?

Prospective voters who did not attend political rallies found the Republican candidate on their thresholds. "I rang a lot of doorbells," La Guardia recalled. He also went "from corner to corner every night in the district." Some of those corners were the scenes of rallies for another candidate (there was a Progressive Party candidate and a Socialist running, as well). As one of their meetings was breaking up, La Guardia arrived in his Ford and bounded out with flyers in hand. They bore a crisp, clear picture of himself and a fuzzy, sinister-looking image of Farley. He spoke in the language of whatever would-be voter he managed to grab.

One man he could not collar was Farley. Adhering to the venerated policy of the front-runner never mentioning the name of an opponent, especially one whose name few had ever heard, Farley stayed above the fray and counted on Tammany Hall to get out the vote.

The tally on election night for Farley was expected to be sixteen thousand votes. The shocker was that he got less than that. He had beaten the upstart La Guardia by only seventeen hundred.

Encouraged by an impressive showing with virtually no party support, La Guardia began planning for the 1916 elections. Based on the near-miracle of 1914, he believed that he'd earned a share of Republican patronage. The post he asked for was "appraiser," with a yearly salary of $4,000. It went to someone else. Offered a lower-paying deputy's position in the office of the attorney general in New York City, he saw it as a means to keep himself politically alive. He accepted the offer. In taking the post he understood that all the important work of the attorney general was handled in the capital, Albany. He also grasped the fact that the New York City office was "a clearinghouse for minor matters and a storeroom for forgotten cases."

One in the latter category was a long-standing complaint by Upper West Side residents, chiefly along Riverside Drive, about noxious fumes flowing across the Hudson from factories on the New Jersey side. Handed the file and told to "do something," he reviewed the details, then dashed off to Washington, D.C. He filed seven lawsuits in the U.S. Supreme Court on behalf of the "State of New York" against the offending New Jersey corporations. To everyone's amazement in the attorney general's office, the Supreme Court announced on February 28, 1915, that it would hear the case, but only against five of the defendants.

Astonished superiors in the state's attorney general's office summoned La Guardia to an urgent meeting.

"Imagine my surprise," La Guardia noted, "when I got a good calling down for acting so precipitously." The Republican Party "big shots," it turned out, "were closely connected with this matter." In a book of memoirs, *The Making of an Insurgent: An Autobiography,* published in 1948, he wrote, "The corporations had used their tremendous influence and I was given orders to take no action from now on."

Presently, the "matter" was settled when the firms elected to avoid costly litigation by installing equipment to reduce emissions.

The next toes stepped on by La Guardia's tiny feet belonged to scallop-harvesting firms on Long Island. He was directed to assist the Long Island Game Commission in the enforcement of laws against individuals gathering scallops that were less than a year old. In customary fashion, he plunged into the details of the litigation. But when he brought cases to court, he was dumbfounded at not getting the jurors to find the scallop harvesters guilty.

"I had plenty of evidence," he said. " I prepared my cases carefully, and I prosecuted them as vigorously as I knew how—but I could not seem to get any convictions. I just could not understand it, and after I became better acquainted with some of the people down there, I asked what was the reason."

A lanky fisherman replied, "Mr. La Guardia, all of us folks that sit on these cases, we know that these fellers are guilty. The reason we won't acquit them is that we ain't going to convict our own neighbors, when the big oyster companies are doing exactly the same thing and getting away with it."

Puzzled, La Guardia asked, "The 'big oyster companies'? What do you mean?"

The incredulous fisherman asked, "You mean you really don't know about them? Well, young feller, you'd better look 'em up."

La Guardia did so and found "three big oyster concerns that were absolutely ignoring the regulations." When he reported this to the fish wardens, they asked, "You don't mean that you are going to prosecute them?"

Expecting to be rebuffed, he answered that he intended to do just that. He was delighted to meet with approval. The wardens gleefully turned over "plenty of evidence."

However, three cases that seemed to be as easy as picking up seashells proved otherwise. Every time he went into court, the cases were adjourned. "The defense always had an excuse," he recorded. "I pressed for trial but I couldn't get anywhere. Finally one bright morning the counsel for the oyster companies rose in court, smiled at me triumphantly, and announced that he was ready to proceed. Then he turned to the judge and asked under what provision of the law I was prosecuting. I quoted the statute."

Reaching into a briefcase, the lawyer produced a telegram. Laying it before the judge, he declared, "That portion of the law which applied to these corporations was repealed by the legislature yesterday. Governor Whitman signed the measure last night. The law under which Mr. La Guardia has brought these cases no longer applies to us."

The Albany lawmakers had inserted three words: "in public waters." The individuals whom La Guardia had prosecuted had looked for scallops in just such places. But the big companies, their lawyer pointed out to the judge, trawled for scallops and oysters in leased, *private* waters.

Stymied, furious, and reinforced in his disdain for "politicians," and ever after suspicious of corporations, La Guardia chalked up the defeat to "experience," went to courtrooms where cases against individual fishermen were pending, and informed the clerks that he was dropping every one of them.

Another lesson in political chicanery arose in a case brought by Deputy Attorney General La Guardia in Magistrates' Court of the City of New York. On behalf of the people of New York he was suing large meatpacking companies for violations of the Weights and Measures Law. It required that the weight of all food and containers be printed on the items. The measure was the work of a dapper, handsome state senator. La Guardia's neighbor in Greenwich Village, he was James J. Walker, known to one and all, East Side, West Side, and all around the town as Jimmy.

On the day the meatpacking cases came to trial, La Guardia was astonished to find that the companies' attorney was Walker. He informed the judge that the ham and bacon in question was not sold in wrappers or containers. Therefore, how and where would its weight be printed?

Case dismissed.

Invited by Walker and the judge to join them for a drink, La Guardia sipped a glass of beer and asked Walker, "Jimmy, how in the world can you possibly appear in a case to defeat your own law?"

Walker looped an arm around La Guardia's shoulder and asked, "Fiorello, when are you going to get wise? Why do you suppose we introduce bills? We introduce them sometimes just to kill them. Other times we *have* to pass a bill because it's smart politics. Right now, you're in the attorney general's office. Are you going to stay there all your life? Of course not. You make your connections now, and later on you can pick up a lot of dough defending the kind of cases you are now prosecuting. What are you in politics for, love?"

One can only imagine Fiorello La Guardia cringing.

Eighteen years later, the mayor known and adored by the voters as "Beau James" would face "the Little Flower" in an election that would answer Walker's question about Fiorello La Guardia's purpose in being "in politics."

5

In the year Deputy Attorney General La Guardia listened to a cynical lecture on public service by Jimmy Walker, one woman of lasting significance left Fiorello's life, and another who would become essential in his future entered it.

His beloved mother, Irene, who had chosen to return to Europe with his sister Gemma to live with relatives, died while in Budapest.

Then, a few days after the new deputy attorney general assumed his post, a slim, flaxen-haired girl walked into his office looking for a job. The pride of German immigrants, she was Marie Fisher. Just graduated from Morris High School, she had taken courses in secretarial work. La Guardia tested her stenography and found it only passable. But she could use a typewriter very well. Hired, Marie was soon improving her shorthand skills, instructed by a man who had once bragged that he was a stenographer *and* a linguist. Presently Marie found herself promoted to his personal secretary. She would hold the job for the next fourteen years.

Immediately caught up in the whirlwind of lawsuits against companies that fouled the air over the Upper West Side, scallop plunderers and meatpackers, Marie soon discovered that her energetic, tireless, and irascible boss had higher aspirations than fighting legal battles for the state of New York. The once-defeated candidate for Congress in the Fourteenth C.D. was gearing up for a rematch with the Democrat who had claimed the seat in 1914.

Consequently, Marie found herself ensconced at a new desk, this one in a vacant store converted to a campaign headquarters in the heart of Tammany country on the Lower East Side. Instead of dealing with government lawyers, Marie was suddenly surrounded by gritty, streetwise campaigners. She met La Guardia's old friends Louis Espresso and Harry Andrews, both of whom knew the territory like the backs of their hands, and John Gugenham, a letter carrier who brought with him pledges of support from his fellow postal workers. Garment workers volunteered in droves. Also into the office came the leaders of the Progressive Party who saw in La Guardia the local embodiment of a liberal cause whose banner had been carried nationally in 1912 by Theodore Roosevelt. Day by day, week after week, others enlisted in the fledgling campaign, drawn to La Guardia for as many reasons as their languages. Leaving the headquarters in Marie's hands, their candidate pounded the sidewalks and spoke in meeting halls to increasingly larger crowds who delighted in the way he went after his opponent and that opponent's bosses in Tammany Hall.

When La Guardia referred to Michael Farley as "the sitting congressman," because he refused to meet La Guardia face-to-face in debate, they roared with laughter. To drive home the point, he showed up one day on the sidewalk in front of Farley's saloon (Farley's headquarters was on the floor above). As an amused crowd gathered, he shook his fists and shouted up at the office windows and challenged Farley to come down and have it out. Farley wisely demurred.

To crowds at meetings to which Farley sent stand-ins ("surrogates" in the parlance of much later campaigns), La Guardia ignored them and flailed away at Farley for "high-hatting" his constituents since becoming a congressman. He noted that Farley hardly ever showed up at his own saloon, and if he did, he forgot to "treat the boys" with drinks on the house. He asserted that Farley was a dealer in "tainted whiskey." He was such an illiterate, he charged, that he couldn't read a speech. To Irish audiences the Italian candidate accused

Farley of disloyalty to the "auld sod" and knowing nothing of Ireland's history. Farley's stand-ins responded by telling the Irish listeners that the man who was attacking one of their own could not care less about them and the Emerald Isle because he was both a dago and a Republican.

Would-be voters of German extraction heard La Guardia's pleas for support in German, along with the blatantly pandering assertion, "Nowadays every educated American should speak German." Regarding the growing debate over whether the United States ought to stay out of the war in Europe, he pledged that when elected—*when,* not *if*—he would not cast his vote in favor of sending American boys to war. But if it came to that, he hoped to be one of the first to fight for America.

Regarding concerns that German Americans might be suspected of disloyalty to their new country if the United States got into a war on the side of Great Britain, he said, "German Americans have as much right to be for Germany as the Plymouth Rockers have to be for England."

This sympathetic rhetoric enticed the owners of the historically pro-Democratic German language newspaper *Staats-Zeitung* to endorse the "son of an American soldier, out of the womb of an Austrian mother."

Painfully recalling how close he had come to beating Farley in 1914, La Guardia and his lieutenants enlisted a sizable army of garment union members, longshoremen, schoolteachers, and others, whom La Guardia later described as "tough guys," to march into boardinghouses and Bowery flophouses to rouse the inhabitants, give them coffee and doughnuts, and lead them to the polling places with the pledge that they would make an X on the paper ballots next to the name of Fiorello La Guardia. Those who said they would do so only in return for a greased palm, got a little money.

To be certain that every vote counted—and only once—La Guardia soldiers stood guard at the polls. When the candidate himself showed up to keep an eye out for any shenanigans in a waterfront voting place notorious for fraudulently stuffed ballot boxes, the startled Tammany district leader, Charles Culkin, blurted, "What the hell are you doing here?"

"What do you think I'm doing here?"

"You shouldn't be here," said the flustered Culkin. "Everything is all right."

"Everything is not all right," La Guardia replied, pulling up a chair, "and what's more, Charlie, you are going to sit here with me and watch the count, and if not, someone is going to jail, and I mean you, Charlie."

In an area that ordinarily went Democrat five-to-one, La Guardia won by a few votes.

Districtwide, he came out ahead by 357, making him the first Italian American to win a seat in the U.S. House of Representatives.

Six weeks after a victory that astonished New Yorkers and shook Tammany Hall to its foundations, the congressman-elect again found himself acting as the people's lawyer, and on familiar ground. On December 12, 1916, alleging that garment manufacturers had reneged on the promises they'd made to settle the 1912 strike, sixty thousand garment workers struck again. Once more La Guardia was called on to go into courts to assist arrested picketers. And again he joined workers on the lines. But this time he and the workers found themselves attacked by thugs, many of them hired gangsters. After an affray in front of the Frank Brothers clothing factory at 318 East 32nd Street on December 16, during which police had stood aside, La Guardia rushed downtown to City Hall to express his outrage to Mayor Mitchel. The mayor summoned Police Commissioner Woods. Orders promptly went forth out of headquarters on Centre Street that instructed police officers on picket-line duty that they had a duty to protect *everyone*.

The congressman-elect then urged Mayor Mitchel to intervene as an arbitrator, along with La Guardia. The result was a settlement of the labor dispute, but not before La Guardia took part in a final round of picketing on Christmas Day. Between then and the convening of the sixty-fifth Congress on March 5, 1917, he made frequent trips to Washington, D.C., to familiarize himself with the layout of the capital city and the Capitol, to find a place to live for the five days a week when the House would be in session, and to locate the best of the city's Italian restaurants.

"Under the rule of courtesy by which members-elect were permitted on the floor," he noted in his autobiography, he went to the House frequently and "liked Congress from the very first day." He was thirty-four years of age, but in the eyes of the venerable Speaker of the House, "Uncle Joe" Cannon, he looked younger. Mistaking La Guardia for a House page, he addressed him as "boy" and ordered him to run an errand for him. Before La Guardia could correct him, Cannon realized his error. Embarrassed, he exclaimed, "Oh, excuse me, I am not in the habit of seeing youngsters as members."

Nor were other senior lawmakers used to witnessing a freshman striding down the center aisle to the front of the House chamber and taking a seat in a row traditionally reserved for the ranking members of both parties. But that is what La Guardia did on March 5, 1917, plunking himself next to James R. Mann, Republican of Illinois, almost twice La Guardia's age, and in the judgment of House observers "the greatest parliamentarian of his or any other period."

Subsequently advised of the protocol, La Guardia took his proper place in the rear of the chamber, except when speaking. If the leaders of the House expected him to be both unseen and unheard, they soon realized that to Representative Fiorello H. La Guardia of New York being a backbencher did not mean sitting down, shutting up, and doing what he was told until he proved himself worthy of being listened to by getting reelected enough times to move up in seniority. To get along, he was advised, go along. And by no means think that a freshman, just by dropping a bill into the hopper, would see it immediately taken up and passed.

Despite this counsel and bitterly remembering the canned embalmed beef of the Spanish-American War of 1898 that Irene Coen La Guardia blamed for the death of her husband Achille in 1904, he presented to the clerk of the House a bill to impose the death penalty on anyone who sold defective supplies to the government in time of war, and long imprisonment for those who did it during peacetime.

⌒≈

As a boy in Arizona in February 1898 after the sinking of an American battleship in the harbor of Havana, Cuba, sixteen-year-old Fiorello La Guardia had enthusiastically joined in the war cry "Remember the *Maine*." One of 435 members of Congress in March 1917, he listened to the outraged speeches on the subject of German submarines engaging in wanton torpedoing of U.S. ships and those of other nonbelligerents. On March 21, while sailing in a "safety zone" in Dutch waters, an American tanker, the *Healdton,* was attacked and sent to the bottom by a German submarine, killing twenty-eight "neutral" American crewmen. Fresh in the memories of the speakers was the British liner *Lusitania,* sunk in May 1915. En route from New York City to Britain, she'd carried 128 Americans. Had not Germany pledged at that time not to send U-boats after ships of neutral countries? So much for the word of a German!

Walking toward the Capitol from the House Office Building on March 21, La Guardia grimly understood that "all the glories of spring could not blot out the knowledge that war was very near the United States." President Wilson on that very day had called on Congress to meet in special session at noon of April 2, twelve days hence, to hear him speak about "serious, very serious, choices of policy to be made, and made immediately."

Once more in Fiorello La Guardia's lifetime the summoning drums of battle were beating across the nation.

Five days before the *Healdton* went down and Wilson sent word from the White House that he would address Congress,

the freshman representative from New York's Fourteenth
C.D. had been home, addressing four large "America First"
meetings. They had been scheduled to give the people, whom
some newspapers termed "the foreign-born," an "opportunity
to demonstrate their loyalty to their adopted country."

The New York–born son of an immigrant from Foggia,
Italy, titled his talk "Confession of Faith." Its essence was
found in two lines: "I have no reason to believe that any considerable number among us will be found wanting in loyalty"
and "These are days when we must renew our love for our
country and the flag that flies over us."

"Congressman La Guardia," reported the *New York Evening World,* "stirred the audience wherever he went."

Progressive by political label, pacifist in philosophy, but
patriotic at heart, he was back in New York following Wilson's call for a special session, but in a different mood. Now
he told the crowds gathered around him that war, if it came,
would be a necessary and just one that in the end would lib-
erate millions of people in Central Europe.

"We've got to fight hard," he said. "We've got to take a
man's part in the war."

He spoke to Thea about the possibility of marriage, and
that he might have to back up his bellicose rhetoric by enlisting in the army. Thea declared, "I shall never marry anybody
while Trieste is Austrian. You may ask me again when the
Italian flag once more waves over it."

At noon on April 2 the House clerk, South Trimble, banged
the gavel to convene the 435 representatives to organize the
special session, beginning with election of a Speaker. Seats in
the spectator galleries were fully occupied. The House chap-
lain, the Reverend Henry N. Couden, implored "God of the
ages" to bless the "extraordinary session under extraordinary
conditions which calls for extraordinary thought, wise coun-
sels, calm and deliberate legislation." When the roll was called
to choose the Speaker, Fiorello La Guardia cast his vote for
James R. Mann, a Republican. The majority favored Champ
Clark, a popular Democrat who had lost his party's presidential nomination in 1912 to Wilson on the forty-sixth ballot.

The urgency felt by the members of the House to hear from the president was not shared by Champ. Presiding by protocol, he led the congressmen step by step through rules and regulations to properly organize the session, each requiring a vote. The housekeeping business took all afternoon and finished at seven forty-seven in the evening. With that, the Senate entered the chamber, along with the justices of the Supreme Court and the diplomatic corps. The only person missing was the president of the United States.

When Woodrow Wilson entered, he was escorted by an honor committee of senators and representatives, many of them carrying small American flags. The procession was led by Vice President Thomas Marshall, whose lasting contribution to American history is his opinion that "What this country needs is a good five-cent cigar."

All the way in the back of the crowded, tense, expectant chamber sat another first-time representative. A Republican whose election by the voters of Montana gave her the distinction of being the first woman elected to Congress, Jeannette Rankin was two years older than La Guardia. A former social worker in New York City and Seattle, she had become a leader in the women's suffrage movement and in that capacity helped gain enactment of suffrage legislation in Montana in 1914. When she entered the House chamber to hear Wilson's address, she carried a bouquet of purple and yellow flowers given to her at a suffragists' breakfast at which she had been guest of honor. A committed pacifist, she would hear Wilson out, then vote no. Had she been able to somehow see herself again serving in the House of Representatives twenty-four years later, she would have observed herself casting a vote on December 8, 1941, to become the only member of Congress on record against American entry in two world wars. While she was one of fifty-six members of Congress who voted against a declaration of war in 1917, her vote on the question of going to war with Japan, taken the day after Pearl Harbor, was the only "nay."

With war declared, Congress was faced with raising troops to fight in it. The number of men in the army in April

1917 was approximately 128,000—less than the toll of French dead in the Battle of Verdun. Few Americans in uniform had ever participated in a real battle. The only time U.S. troops had boarded ships to go off to war was 1898, bound for Cuba. Casualties had been so light that America's ambassador to England, John Hay, called it "a splendid little war."

To have any effect on the present war, Congress would have to resort to a draft. The last conscription had been in the Civil War. Although La Guardia understood that men would have to be called up, he felt an obligation to his constituents, many of whom were pacifists, to poll them. In a mailing he explained, "I think conscription is needed and I am trying to educate the people up to it. It is up to you to respond; don't blame me if you do not like the way I vote."

A majority responded in the negative. He voted for the draft, but he appealed for a total mobilization, including physically handicapped and conscientious objectors to work behind the lines. It was, he said, "only fair." But he took to the floor of the House to declare that a country that required immigrants and the sons of immigrants to take up arms in the cause of American values owed it to them to change "obnoxious and unwise" laws that restricted immigration and decreed who could enter the country and who could not on the basis of their ethnicity and place of origin. To assertions that Italians were dodging the draft he pointed out that "the first soldier in the service of the American government in this war who gave his life for his adopted country was an Italian, John E. Epolucci."

While defending Italians on the floor of the House, he warned the Italian Americans in his district that they owed their allegiance to the Stars and Stripes. "Those who prefer Italy to America," he advised, "should return to Italy."

Again remembering the embalmed beef of 1898, he called the House's attention to his bill that would punish war profiteers. He asked, "Do you know that American warehouses are bulging with defective arms and ammunition that has been rejected by the Allies in the last two years? And are we going to make our army and navy a dumping ground for these defective arms and this defective ammunition? We must keep our eyes open."

A sure way to ensure this vigilance, he argued, was to reject a pending proposal for press censorship. The way to prevent the "scandals, abuses, graft, and incompetency of 1898" was through an unhampered press. Championing the First Amendment, he said it was Congress's duty "to do nothing which will impair, restrict, or limit the press." He demanded that "this bill be sent back to committee, where it should die in shame and neglect."

A diminutive figure, he stood in the majesty of a chamber accustomed by history to the soaring eloquence of great orators—Henry Clay, John C. Calhoun, Stephen Douglas, Daniel Webster, William Jennings Bryan, and others whose memories and portraits in oil and marble adorned the halls of the Capitol. He referred to men in the current House of Representatives who "have spoken about the protection of the American boy." With high-pitched voice and waving his arms, he declared:

> We all want to protect him. It is for his protection that I oppose this bill. You have spoken about the vicious enemy. I know the enemy is vicious. We all know that, and prepare accordingly. When the American Army meets the enemy, whenever that may be, leave it to the American Army to crush him. But what is more vicious, dangerous and cowardly than the friendly domestic enemy who is willing to turn American blood into gold and sell rotten corn beef, wormy beans, paper shoes, defective arms for our American boys? And when the American press ferrets him out they will likewise crush *that* enemy.

Going to war necessarily meant that the president would be granted powers of a despot, he agreed, but the American people did so with "comforting assurance that the despot about to be created has the present expectation to be a very lenient, benevolent despot."

A need to guarantee American security was no excuse for abandoning basic rights. We have our "heart and soul in this war," he said, "but because we have our heart in it is no reason why we should lose our head."

The censorship bill passed, along with the "Espionage Act." Observing ensuing arrests on charges of disloyalty, amounting to two thousand prosecutions, including the Socialist Eugene V. Debs, for opposing America entering the war, Max Eastman, author and editor of the Socialist magazine *Masses,* cracked to a Greenwich Village audience in July, "You can't even collect your thoughts without getting arrested for unlawful assemblage." He added, "They give you ninety days for quoting the Declaration of Independence, six months for quoting the Bible, and pretty soon somebody is going to get a life sentence for quoting Woodrow Wilson in the wrong direction."

Perfectly summing up Fiorello La Guardia's activities during that anxious springtime, biographer Thomas Kessner wrote, "The impertinent new voice, edged with suspicion and a sense of grievance, had in a very brief time made himself familiar in the halls of Congress." As the "lone Italian-descended legislator [he] had come to Washington and made them take notice of him. Now it would be up to him to convert that attention into power, into an agenda for his constituents."

It was time, La Guardia decided, to stop talking and "take a man's part."

6

The next sixteen months of Fiorello La Guardia's life tran-
spired as if someone had scrambled the pages, plots, and
characters from a second-rate Italian opera, Gilbert and Sullivan, a French farce, Weber and Fields's vaudeville act, and
a dime novel crammed with villains and acts of derring-do.
The hero of the tale was a swashbuckling young aviator made
of spit and vinegar who zipped through the skies in a rickety
airplane held together by baling wire and kept aloft by his
patriotism, prayer, and pure American willpower.

The curtain rose on July 25, 1917. The scene: the Southern Building, Washington, D.C. Seated at a desk interviewing prospective recruits for the U.S. Army, Major Benjamin
D. Foulois looked up at a slight, black-haired young man
gripping a black Stetson hat. The major asked, "What's your
name?"

"Fiorello H. La Guardia."

"Any relation to the congressman?"

"I *am* the congressman."

"What can I do for you, sir?"

"I know how to handle airplanes. You can sign me up for
the Army Air Service."

Commissioned a first lieutenant on August 16, 1917, and
put on active duty, La Guardia held the rank for only sixteen
days. The first of September found him promoted to captain.
The rapid elevation was the result of his proven flying ability
and the recognition by the army of the prospective advantages of having a member of Congress in its officer corps.

However, being both congressman and army officer, and getting paid twice from government coffers, were impermissible in federal law. Consequently, La Guardia's compensation from both jobs was cut off, leaving him without money. To resolve his financial dilemma he went to Riggs National Bank and got a loan of a hundred dollars a month on the strength of his signature.

Declaring that he was entitled to either $2,500 a year as a captain or $7,500 annually as a member of Congress, he vowed to ultimately collect one or the other. "If the Germans don't get me," he said, "I'll get that pay."

Next came the problem presented by a member of the House being absent at roll calls for who could say how long. Was it legal for a House seat of a living member to remain unfilled, or must the House declare it vacant and require a special election to provide a replacement for "the gentleman from New York"?

La Guardia's answer was blunt: "Congress will have to go on record. I cannot think that the House will expel a member for doing just what it is advocating as the duty of every young man in the country!"

A recent *New York World* editorial had raised the embarrassing fact that members of a Congress that had voted a draft law (but dulled its compulsory edge by titling it the "Selective Service Act") had not rushed off to volunteer for duty. The headline was:

SOLONS OF NATION CAN'T SEEM TO HEAR THE
BUGLE CALL

Regarding Captain La Guardia, the House ducked the issue by officially granting him a leave of absence. Which branch of the government owed him money was left unresolved, but La Guardia let the issue lie, except to pledge, "I'll take up the matter at the close of the war." A few months later, the House agreed to pay him. Ironically, as the conscription measure was debated, Representative La Guardia had offered a bill "to continue the pay of employees in the service of the U.S. Government or Departments thereof" who enlisted in the army or the navy. If La Guardia had gone into the Flying Service as an enlisted man, his congressional salary would not have been an issue.

In rushing to don the uniform of his country and of his father, La Guardia acknowledged that he was motivated and inspired in part by Theodore Roosevelt's example in the Spanish-American War. As TR could have continued in office as assistant secretary of the navy without being faulted as lacking the courage of his convictions, La Guardia could have stayed in the House. But TR had given up his swivel chair and desk for a cavalryman's saddle to know, as TR described the thrilling experience of battle in his recently published autobiography, the feeling of "the wolf rising in the heart."

The Fiorello La Guardia who had been denied enlistment in 1898 because he was too young and too short to join TR and Achille La Guardia's war was not about to sit out this one in the House of Representatives.

Lieutenant Colonel Roosevelt reported to the Rough Riders' camp near San Antonio in a uniform tailor-made by Brooks Brothers. Captain La Guardia went to the army aviation post at Mineola, Long Island, wearing an outfit with bulging and baggy puttees that an early La Guardia biographer described as looking as if it had been "designed for a stable orderly."

When he arrived at the start of September, he was seven weeks too late to encounter TR's youngest son. Twenty-year-old Quentin Roosevelt had completed his flight training in July and shipped out to France. But stories about the handsome, dashing offspring of the hero of San Juan Hill abounded around the training school. La Guardia heard tales of the young Roosevelt's aerobatics that reminded him of himself. His takeoffs were often "cockeyed" and the landings "brutish." But he loved to fly. Whatever their shortcomings, the plain fact was that Quentin and he were of a unique breed. When Woodrow Wilson finally asked Congress for a declaration of war, the U.S. Army had only thirty-five qualified pilots and fifty-five planes for them to fly.

Captain La Guardia was under no grandiose illusions regarding his piloting skills. "I had been enrolled as an aviator," he said, "but that did not mean I was ready for action."

There was a great deal of difference between flying at Giuseppi Bellanca's school and the aviation required to fight Germans in the skies above Europe.

Expecting to follow Quentin Roosevelt and his comrades to France, La Guardia and his fellow novice aviators completed their training with orders to proceed to Oxford, England, for a course of further instruction at the School of Military Aeronautics. The problem was, the orders said nothing about how they were to get there. No one knew anything about sailing plans.

Frustrated by the red tape, the former customs official took matters in hand. Learning that a Cunard liner, the *Carmania*, was set to sail on September 15 from New York, he rushed to the city and demanded 152 first-class passages.

The Cunard ticket agent wanted to know who was paying for them.

The Fourteenth C.D. congressman said, "Charge them to the U.S. government."

When he marched the men aboard, Major John E. Hunt, whose job was to assign billets, directed Captain La Guardia to send his men "below."

"It's all right, Major," said La Guardia with the self-confidence of the "ruler of the king's nay-vee" in Gilbert and Sullivan's *H.M.S. Pinafore,* and waving the 152 first-class tickets, "my men know where their rooms are."

Soon after he reported to Oxford, a twist occurred in his army service that was worthy of any turn taken by the plot in an Italian opera libretto. Orders directed him forthwith to the Eighth Aviation Center School at Foggia, Italy.

"Foggia! The very name gave me a thrill as I stood looking at my orders," Fiorello wrote. "I had heard about Foggia all my life. I was returning not only to the land of my ancestors but the birthplace of my father. Generations of La Guardias had lived at Foggia—that bustling little city of Apulia, just above the 'heel of the boot,' a few miles from the Adriatic Sea."

He reported for duty on October 16 to begin training under Italian instructors. As the senior American officer, he assumed command of a few hundred other Americans at the school. His title was "instructor," but he recognized "that meant nothing. I was simply in charge of the administrative details. When it came to flying, I was just as much a student as any of them. We all took instruction from experienced Italians aces."

He would not be "officially placed on flying status" until December 10, 1917.

In the meantime, he was in charge of patriotic young Americans stationed more than one thousand miles from the nearest U.S. Army quartermaster. This meant that "doughboys" who had grown up savoring New York steaks, Iowa corn, and Idaho and Long Island potatoes had to eat meals that consisted almost entirely of spaghetti. Meat was on the menu twice a month.

Captain La Guardia's response to his men's complaints was to go into Foggia to call on a civilian provisioner. Ordering large quantities of food equivalent to that being served to American soldiers in other places, he directed the bill to Army Service of Supply headquarters at Tours, France.

The quick response to this "unprecedented action" was a summons from the colonel in charge of disbursements at Tours. The irate officer delivered a lecture on regulations and ended by telling Captain La Guardia that for blatantly flouting them, he was to be brought before a court-martial as soon as possible.

"If the Articles of War won't permit me to feed my men when they are hungry," replied *Congressman* La Guardia, "I will go back to Washington and see to it that the secretary of war makes out some new ones."

The representative of New York's Fourteenth C.D. would pull his political rank only twice more as an army officer. "I did it a second time to get to the front," he later explained.

"And I resorted to it for a third time when we needed gasoline, while we were fighting the Austrians."

La Guardia's grocery bill made its way up the chain of command to the American Expeditionary Force's general purchasing agent, Brigadier General Charles G. Dawes. "Hell, this man La Guardia is right," said the general (and future vice president of the United States). "Tell the people in Foggia to send the bill to the Italian government, and tell the people in Rome to pass it along to me."

In the unfolding of Fiorello La Guardia's military career, Gilbert and Sullivan and Italian opera now turned into a kind of French bedroom farce.

Having escaped a court-martial, Captain La Guardia returned to Foggia in anticipation of providing a Christmas holiday for his now well-fed men amid the splendors of Rome.

Appreciating that they would be more interested in wooing Italian women than spending their furloughs exploring the ruins of the capital of the Caesars, but worried about the frolicking men's health, he consulted a junior medical officer, First Lieutenant Oliver Kiel. In civilian life he'd been a physician in Wichita Falls, Texas. They agreed that the means of protecting the men from the possible perils of sexual intercourse would be to set up within the Roman "red-light districts" a "mobile prophylaxis station."

The senior medical officer vetoed the scheme, citing Department of the Army reports that giving out prophylactics would only encourage "immorality." La Guardia and the lieutenant were scolded and sent back to their quarters. But after pondering the decision, La Guardia put on his pistol belt and holstered Colt automatic, marched back to the senior surgeon's quarters, and placed him "under arrest."

The charge was that his reports were out of date and, therefore, his order against a mobile prophylaxis station was "illegal."

While Captain La Guardia's men went to Rome with assurances that the means were at hand to guard them against infection, word of La Guardia's actions reached General John J. Pershing's A.E.F. headquarters at Chaumont, France. The report landed on the desk of Major General Meritt W. Ireland, the Army's surgeon general. A telegram in his name was soon on its way to Foggia, ordering La Guardia to G.H.Q. immediately.

Recounting this as related by La Guardia, biographer Lowell Limpus wrote:

> His arrival at Chaumont was an event. The commander of American flyers in Italy had achieved a questionable notoriety. Wide-eyed Second Lieutenants gazed after him, staring at the Captain in a kind of horrified fascination. His superiors were coldly formal. He moved in an atmosphere of awe and pity. It was known that the medical corps was raging at the treatment accorded the senior surgeon, and the offender could expect no mercy. Buoyant as ever, La Guardia entered the lion's den.

General Ireland asked, "Captain, just *what* did you do to the senior medical officer?"

La Guardia answered, "I placed him under arrest."

"And *why* did you place him under arrest, Captain?"

"He refused to permit us to send our mobile prophylaxis station to Rome."

General Ireland's eyebrows arched. He leaned forward. "Mobile prophylaxis station? What in blazes is that?"

La Guardia explained in detail.

Ireland asked, "How did it work out? Was it successful?"

"Entirely so, sir," said La Guardia, presenting Ireland with a report that had been prepared by Lieutenant Kiel. "It's all in there."

"I'll read this later, but I'll take your word now that this idea worked," said the general. "If what you say is true, it's something worth considering throughout the A.E.F. Congratulations on thinking of it."

La Guardia saluted and turned to leave the office.

"About the surgeon you arrested," said Ireland. "Would it make things easier for you at Foggia if I were to transfer him?"

"Why, yes, sir," La Guardia replied, "I think it would."

The general smiled. "He'll be gone by the time you get back." He was.

⚬⚮

Shortly after New Year's Day, leave-of-absence congressman La Guardia found himself being asked to temporarily set aside his role as captain, U.S. Army Air Service, to represent his country by making a speech to Italian citizens in the city of Genoa. The request was made by the American ambassador to Rome, Thomas Nelson Page. A novelist from Virginia with a courtly manner, he had earned a nickname among the embassy staff. They called him "Sir Thomas of Shenandoah." The purpose of the speech, he explained, was to warm Italian feelings toward the United States. "The audience will be large," Page advised. "We anticipate somewhere around three hundred thousand people. I can't think of a better representative of all that the United States stands for than an Italian-speaking congressman who's the son of an Italian immigrant."

That was very nice, Fiorello replied, but there was Genoese Italian, northern Italian, the Italian of Rome, Venice, and who knew how many other local dialects. He spoke the Italian of the streets of New York. Very colloquial and totally Lower East Side! He joked that he might end up doing more damage than good.

Were that to happen, Page replied, as U.S. ambassador he would, of course, state that he'd known nothing about the speech by Captain La Guardia. If the address went over well, he would naturally claim credit for a brilliant public relations stroke.

An American observer of the speech noted that La Guardia began haltingly, but in a few minutes "he seemed to grow from a man into an Alp." In fact, Captain La Guardia became the Fiorello of countless street-corner stump speeches and smoke-filled meeting halls in the Fourteenth C.D. He assured his Italian listeners that America's purpose was theirs. The United States wanted the war over quickly and Italy's "lost territories" of Trentino Alto Adige, Trieste, and the Fiume that he knew so well returned. The biggest audience he had ever addressed cheered.

Delighted by the result, Ambassador Page arranged more speeches, but in the capital. The Roman crowds proved equally welcoming and approving of what they heard. One of the American listeners was Teddy Roosevelt's cousin Assistant Secretary of the Navy Franklin D. Roosevelt. He grinned and joined in the applause as La Guardia exclaimed, "Viva Wilson! Viva America!" The Italian newspaper *Giornale d'Italia* dipped into ancient Roman history to laud La Guardia as a man "harnessed in Uncle Sam's chariot in the vital and chief pursuit of the day."

The *New York Times* asserted, "President Wilson could not have chosen a better representative in Italy than this brave soldier."

Officially designated the army's man on the Joint Army and Navy Aircraft Committee, he pressed General Pershing's G.H.Q. to allow a greater participation in combat by the Army Air Service. Ordered to "collaborate with Captain La Guardia," the brash young officer's superior, Major William Ryan, seethed with resentment. He complained to his superiors that La Guardia seemed to have forgotten who was in charge in Foggia.

That La Guardia got a little carried away with his importance was evidenced on the day he left for Paris to inform the Inter-Allied Purchasing Commission that a newly designed Italian plane, five hundred of which were due to be provided to the Air Service, was not only defective, it was a "flying coffin." When the first plane was delivered, he had "looked it over carefully" and "didn't like it at all." He decided it was not fit to fly. "It was structurally unsound, and I felt it might come apart in the air."

He demanded that the purchasing commission cancel the order.

"My superiors stepped on me," he bitterly recalled for an interviewer a few years later, "and they stepped on me hard."

Was he an aviation engineer? What did he know about "stresses" and "strains" and what was "structurally unsound"?

And by the way, who the hell did he think he was, dashing to Paris without permission? It was his job to fly planes, not criticize. "Go back to Foggia and do it!"

On March 14, 1918, he took one of the planes for a practice flight. Running into a storm at fifteen thousand feet, he found the engine so underpowered in forging through the bad weather that it failed. Struggling to control it in a wind-buffeted glide, he descended to twenty-four hundred feet. Strapped in his seat "good and tight," he braced for a crash and the likelihood of being killed.

The plane hit the ground at a slight angle and somersaulted twice. One of the straps that was to have kept him in his seat snapped. He hurtled out, landed on his back, and passed out.

"My plane was wrecked, and I would have been, too," he recalled, "had it not been for that strap breaking at the critical moment."

When he awoke in a hospital the next day, one of his "pet pupils" was seated next to the bed, keeping a vigil. He was Lieutenant Marcus Jordan of Washington, D.C.

"What a flyer our C.O. turned out to be," Marcus jibed, "busting up planes!"

La Guardia conceded that if he'd been a better pilot, the crash might not have occurred. "But I don't think much of that plane."

The lieutenant and his captain chatted for a while. Marcus returned to base. Two hours later, La Guardia was informed that Marcus had taken up one of the planes. It came apart in the air and crashed, killing Marcus.

Though only a captain, and hobbling on crutches into the offices of the manufacturer, La Guardia declared that he was head of all American forces in Italy and canceled a three-million-dollar deal for delivery of the rest of the planes to Foggia.

Again summoned to Paris, he leaned on the crutches and faced more stars on shoulders of generals and eagled colonels than he'd ever seen in one place. Part of the inquisition that he recorded for posterity went:

Major La Guardia,
bomber pilot, U.S.
Army Air Services,
Foggia, Italy, 1918.

"*Who* canceled this order?"

"I did."

"By what authority?"

"By the authority vested in me to take every precaution to safeguard the lives of my men."

"Will you go back to Italy and direct the manufacturer to continue?"

"I cannot do that."

"Well, then, will you go back to Italy and attend to your own business?"

"I don't see how I can do that either."

Warned that he would be stripped of his captain's bars and uniform and sent back to the United States, he answered that should such a thing occur, he would resume his seat in

Congress and "stump the country from one end to the other" on the subject of defective, deadly airplanes.

Support for his cause came unexpectedly from a dozen Italian aviators, including some of the leading aces of Italy's air force. They signed a round-robin letter in which they threatened to resign their commissions rather than go up in the questionable aircraft. The Italian government in turn condemned the plane and canceled orders.

Red-faced Americans in Paris not only followed suit, they also asked La Guardia to advise on finding a replacement for the discredited plane. He remained at G.H.Q. for that purpose and went back to Foggia to resume recovering from his back injury, though refusing to undergo surgery. When he found orders to return to France for a post on General Pershing's staff, he blurted that he did not want to be "a brass hat." A demand to see action was backed up with a reminder that he was a member of Congress.

The result of this bluster was promotion to major and command of a large, twin-engine Caproni biplane bomber. La Guardia named it *The Congressional Limited*. His copilot was a famous Italian bombing ace, Captain Frederick Zapollini. The "observer" was Major Piettro Nigrotto, himself a legislator in civilian life. Manning the machine gun was Private Giovanni Fiumanni, a recognized marksman. When the bomber took to the air for the first time, it headed for Austria. Along with a couple of bombs went a note, written in Italian, informing those below of the special nature of the plane with its unique emblems and famous crew, and telling them they were "free to try to bring it down."

On September 15 the targets were the towns of Bellico, Runcti, and Buso. Weather was good. The plane flew at thirty-five hundred feet and scattered *manifestini* (propaganda and demands for surrender). La Guardia was "right-hand pilot." He noted in his report, "Motors worked badly all the way over enemy territory, but picked up on way back. Enemy fire, wild."

The next night flying conditions were good, altitude twenty-eight hundred feet; the objective, an aviation camp at Gedega. He found not being in control "unsatisfactory." He reported:

All bombs landed in field and hangars. Bombed at 1400 metres. Enemy territory well lighted with searchlights, owing to their machines [planes] being out on an expedition. Saw one enemy machine, which did not give us battle; exchanged shots in passing. Enemy searchlights very efficient.

On another night mission, on September 17, the objective was Mansue, but in "very bad" flying conditions. This time La Guardia was flying the plane. He reported:

Weather made navigation extremely difficult. One of my bombs caused a large fire. I doubt whether it was on an aviation field. Personally, I believe it was military supplies. Flying partners and Observer contend that aviation field and hangars were hit. Enemy fire intense and well-placed.

For his actions as a combat aviator the Italian government awarded him its three highest medals, *Croce di Guerra, Commendatore,* and Crown of Italy.

Plaudits also showered on him from home. On July 13, 1918, Republican members of the New York congressional delegation, eager to see that he was reelected, had resolved,

Whereas, Fiorello H. La Guardia, a representative in Congress from the Fourteenth District of New York, has been serving his country as an officer in Italy, and

Whereas, by his patriotism in giving his services to his country, and by the splendid work he has been able to do by reason of the fact that he speaks fluently the Italian language, and also by reason of his position as a Representative in the Congress of the United States, in cementing more closely the friendly relations between Italy and this country, and by reason, furthermore, of the valiant services he has rendered since he volunteered, be it unanimously

Resolved . . . that his course entitles him to the enthusiastic approval of all Americans . . . and the loyal support of the constituents he now represents in his campaign for a return to Congress at the election this fall.

To the public's astonishment, but not to New York City politicians, for the first time in the history of Tammany Hall, the bosses announced their preparedness to join a fusion ticket with the Republicans "so that La Guardia would not be opposed."

Except, of course, by pacifists and Socialists. They railed about an "absentee congressman" and nominated a college professor, Scott Nearing, who was under indictment for violation of the Espionage Act for his opposition to American participation in the war.

On June 30, the *Times* devoted considerable print to praise the "Flying Congressman" as a soldier, orator, and patriot, and "American by birth and heart, who has shown himself to be the best mouthpiece of the White House's diplomacy and indefatigable heart of the Government's Democracy, who had gone to the Piave trenches with the assurance that America stands behind Italy. Let's not forget Fiorella H. La Guardia, the soldier-Congressman of the United States."

The *Times* noted, "Up to a year ago he was unknown."

Now he was a heroic figure with the endorsement of the Tammany tiger and, apparently, everyone else, with the usual exceptions of the pacifists and Socialists. Tracked down in Italy by a *Times* reporter, he was asked if he planned to return to New York to campaign. He ducked by replying, "Naturally, being in the military service, I cannot leave my post without proper orders."

Surely no one in the high command or in Washington would stand in his way?

"Personally, it is far more pleasant to remain here, to fight with the men trained by me, and to take a direct part in the fight," he replied. "I admit it is also a source of personal pleasure to know, after a successful bombing raid, that one has played a small part in advancing the line, in hastening a victorious end to this struggle."

However!

"If the people of my district desire me to resume my seat in the new Congress, I shall certainly do so."

On the other hand, "I know that they would not ask me to come back, unless convinced that my experience in the air for over a year, and knowledge which I have necessarily acquired concerning aviation matters, would be more useful to my present duties here."

But in a letter to Harlem congressman Isaac Siegel, he wrote that he intended to come home to campaign. He promised to conduct an "anti-socialistic, true blood American platform."

In the meantime, work on behalf of the Fourteenth C.D. constituents and the campaign rested in the hands of Harry Andrews and Marie Fisher, assisted by Siegel on matters beyond their power to act in governmental matters.

Recognizing a war policy ally in La Guardia, even if he was Republican, and tuned to the sentiments of public and press that the diminutive hero belonged at home and back in Congress, the Wilson administration was content to have General Pershing order Major La Guardia back to the United States "for duty" in connection with "bombing training." Slim, tan, and smart in his uniform, he stepped onto a Manhattan dock and into a swarm of reporters on October 18, 1918.

The *New York American* scribe noted, "Congressman Fiorello La Guardia, Major of Aviation in Uncle Sam's forces on the Italian Front, slipped into port last evening as if he had been gliding over Austrian lines in his bombing plane. The subsequent effect was also a good deal like a bomb explosion!"

A reporter asked La Guardia, "What do you think of Nearing?"

The major puzzled for a moment. "Nearing? What regiment does he belong to?"

Told of the Socialist candidate's legal problems, the man who always disdained the label of "politician" gave a politician's answer. "I did not know he was under indictment. But remember this: Under the laws of this country a man is innocent until he is proven guilty."

On November 2 he met Nearing for a debate at Cooper Union. The audience was mostly composed of pacifists and Socialists. Even the friend who introduced him, Judge Jacob Franken, was a Socialist. Declared La Guardia, "I am personally opposed to militarism, imperialism, and all manner of oppression. I am against war, and because I am against war, I went to war to fight against war."

The audience hissed and booed.

"I don't think we can end war by merely talking against it on East Side corners."

Against a continuous tide of shouting that often drowned his words, he assailed German Socialists "who did not protest against the orgies of butchery to which their government had committed them."

Pandemonium!

Judge Franken feared a riot between a mass of red flag–wavers and a small number of La Guardia loyalists hoisting American and Italian flags. Fists also flew. The uproar raged for more than a quarter of an hour. It subsided only when Nearing got up to speak.

"I know a war is on," he said, "the war between plutocracy and the plain people. That war is raging in every country on the earth."

Recognizing the futility of going on, La Guardia said, "I can't debate this man. I understood he was a professor of economics. It is a mistake—he is a poet."

While Nearing had the Cooper Union crowd and the votes of Socialists, La Guardia had the backing of Tammany Hall. In the history of the Fourteenth C.D., it was all that was needed. He beat Nearing fourteen thousand to six thousand. A week later came the Armistice, ending the "war to end all wars" but planting seeds of the next when Fiorello H. La Guardia would be "Hizzoner," the mayor of New York, but happiest if someone still addressed him as "Major."

7

Of all the stories Mayor La Guardia liked to tell about his participation in "the Great War," none amused him and his listeners more than an escapade in Spain, which in the telling had aspects of the antics of comedians Abbott and Costello or a Bob Hope and Bing Crosby movie that could have been titled *Road to Barcelona.* It was undertaken with civilian clothes, phony identification papers, forged travel documents, and a flagrant violation of the rules of war that could have classified him as a spy.

The purpose was to overcome a serious shortage of materials for the manufacture of airplanes. The factories of Fiat, Isotta Faschini, and Caproni, maker of *The Congressional Limited,* found themselves lacking sufficient steel, copper, other vital metals, and ash wood for making propellers. Much of this was to have been acquired from the United States, but a bureaucratic mixup had sent it to England and France. Contemplating the problem, Captain La Guardia came up with a plan to acquire the stuff surreptitiously in Spain and smuggle it out. But when he sent the idea through proper channels to G.H.Q., he was advised that approval could take weeks, if it came at all.

Unwilling to wait for the go-ahead, La Guardia gleefully said to a prospective accomplice, "Smuggling is an ancient art."

The collaborator he had chosen was his adjutant, Albert Spalding. A talented violinist who yearned for air combat, he was kept grounded because La Guardia said he was "too old," even though he was six years younger than his commander. Music-lover La Guardia's reason for denying him his wings was a desire to keep Spalding "fiddling."

As a collaborator in a cloak-and-dagger adventure, Spalding was just the man.

"We leave tomorrow night," La Guardia exclaimed. "Tickets, clothes, orders, those are your affair. You have an imagination—use it! Any kind of orders that will do the trick!"

Spalding proved to be a deft forger. As clothier for the mission, he decided he did not have to worry about outfitting a man whose uniforms always seemed to have been tailored for someone else. While "touristy-looking" civilian raiment and the phony documents were being obtained, La Guardia was busy collecting letters of credit from an Italian bank in the amount of $5 million.

According to Spalding's account of the adventure, while traveling by train through the south of France La Guardia was more relaxed than Spalding had ever seen him. He realized that his boss "rests as intensely as he works." The "galvanic energy" could be "shut off at will."

"La Guardia talked about home, about the girl to whom, once the war was over, he was to be married," Spalding recalled. Looking at a photograph of Thea, he "could not imagine two greater opposites" than the lovely girl in the picture and "the volcano of virility at my side."

Upon arrival in Barcelona, La Guardia whispered to Spalding, "There's no doubt we will be watched, and not by friendly eyes. We'd better take in a bullfight. It's one of the sights."

Next to spending a diversionary afternoon of blood and sand that could have been taken from a page in Ernest Hemingway's yet-to-be-written *The Sun Also Rises,* the top priority of the La Guardia scheme was finding a shipping company willing to join in the smuggling operation. This meant researching past newspapers for reports of ships lost to German submarines. By far the greatest Spanish victim of U-boats was the Taja line. Even better for La Guardia's purpose, its owner's only son had gone down with one of the torpedoed ships.

Señor Taja happily extracted revenge on the Germans by assisting in obtaining the steel and port clearances. Eventually the little Spaniard and his ships came through with more than $1.5 million worth of steel and other materials delivered to Italian ports.

A few days after returning to Italy, and two weeks after he and Spalding had launched their enterprise, La Guardia found an order from General Pershing authorizing it. He also received an invitation to lunch with Italian general Armando Diaz. The supreme commander of the Italian Army was so pleased with La Guardia's exploit that he took him to see King Victor Emmanuel.

Observers of the meeting between the grandson of a former Garibaldi redshirt and the king were amused to hear La Guardia call the monarch "Manny." They were shocked when he told His Majesty that "the days of monarchies are numbered."

Five years later, Victor Emmanuel III was king in name only, his powers usurped by the fascist dictator Benito Mussolini. The result of that turn of events would eventually skewer the first Italian mayor of New York City on the horns of a political dilemma.

Reelected to Congress in November 1918, and with the war over and Trieste again to be part of Italy, Fiorello La Guardia announced his betrothal to Thea in January and set March 8 for the nuptials. The morning ceremony was held in the Madison Avenue office of Cathedral College behind St. Patrick's Cathedral. The ceremony was conducted by Monsignor Gerardo Ferrante before a small group of friends, Thea's brother in a U.S. Navy uniform, Louis Espresso as best man, the groom in his uniform (cap tilted rakishly), and the bride in a stylish fur-trimmed suit. Following a breakfast celebration at the Hotel Netherlands, the couple departed for their honeymoon. He was thirty-five, she was twenty four.

In contemplating the marriage of a devout Roman Catholic and an at-best lukewarm Episcopalian, La Guardia biographer Thomas Kessner noted a "hint" of Achille La Guardia's "enduring influence on his son." With the caveat that too much might be made of what could have been a simple coincidence, Kessner pointed out that Achille also had married a woman who was ten years younger than he, and of a different faith. Like Irene, Thea desired nothing more than to share the private life of a public husband. Each wife was as withdrawn as her husband was outgoing, as calm and frail as he was volcanic and unrelentingly ambitious.

Fiorello and Thea set up housekeeping in his Charles Street apartment, but five days a week he was in Washington and once again vexing the potentates and rank-and-file members of the House of Representatives, the majority of them Republicans who were swept into office on a tide driven by voters' repulsion against the bloodbath in a war that President Wilson had vowed to keep America from joining. Now Wilson favored a continuing role for the United States in a world "League of Nations," and a standing army a million strong.

In step with popular sentiment, La Guardia wanted "the boys" home as soon as possible. As to Wilson's "League," La Guardia declared, "If you will consult the two million American men who fought overseas, you will find no difference of opinion among them. They are all for an arrangement—I do not care what you call it, a League of Nations or anything else—which will make impossible another world war."

While debate raged over the size of an army (it was settled at half of Wilson's idea) and the proper place of the United States on the world stage (the U.S. Senate decided that American security was better preserved by two oceans than a seat in the League of Nations), most Americans were more interested in a pending proposal by a Republican congressman from Minnesota. Andrew John Volstead had introduced an amendment to the Constitution to prohibit the making and sale of alcoholic beverages. A man who once asserted "one drink never hurt nobody" was now wholeheartedly enlisted in the ranks of Prohibitionists who had been fighting for decades against "demon rum" and "John Barleycorn" in the belief that bad private behavior should be restrained by federal statute. Now they had a powerful congressman who justified curbing the national thirst by declaring, "Law has regulated morality since the Ten Commandments."

Representative Fiorello La Guardia responded, "I maintain this law will be almost impossible of enforcement. And if this law fails to be enforced—as it certainly will be, as it is drawn—it will create contempt and disregard for law all over the country."

The cocky Army aviator who in Victor Emmanuel's palace in Rome had pronounced the twilight of monarchies and eventually became mayor of New York would see vindication of his forecast of the foolhardiness of the Eighteenth Amendment and the Volstead Act in the sinister gangsters who caught the tide of Prohibition and rode it to riches and corrupting power. Many of them, unfortunately, had Italian names—Maranzano, Masseria, Luciano, Genovese, Costello, and Ciro "the Artichoke King of New York" Terranova, among other tinhorns and chiselers.

In the spring of 1919 La Guardia found himself still way down on the seniority list in a Congress described by muckraking editor H. L. Mencken as "petty lawyers and small-town bankers" and a "depressing gang of incompetents." All La Guardia could do was rail at "outrages" in speeches that few people paid attention to and cast votes that changed nothing. Not even the "progressives," such as Robert La Follette and George Norris, took him seriously.

Recognized by "wets" as their congressional champion in the struggle with the "drys" to bottle up the Volstead Act, the gentleman from the New York Fourteenth C.D. (where, he said, "there are no drunks on the streets") also considered himself a fighter for veterans of the war and wives and "Gold Star mothers" whose men had been killed. While he opposed proposals to disinter the fallen and bring them back for burial in American soil, he advocated appropriating funds to pay for the women to visit the military graveyards in Europe.

Among other La Guardia measures were repeal of the
Espionage Act, reinstatement of jobs to government employees who'd gone off to war, and reintroduction of his defeated
bill to impose the death penalty on war racketeers. He also
proposed a measure for the rehabilitation of "cripples" who
wished to return to prewar industrial jobs.

Reminding the House and the white people of the country
that "Negro soldiers fought alongside us," he ranted against
racial discrimination.

Going against the grain of a prevailing probusiness sentiment, he pointed out that by profiting from the war, forty-two
thousand businessmen had become millionaires.

When the American Red Cross and the YMCA billed the
government for soldier clubhouses that they'd set up and run
during the war, he took to the floor in high dudgeon. When
the American people gave donations to those organizations,
he said, they'd given the money to be spent for American soldiers. "They are a direct gift of the American people to the
soldier boys of this country."

Yet his flamboyant style and war record overcame a growing reputation as "too liberal" and made him a sought-after
guest at dinner tables and cocktail parties (despite Congressman Volstead's pending constitutional amendment). If
La Guardia was invited on the basis of his reputation for saying what was on his mind, he did not disappoint.

Three stories of La Guardia as invitee became legendary
in the lore of capital society.

After going on at length with a man seated next to him
on the subject of the Balkans, he boasted, "I've lived in that
part of the world for three years, and I know what I'm talking about." Finally pausing, he asked the gentleman what he
did for a living. The patient listener smiled and replied, "I
am the Serbian ambassador."

To a woman at dinner he denounced the quality of aircraft engines made by General Electric Company. The lady
was the wife of a GE executive.

During a break in the festivities at a party in a posh hotel,
he retired to the men's room. A man on the way out asked if
he was enjoying the evening's company.

"I've never seen such a bunch of nuts," La Guardia replied. "I'm clearing out of here. What about you?"

"I can't. I'm the host."

Presently, a leading figure of another party—the Republican—extended an invitation to Congressman La Guardia that he felt he could not refuse. This request for his presence came from New York Republican kingpin Samuel Koenig. Never a man to miss an opportunity, Koenig wondered if La Guardia would be interested in giving up his seat in the House for a chair on the New York Board of Aldermen. But not *any* chair; the *presidency* of the board.

The position had suddenly become available as a result of the incumbent running to be the next governor of New York. Suddenly Fiorello H. La Guardia was being courted by the Republican Party in an attempt to replace a giant among Democrats, a gritty, Lower East Side, Irish "pol" with hallmark bowler hat and an ever-present cigar.

Alfred E. Smith, universally called "Al," was the second-most-popular political figure in the recent history of the Empire State. The first was the late Theodore Roosevelt, who had died on January 6, 1919, because, it was widely believed, he had never recovered from the loss of his beloved youngest son. Quentin Roosevelt, age twenty, had been killed when his plane was shot down over France in the waning months of the war. Three other scions of the former president, the "lion's pride" of Theodore Jr. (Ted), Kermit, and Archibald, had been seriously wounded. Ted had come back to lead in the formation of the American Legion and find himself a favorite among New York Republicans who saw him following TR to the governorship and then to TR's former "bully pulpit" in the White House. The brightest dream of men such as Koenig was Ted Roosevelt beating Al Smith either for the governorship or the presidency in the 1924 elections, with La Guardia occupying Smith's former place as president of the Board of Aldermen.

This was the scenario that was to be laid before Fiorello at a meeting with Koenig; Paul Windels, another Republican leader; and others. The plan leaked to the press. When the Capitol reporter for the *New York American* showed

Congressman La Guardia a story based on the leak, La Guardia said, "This is the first time I have heard about being selected to run for president of the Board of Aldermen of my city. It is indeed very kind and complimentary to mention me in this regard. I really have not given the matter any thought. I am too busy with my congressional work to think about any other position at this time."

He was not the first nor the last politician to qualify a statement with "at this time."

The reporter was asked, "Don't you think there is enough to be done here to keep any representative busy without looking for other jobs?"

A pause. Then, "Of course," La Guardia continued, speaking like a man with a Stetson hat to throw into the ring while hedging his bet, "the campaign will be exciting and interesting, but the job [of aldermanic board president] is too inactive."

The reporter and the congressman knew otherwise. President of the Board of Alderman was second to being mayor. If the mayor could not act—two had recently been shot at—the city government fell into the hands of the board's president. As congressman, he was one of 435, and a very junior one at that. The 65-member Board of Aldermen was the city's legislature, whose president was, in a later political parlance, "high-profile."

But La Guardia told the reporter, "I like the House, and I don't want to leave it."

The newsman filed a story to that effect. Few people in New York who understood the game of politics believed a word of it.

Neither did Koenig and Windels, nor Will Hays. Chairman of the Republican National Committee, Hays was famous for asserting a political platform based on "faith in God, in folks, in the nation, and the Republican Party." He went down to Washington, D.C., and gave his word as a gentleman that if La Guardia would run for president of the Board of Aldermen in the special election to replace Smith, and win it, he would see to it that the next GOP candidate for mayor of New York would be Fiorello La Guardia. Hays added, "You would be the first person of Italian ancestry to attain that office."

A black Stetson hat sailed into the ring as candidate for aldermanic president.

The head that wore it was quickly anointed GOP candidate in a race against Robert L. Moran, an ailing Bronx florist and choice of Democratic mayor John F. Hylan. Soon after Fiorello decided that there was a job with a future that was brighter than staying in Congress, the boss of the Republicans in Brooklyn, Senator William Calder, sent an emissary to invite La Guardia to the annual banquet of the Kings County GOP.

The man delegated to extend the invitation telephoned Calder in a panic. "We can't have La Guardia at that meeting," he exclaimed. "If he comes, he'll ruin his chance for election."

Astonished, Calder asked, "What do you mean?"

"La Guardia just had his head shaved and he looks like hell. We can't let him be seen in public until his hair grows back."

The only thing more lacking than Fiorello's hair was money. When he agreed to run for president of the Board of Alderman, he had $35 in the bank. To oversee the campaign and counsel La Guardia on the vicissitudes of a run for a citywide office, the Republican bosses assigned Paul Windels the job of campaign manager. The veteran politician's advice was that La Guardia ignore his direct opponent and run against the record of Mayor Hylan. Fiorello took to the task by turning on the "galvanic energy" that Albert Spalding and everyone else who knew LaGuadia in action in Italy came to expect.

With the exception of Theodore Roosevelt, New York City voters had never seen the like of Fiorello La Guardia. Certainly, no Italian voter and no one Jewish had witnessed a candidate who could talk to Italians in Italian and to Jews in Yiddish. And not since Teddy Roosevelt ran for mayor in 1886 had a *Republican* commanded such attention, or deserved it. He ranged up and down Manhattan Island, into Queens, Brooklyn, and the Bronx, and even across the harbor to Staten Island to denounce Mayor Hylan's 1920 city budget as a document "conceived in the bowels of darkness."

He assailed the administration for tolerating "firetrap" school buildings. "The Tammany Board of Estimate," he charged, "has been more interested in grabbing greater power than in making first [a school system] adequate to the pressing needs that crowd it."

He targeted the costly and "useless office of city chamberlain" and city spending of extravagant amounts on "ornate celebrations" for returning veterans. "Under the guise of 'patriotism,'" he said, "the people's money was squandered, to a large extent through blunders and other wastages, and some of the items of expense are an insult to the soldiers, some of whom, as taxpayers, must bear their share of this financial burden."

Discussing the city transit system of trolleycars and subways (known then as "traction"), he lambasted Hylan for speaking on a subject Hylan "knows absolutely nothing about." The least the mayor could do, he proposed, was "keep quiet and remain in hiding."

With the experienced assistance of the old La Guardia "hands"—Louis Espresso, Harry Andrews, and the indomitable Marie Fisher—Paul Windels could count on mobilization of the same stalwarts in the garment unions, postal workers, Greenwich Village "radicals," teachers, and, of course, Italians who had previously rallied to elect "the Little Flower."

Financially it was a campaign run "on the cuff." As election day neared, the debt was more than a thousand times the $35 in the LaGuardia bank account at the start. How the money was to be repaid, win or lose, was an overwielding, ominous cloud. But a few days before election day, Frank Munsey, a Democratic stalwart and friend of Louis Espresso, offered Espresso a bet. "Three to one," said Munsey, "that Moran wins."

Espresso was reluctant to bet any amount, but the same was not true of Mrs. Fiorello La Guardia. Thea told Espresso that her husband was going to win and that she had $1,050 of her own that she was willing to wager. Other La Guardia supporters volunteered to chip in whatever they had. On the Saturday before election day the "kitty" amounted to $12,000. At odds of three to one, the winnings could retire the campaign debt. Espresso tracked down Munsey and made the bet. Should Fiorello fail, of course, they would be out the $12,000 and still have to come up with the more than $35,000 the campaign owed. Whether the candidate knew about the gamble was not recorded. Given his long-standing disapproval of wagering, learned by watching the tinhorns who had financially scalped poor people in Arizona, including his mother, it is unlikely that he would have approved.

At two in the morning on the day after the election, Sam Koenig telephoned to report to the candidate, "FH, you're in."

He'd won by 145,000 votes.

On December 31, 1919, he resigned from the House. At midnight he took the oath of office as president of the Board of Aldermen.

The City Hall fireworks commenced.

8

To signify the arrival of its new president, the Board of Aldermen gave La Guardia a new gavel. Although he occupied the head chair and wielded considerable authority, he was in the minority. Acutely conscious of this fact, he put a typical La Guardia spin on the reality. "My understanding of the function of the minority," he declared with a straight face "is that it is to set the pace for the *majority*."

The role of the minority, he continued, was to "first point out to the majority when the majority is headed in the wrong direction." Only then "can it possibly criticize the majority for any error committed or mistake made."

During the proceedings of the board, he said to the majority and the minority, "Every member present must behave as a gentleman, and those who are not must try to."

Newly elected to the sixty-five-man board were four Socialists. Manhattan voters had also sent five to the New York legislature, only to see the State Assembly refuse to seat them. Outraged, and fearing an attempt might be made to block the four Socialists from the Board of Aldermen, La Guardia warned, "In ousting the five Socialist assemblymen, a dangerous precedent has been created. If we deprive the Socialists of their legal rights after legitimate use of the ballot; if we deprive them of free speech and of the free press, they will be compelled to resort to the same sorts of methods used in Russia. With grain, eggs, and oatmeal becoming luxuries in the average family, these Socialists, along with the general public, are right in demanding a radical change in conditions."

The aldermanic Socialists remained, and in the following elections for the Assembly, the five who'd been denied their seats were reelected and accepted in Albany without challenge. The Socialist who ran for governor the next year lauded La Guardia's stance, saying that it had "required courage—and you displayed it."

As president of the Board of Aldermen, La Guardia had three votes on the body that had responsibility for the city's finances, the Board of Estimate. Mayor John Hylan (presiding officer of the board) also had three, as did City Comptroller Charles L. Craig. Five borough presidents were entitled to two each, for a grand total of sixteen votes. The party divide was Democrats eleven, Republicans five. The GOP had managed to win the Manhattan Borough presidency for Henry H. Curran, also a war veteran with the rank of major, and a former alderman. During the campaign, a *Times* editorial had ridiculed the Board of Estimate for so much quarreling that it was "impotent" and worthy of Gilbert and Sullivan.

In the sometimes strange alchemy of party politics, Democrat mayor Hylan despised the Democrat comptroller and therefore welcomed a discreet alliance with the new president of the Board of Aldermen in battling Craig. With Hylan's assistance, La Guardia was able to attack his pet projects, including a contract for a new courthouse. At one point Craig was so furious with La Guardia during a meeting of the Board of Estimate that he shouted to Hylan, "Will you please hit the little wop over the head with your gavel?"

Concerning the proposed new courthouse and La Guardia's opposition to it, Hylan recalled, "A site had been selected and purchased by the previous administration. When the matter first came before the Board of Estimate, I expected unanimity of opinion in favor. Much to my surprise, La Guardia commenced opposing every move."

City Hall veterans had not known such a battle since 1896, when Police Commissioner Theodore Roosevelt dared another city comptroller to settle a rancorous dispute "with pistols or anything else."

La Guardia told Mayor Hylan, "This courthouse business stinks. It's ROTTEN. You can't stand for it. Mr. Mayor, you look into it as much as I have, and you will find that the city is being robbed. The price of the limestone is ridiculously high, and not only that, but the specifications call for about three hundred cubic feet more than they need."

Hylan accused La Guardia of using figures provided by the opposition *New York World*.

"No," replied La Guardia, "the *World* is getting its figures from me."

Hylan ordered an investigation by the commissioner of accounts. When confronted with La Guardia's figures, representatives of "the limestone people" became panic-stricken and walked out of the hearing. Hylan called a special meeting of the Board of Estimate and announced cancellation of construction contracts, except for the foundation, which was already being dug.

La Guardia later recalled the huge cost overruns of the courthouse built by the late boss William Marcy Tweed, located behind City Hall, and said that Comptroller Craig's "limestone courthouse out-Tweeded Tweed."

La Guardia also remembered, "Some of my political friends criticized me very severely for my action in this respect. It was suggested that I might have a great campaign issue had I waited and pointed out the terrific wastefulness of the limestone purchases. That is the doctrine of the old school of politics. It might have been good campaign material, but it would have been far too costly to the City of New York. I considered it my duty to serve the city first and look for campaign issues afterward. That is the teaching of the new school of politics."

La Guardia practiced it in fighting another Craig proposal to increase the pay of all the city's employees, as authorized by the state legislature "to meet the constantly growing cost of living." Craig wanted a 20 percent hike. La Guardia noted that the bulk of the funds were not earmarked for rank-and-file employees but "appointed high officials."

"President La Guardia was right on the jump," said Hylan, "and fought it."

The Board of Estimate approved the measure and so did the aldermen, but when it got to Hylan's desk, he listened to La Guardia's objections and vetoed it. A revised measure giving the raises to workers, rather than politicians, passed, to "the displeasure of many of the high and mighty in political circles."

When Craig attempted to exempt members of his staff from taking civil service exams, La Guardia issued a press release. It called Craig's move "a brazen attempt" to appoint "riffraff who could not pass the civil service test." Again, Craig was stymied.

The La Guardia opinion was not confined to city affairs. When the state legislature was proposing daylight saving time, he came out in favor of sticking to "God's own sunshine."

As acting mayor one day, he vetoed a measure to erect a fountain in Crotona Park. Calling the proposed fountain "inartistic and grotesque," he said it would be "a pity to mar" the park, and suggested an art competition limited to residents of the Bronx.

Still on the subject of public art, he proposed formation of a committee to be headed by the artist Charles Dana Gibson to encourage talented high school students to pursue art. As the mayor, he would oversee creation of the first High School of Art and Design in the nation.

In May 1921 he went to Connecticut to urge ratification of the women's suffrage amendment. "The hope of American politics," he said, "is the woman's movement."

On July 19 he wrote to Hylan that the higher officers in the Police Department be made to undergo the same physical tests given to army officers. He suggested that all lieutenants, captains, and inspectors be fit to walk ten miles a day on three consecutive days, or in some cases that they ride thirty miles a day for the same period. Fourteen years later, as Mayor La Guardia went on the radio to read "Dick Tracy" to "the kiddies" during a newspaper strike, he offered an aside to Police Commissioner Lewis Valentine, wondering why Dick Tracy was slim and trim and so many New York police detectives were fat.

Called upon to mediate to stave off a strike in the Housewreckers' Union, he got a crash course in the problems of housing. Providing it to as many city inhabitants as possible would be a dominant theme of his mayoralty.

He provided a foreshadowing of his mayoralty policy on gratuities. He turned down a season pass (No. 507) from the American Baseball League of New York. Sending it back, he wrote, "I wish to make it clear that I understand fully the kind of spirit in which it was sent; but inasmuch as I have made it an ironclad rule not to accept any passes, or favors of any kind, while in public office, I am compelled to return it to you." He noted he was "very fond of the game" and knew no better way to spend "a disengaged afternoon."

Invited to become vice chairman of his American Legion Post, he declined, stating that "if the American Legion is to attain its potential strength, nothing should be permitted which would give the impression the Legion is to become an instrument in the hands of politicians." In doing so, he followed the example of his friend and fellow Republican Theodore (Ted) Roosevelt Jr., who had helped found the Legion, but turned down a leadership title because he meant to run for elective office.

Roosevelt and the state Republicans had their sights set on the governorship in 1924. Fiorello La Guardia had the pledge of the party's chairman that in 1921 he would be the party's candidate for mayor. But he also had ringing in his ears the voice of the Republican governor. He complained of La Guardia's "tendency to go whooping off the reservation, his fiery antics, radicalism, and demagoguery."

But in the autumn of 1920, a year before the next mayoralty election, La Guardia's job as aldermanic president and thoughts of taking the next step up in city politics took a backseat to Fiorello the proud prospective father. Relocated from Charles to Christopher Street in Greenwich Village, he was still a host to Italian friends and his circle of political advisers. Now and then after the spaghetti he dusted off his cornet to entertain, but most of the time he left music to Albert Spalding's violin and Enrico Caruso when the opera star wasn't singing at the Met or on the road. When Thea announced that she was pregnant, the happy news was saluted with many a glass of chianti.

The baby was born in November and named Fioretta Thea. But her always frail mother did not fare well. Hoping that the fresh air of Long Island would help her rebound, La Guardia rented a house in Huntington. This required him to spend hours commuting by train. But Thea showed no improvement. Then she was diagnosed with tuberculosis. Seeking an even better place for her to get well, he took her and the baby to Saranac Lake, but this meant he could be there only on weekends. Thea asked to return to the city. Borrowing money and pawning everything he had, Fiorello bought a house on University Avenue in the Bronx.

In the midst of this personal turmoil and worry he was in the heat of his battles with the comptroller. He was also on the receiving end of criticism from parts of the press, but more importantly, in the ruling circle of the Republican Party, sparked by Governor Miller. Early in the spring of 1921 the party potentates announced that they would bestow the nomination for mayor on Manhattan Borough president Curran.

Betrayed and furious, La Guardia declared that he would go after the nomination in a party primary. But he found himself in a four-man race. Also contesting the crowning of Curran would be Brooklyn judge Reuben L. Haskell and Senator William L. Bennett. (The latter's plan to run for Congress in the Fourteenth C.D. had been derailed by the party in favor of La Guardia.) All astute observers felt that the primary contest for mayor would actually be a two-man race, La Guardia versus Curran.

Although La Guardia tackled the challenge with expected verve, he could not give all his time to the race. On most evenings he rushed to the Bronx to be with his ailing wife and child.

Telling the press, "I looked forward to a pleasant, intelligent campaign with my opponents on the issues," he expressed dismay at being attacked by his opponents. After he fired two Republican district leaders from the staff of the aldermanic president for "neglect of duty," but really for not backing his candidacy, he found himself assailed by Curran and Bennett, and in newspaper editorials. The dismissals, said the *Evening Post,* were "the kind of performance we would expect from a Tammany official." On the same day the *Evening Mail* ran an editorial with the headline "La Guardia Rules Himself Out." It predicted that "scores of Republicans who have hitherto held him in esteem" would defect.

The paper was right. He lost to Curran by just over sixty-five thousand votes.

To make matters worse, two weeks after the defeat, the back injury in the plane crash in Italy sent him to the hospital. Doctors urged surgery. He refused and went to visit Thea and the baby in a sanitorium in Croton, New York. After two days of excruciating pain, he yielded to Thea's pleas that he go back to the hospital for the operation. It was done on October 3 at Roosevelt Hospital. In the eight days while the house in the Bronx was unoccupied, burglars broke in and pillaged it of everything, including Major La Guardia's record of war service.

On October 13, Fioretta Thea La Guardia died of spinal meningitis. Her mother was so ill that her devastated father had to go to the funeral without his wife. Thea died on the fifteenth.

A few weeks later, the Republican candidate for mayor went down to defeat by what a newspaper called a "prodigious plurality" to La Guardia's sometimes ally John Hylan. Tammany boss Charles Murphy crowed that the reelection of "Honest John" proved it was "foolish for our enemies to charge that there is nothing good, but everything corrupt in Tammany." Pointing to a large "women's vote" for Hylan, in the first election in which they were allowed to cast ballots, Murphy added that the women were "a great moral force and their votes have shown it."

With a cynicism that remains repulsive eighty years later, Comptroller Craig said of the grieving and often sullen La Guardia, "The trouble is that he wanted to be mayor and the people gave him their answer. Now he is sore. He's the 'late lamented La Guardia.'"

When La Guardia eschewed serving the last two weeks of his aldermanic presidency and said he was leaving for a two-week vacation in Havana, Cuba, Mayor Hylan wrote him a note. Delivered on La Guardia's final day, it said, "I could not let this, your last day at City Hall, pass without writing you how sorry I am that you are leaving, and particularly that the people of this city are losing your services."

As politicians and newspaper editors were pronouncing Fiorello H. La Guardia dead in politics, Hylan wrote, "There is no gift of the people that is too good for you."

In the gloomy aftermath of so much death in the life of Fiorello La Guardia there came a flicker of hope that the people who found glee in the evident demise of "the Little Flower" were wrong. Their chortles that La Guardia had no political constituency were premature.

On March 16, 1922, over plates of spaghetti and between discussions of the glory that was Rome in a home that La Guardia called "Villa Thea," there was born the League of Italian American Republican Clubs.

With astonishing speed, scion groups blossomed in the Italian neighborhoods like the flowers in Central Park. To mark each birth there appeared to speak to the members the first Italian American to serve in Congress, the only Italian American to be the "number two" official in City Hall, the Italian American hero of the Army Air Service in the motherland, the Italian American who'd once called King Victor Emmanuel III "Manny" and told him the days of kings were numbered—a voice not only for themselves, but all with a hyphenated identity.

When Fiorello La Guardia informed the clubs, and the general public, that he was thinking of running for governor that year as an independent Republican, the GOP bosses rushed to see him with "a better idea." If he did not run for governor, they pledged, they'd be happy to back him in a bid to return to Congress. But not for his old seat from the Fourteenth C.D. What they had in mind was the GOP stronghold of La Guardia's friend and ally Congressman Siegel, who was retiring. Why not run in an area where he'd be certain of victory, they asked, on the Upper East Side, in the richly Italian American Twentieth Congressional District?

La Guardia said "Yes."

BUT. Only if he did not have to stand on the Republican state platform. Only if he could publish his own platform. Only if they left him to his own devices.

If the potentates did not agree, he would challenge their anointed gubernatorial choice in a primary, which La Guardia might win, but if not, in losing he would certainly doom their man in November.

The bosses agreed. On August 30 he accepted the party's nomination in the Twentieth C.D. It ran from Central Park to the East River, from 99th to 120th Streets. He was again a candidate in a city whose geography was described in an enduringly popular 1890s song called "The Sidewalks of New York," but more widely known as "East Side, West Side."

What would the people of "East Harlem" think of this "downtowner" who now had a house in the Bronx invading their territory? One answer came immediately from Tammany's choice in the race. A Jewish lawyer named Henry Frank, he cried, "Carpetbagger!"

Frank immediately launched a campaign to discredit La Guardia among Jewish voters. Mass-mailed postcards warned, "Beware how you vote." It labeled La Guardia "the Italian" and a "pronounced anti-Semite and Jew-hater."

La Guardia's response was a widely handed-out broadside "Open Letter to Frank" that was printed in Yiddish. Accusing Frank of resorting to "the kind of campaigning which was discredited in American politics over twenty years ago," it continued, "You, your captains, and your canvassers are making a strong, racial-religious appeal for sympathy votes, based entirely upon religion. I regret exceedingly that this has happened. However, I have always met a fight on any issue openly. I will take combat wherever it is offered me."

Knowing that Frank did not speak Yiddish, La Guardia said, "I hereby challenge you to publicly and openly debate the issues of the campaign, THE DEBATE TO BE CONDUCTED BY YOU AND ME *ENTIRELY IN THE YIDDISH LANGUAGE.*"

The debate subject was to be, "Who Is Best Qualified to Represent All the People of the Twentieth Congressional District?"

Frank's reply was a letter to La Guardia, also published, stating that because of Major La Guardia's "well-known anti-Semitic tendencies," the challenge to debate in Yiddish "is an insult and an affront to the Jewish electives in our community."

Frank predicted "the day when the people send you back, bag and baggage, to your little cottage and sun-parlor on University Avenue in the Bronx."

Bristling from the "sun-parlor" snipe, La Guardia retorted that Frank was expecting to be elected simply because he was a Jew. Was Frank running for Congress, he asked, or "looking for a job as a *schamas*?" (Yiddish for a caretaker in a synagogue).

"From that point on," cracked a political wag, "things really got personal."

As La Guardia continued to press Frank to debate, his opponent's press spokesman said that Frank was not feeling well. Frank was a man of fragile health, but La Guardia snapped, "His is a diplomatic illness."

The day before election, sensing the tide running against him, Frank announced that he'd gotten a letter from the "Black Hand," forerunner of the Mafia. He said it warned him to quit the race, implying bad things would happen to him if he did not.

Only Frank backers believed it. Italian American voters took it as a slur.

When La Guardia squeaked out a victory by 254 votes, Frank charged that bands of La Guardia's supporters intimidated the poll inspectors.

In one instance, Frank declared, "one of our watchers was threatened with bodily harm by Mr. La Guardia himself."

Fiorello had a one-word reply: "Silly."

Frank filed an official challenge to the outcome and demanded a recount.

La Guardia made plans to return to Congress.

⊘⟋⟍

"I am a Republican," he had declared at the start of the campaign, "but I am not running on the Republican platform. I stand for the Republicanism of Abraham Lincoln, and let me tell you now that the average Republican leader east of the Mississippi doesn't know any more about Abraham Lincoln than Henry Ford (notorious for his anti-Semitism) knows about the Talmud. I may as well tell you now, for it wouldn't be fair to put it off until after I am elected, that I don't fit in at all with the average so-called Republican in the East. I am a progressive. I want to work with such men as Senator [William E.] Borah, Senator [Hiram] Johnson, and Senator [Robert] La Follette." This meant that he stood for a federal minimum-wage law, old-age pensions, restricting child labor, national maternity legislation, direct primaries, equal opportunity on the job for women, and modifying the Volstead Act to legalize light wines and beers. He was also for a soldiers' bonus, good roads, decent pay for federal employees, development of water power, and sale of electricity at cost.

What the representative-elect from New York's Twentieth C.D. believed was spelled out to a conclave of congressional progressives at the U.S. Capitol. He decried "powers that have heretofore controlled the government." He proposed, "Let's clean out both parties so that the American people may be voting *for* decent government, instead of against it."

On December 11 he spoke at New York's International Synagogue and took aim at the state GOP: "We have witnessed in our state, in the past two years, a wicked and heartless government, controlled by the connivance of the privileged few, for their benefit, disregarding the rights of the many and the comfort and happiness of the population of the entire state."

He titled the speech "The Awakening of the Progressive Spirit in This Country."

Four months later in Erasmus Hall in Flushing, Queens, he publicly declared that he was no longer a "regular" party man. The address defined who he had been, who he was, and who he would be in the future. He said:

> There comes a time in the life of every public official, when he must decide between right and irregularity. Of late such times have come to public officials at shorter intervals and with unusual frequency. At times it seems difficult to oppose your own political family and take issue with close political friends. In the long run, however, even in politics, right conquers, and we have seen in the last fifteen years, strong and powerful political machines entirely beaten, destroyed, and put out of commission.
>
> In 1921, I was confronted with just such a situation. I had to decide whether I would be faithful and true to my oath of office as a city official elected by the entire city, and take a stand according to what I believed was for the best interests of the city—the protection of its resources and property and the welfare of the six million people residing in New York—or whether I would line up with the individuals then in absolute control of the party, submit to the will of my governor; be a "good fellow," as it were, and not cause any trouble or "agitate," but just go along with the crowd and be a "regular guy."
>
> I made my choice.

9

The election of a "progressive" in the Twentieth C.D. was a close thing. The recounting of the votes reduced the La Guardia margin, first to 168 and finally to 11. It mattered not to the winner. He saw the cause of progressivism in the ascendency. He wrote to its recognized leader, Senator La Follette, "I am quite convinced that there will be a rush to get on the Progressive bandwagon at the next session of Congress."

In the meantime, there was plenty for La Guardia to do at home. The veteran of the labor movement joined in organizing a Harlem "meat strike" to force reduction of the price of meat from fifteen to ten cents a pound. The protest quickly went citywide. Next, he encouraged and spoke to meetings, including a mass demonstration in the great hall of City College, for lower rents in tenements. Governor Al Smith asked "the major" to assist a legislative Housing Commission during hearings on the dismal living conditions in slum areas.

Thirty years earlier, newspaperman Jacob Riis had taken a camera into slums and published *How the Other Half Lives*. The book had shocked the city and the nation and had sparked Theodore Roosevelt to join the cause of housing reform. But after three decades, the Housing Committee found that little had changed. Families of eight and nine were living in two-room flats, and in some cases, in cellars and coal bins. La Guardia personally collared every candidate for the legislature in the 1923 elections and extracted promises of votes for housing reform.

On January 18, 1923, he sponsored a meeting at Town Hall in the cause of disabled war veterans whose cases had become bogged down in the bureaucracy of the new federal Veterans' Bureau. He dictated to Marie Fisher a letter to its chief: "So, after much heralding and publicity about systemizing the work of the bureau, we find it has so been so scientifically systematized as not to be able to find a veteran's papers! It's a damn shame."

On February 24 Marie took down a letter to Congressman Frank W. Mondell, the GOP floor leader in the House, on the topic of immigration statistics. The son of an Italian and a Jew, and former immigration official on both sides of the Atlantic, found the numbers "artificial and arbitrary, and solely for the purposes of excluding Italian and Jewish immigrants."

Before going to the capital to take his seat he headed a committee to raise funds for relief of sufferers from a fire at the Ward's Island hospital on February 18. In the Capitol on March 12 he named his secretarial staff: Mr. Patsy Bruno, Robert Levy, and, of course, Marie Fisher. In a newspaper story on the appointments, the reporter noted that in working for La Guardia during two terms as the congressman in the Fourteenth C.D., the aldermanic presidency, and several election campaigns, she earned a reputation as a "practical politician" with "a host of friends among the leaders throughout the city." The item also noted, "She is known to be more progressive than the major himself."

The president of the United States was a Republican, Warren G. Harding. Except for the official party label, he had nothing in common with "the gentleman from New York" who now represented its Twentieth Congressional District. La Guardia hoped to keep a check on Harding from a seat on the House Judiciary Committee. Any chance of that happening went out the window on the first day of the Sixty-eighth Congress's session. He declared that he would introduce Senator Borah's bill to let only seven of the nine justices of the U.S. Supreme Court concur to strike down an Act of Congress as unconstitutional.

He asserted that the Constitution "today must necessarily be construed in the light of new conditions and the advanced age we are living in."

The Judiciary seat went to someone else. Aligning himself with the Progressives did not help. The majority leader of the House, Nicholas Longworth, refused to recognize the twenty-three House "liberals" as a group. They retaliated by holding up election of a Speaker. Longworth was forced to negotiate with a committee of the rebels, including La Guardia. The result was a compromise in which the old House rules would expire after thirty days and be replaced by more liberal regulations.

But nothing concerning La Guardia's activities in the House drew more attention than the day he took the floor to denounce automobile manufacturer and American popular icon Henry Ford for an anti-Semitism that had helped to foster a rebirth of the Ku Klux Klan, to which some members of Congress belonged. "The wealth and ignorance of Henry Ford combined," he said, "has made it possible for vicious men to carry on a nefarious warfare against the Jews, not only of America but of the whole world. . . . Henry Ford has done more, owing to his bigoted hatred, to create strife in this country than any other man in the United States."

To a House colleague who in a debate on immigration spoke of his pride that he had ancestors who came to America on the *Mayflower,* the former consular official at Fiume replied, "I hope you can understand *my* pride when I say the distinguished navigator of the race of my ancestors came to this continent two hundred years before yours landed at Plymouth Rock. For every year by which your ancestors preceded mine to this country, mine can boast an additional century of civilization."

No issue provoked as much colorful oratory from the five-foot-two, unruly black-haired, chubby, arm-waving, squeaky-voiced champion of a Progressive agenda than the immigration legislation that he saw as anti-Italian and anti-Jew. Standing in the well of the House on April 8, 1924, he asked, "Where will you find the average Jewish immigrant?" His answer was:

> You will find him in the shop. You will find him back of the pushcart. You will find him doing the most laborious work from the moment he lands until he is laid away. What is he doing it for? He is doing it because he has come here with one great purpose, and that is to give his children the opportunity which was denied him and to his ancestors for centuries.
>
> His children know no other land, and allegiance to no other flag—love no other country but the United States. The children of the Jewish immigrant will have an opportunity of an education, will take their places in the community. And in every city in which the Jewish immigrants have settled, I will show you development, business industry, as the result of their labor, determination, and efforts.

And of the Italian immigrant, "Where do you find him?"

> You soon find him with the pick and shovel, building our railroads, digging our canals, boring our subways, or in the depths of our mines. He saves his money, you say? Yes, saves money so that he may send it to the other side to bring over his wife and babies.
>
> Then he establishes his little home. You show me the house of an Italian laborer, no matter how humble, and I will show you every inch of the ground of his backyard cultivated as a garden. I will show you every place where there is space enough—a beautiful flower. Come to our schools in New York and you will see hundreds of thousands of little black-headed sons of Rome, poring over their ABCs in the grade schools. In the high schools, preparing thsemelves for the duties and responsibilities of American citizenship.

La Guardia could have told the House about just such a youth whom La Guardia had met while making a speech to the student body of De Witt Clinton High School. One of the students who preceded him on the podium was Vito Marcantonio. He'd surprised La Guardia by talking about old-age pensions and Social Security. His goal was to be a lawyer.

Fiorello had advised the handsome teenager to "cut out your evening appointments, your dances, your midnight philosophers for the next five years and devote yourself to the study of the law. Be careful of your personal appearance. Get a Gillette razor and keep yourself well groomed at all times. Be always respectful and courteous to all, the humble as well as the high and for goodness' sake keep your ears and eyes open and keep your mouth closed for at least the next twenty years."

It was not the poetry of Shakespeare's Polonius giving advice to Laertes in *Hamlet,* but Vito took it to heart. When the Republican machine set up shop in East Harlem after La Guardia had shown the district was not in Tammany Hall's pocket, Marcantonio countered the GOP by organizing a "La Guardia machine" and working in La Guardia's congressional office in the area to assist constituents.

Much would be heard of Vito Marcantonio when his early mentor presided at City Hall as mayor, including Marcantonio being arrested personally by Police Commissioner Lewis J. Valentine during a Marcantonio-led unruly protest against the way in which President Franklin Roosevelt's New Deal Works Progress Administration (WPA) was being run in New York. Young Vito had learned about demonstrating from a master. La Guardia had initiated him to picketing. The protégé would eventually be elected to Mayor La Guardia's former seat in the House.

Meanwhile, as the most famous Italian American in the country, La Guardia found himself recruited in the cause of two Italians whose names became as notorious in the 1920s as that of Al "Scarface" Capone. On June 10, 1923, he was retained as the counsel for a committee organized to spare the lives of a pair of "anarchist" immigrants who had been convicted of a holdup-murder in South Braintree, Massachusetts, on April 15, 1920. As the case of Nicola Sacco and Bartolomeo Vanzetti went through the appeals process, a movement materialized to protest the trial for being unfair and to gain their release. Among the critics of how the case had been handled were the famed wits of the Algonquin Round Table Robert Benchley, Dorothy Parker, and Heywood Broun, along with writers John Dos Passos and Edna St. Vincent Millay. La Guardia prepared an appeal brief that was to be argued before trial judge Webster Thayer. La Guardia and the Sacco-Vanzetti Committee did their best, but to no avail. Thayer imposed the death sentence. It was carried out on August 23, 1927.

La Guardia was never certain that Sacco and Vanzetti were not involved in the robbery and murder, but he believed they'd not gotten a fair shake in court. He thought the pair were "demented" in their anarchist views. Regretting that the affair contributed to the anti-Italian sentiments against which he was fighting, he tried to shift the public's focus toward exemplary Italian Americans, from Caruso to Tony Lazzeri of the New York Yankees.

In standing up for Italians, he did not overlook the concerns of constituents with ties to Ireland. When the British imprisoned Irish president Eamon De Valera without specific charge, the representative from East Harlem rose in the House to introduce a resolution to express the sentiment of Congress that his "continued imprisonment, without a trial, is against the morality, customs, and policy of liberty-loving people."

Told by another member that what happened between England and one citizen of the United Kingdom in Ireland was not the business of Congress, La Guardia pointed out that De Valera had been born in New York State, his mother "is a resident of Rochester," and that De Valera's "gallantry, courage, and noble purposes in fighting for the freedom of the people of Ireland, is a guarantee that he never took an oath of allegiance to the king of England."

The resolution was voted down. Letters of gratitude and praise from Irish Americans all over the United States flooded into an office that was, by all accounts, the most untidy place in the nation's capital. Only Marie Fisher was able to periodically restore order. Biographer Lowell Limpus quoted La Guardia on the subject: "The only efficient secretary I ever saw."

Files were opened and rapidly expanded. Every piece of correspondence had to be kept. Card indexes ranged from turning Governor's Island in New York Harbor into an airport, a drug control program of the League of Nations, grounds for impeaching several federal judges, all the pending legislation, information deemed potentially useful in floor debates, and interpretation of the teachings of Christ, to the proper way to cook macaroni.

When Limpus inquired about the Jesus file being the only one on religion, La Guardia said that it was strictly for reference. "Free Masonry is my religion," he said. "A man who could live up to the teachings of the Order would do no other." (He had become a Mason in 1912.)

Dutifully filed in one of Marie's neat cabinets was the text of a "Resolution for the Outlawry of War," introduced on May 17, 1924, along with a copy of a letter on the subject to the editor of the *Christian Science Monitor*, commending the newspaper for having "done more intelligent and constructive work for the cause of peace than all other forces of the country put together."

Data also accumulated on the subject of radio, then reaching more and more people as makers of phonographs, such as the RCA Victor company, promoted sales of players and the records to put on them. While a music lover, La Guardia was more interested in the potential of radio for getting out his ideas on good government.

Radio would be a staple of governance and a means of garnering public support in all the years of the Fiorello La Guardia mayoralty, and emulated by mayors who succeeded him, even in the era of television.

The issues dearest to Representative La Guardia in the Sixty-eighth Congress were the righteous causes of pacifism and abolition of the "great experiment," and total failure, in his opinion, of the Eighteenth Amendment and its implementing Volstead Act.

The 100 percent proof that banning John Barleycorn had "come a cropper," as La Guardia's "dry" allies from the West would put it, was to be found everywhere, including the language of the average American. To give the lie to the Prohibitionists' dream of an abstemious nation one need only utter the terms "bathtub gin," "hooch," "cocktail," "high ball," "blotto," "rum runner," "bootlegging," and "speakeasy."

Seven years after the ratification of the Prohibition amendment, to demonstrate the law's absurdity, La Guardia invited reporters into Room 500 in the House Office Building to observe him mix and drink an illegal brew. The libation was a combination of two legal liquids, malt extract and near beer. Stirring them together created an outlawed level of alcohol. His stunt was dismissed by "drys" as a farce because congressional immunity prevented him from being put under arrest. He promptly went back to New York to announce that at nine in the morning of June 17, 1926, he would be found in Kaufman's Drug Store, at 95 Lenox Avenue, mixing the same ingredients, quaffing the result, and waiting to be arrested. Newspaper reporters flocked to the show, but not cops to haul him to jail. As a result of the publicity, it was said, sales of the malt extract and near beer skyrocketed. A New York editor shot off a wire:

YOUR BEER A SENSATION. WHOLE STAFF TRYING EXPERI-MENTATION. REMARKABLE RESULTS

Acknowledged leader of the "wets" on Capitol Hill and hero to imbibers everywhere, he asserted that Prohibition would work only "when Congress by an act or by law will be able to stop fermentation, or to repeal the law of gravity." Upon ratification of the Eighteenth Amendment he had predicted that there were not enough policemen in the entire country to prevent anyone who wanted a distilled or fermented drink from having one, or two, or three. To enforce the law in New York alone, he said, "it will require a police

Prohibition
Congressman
La Guardia daring
arrest while mixing
malt extract and
near beer to make
an illegal drink in
New York City
drugstore in 1926.

force of 250,000 men and a force of 250,000 to police the police."

He backed up this allusion to the corruption that would flow from outlawing drink by noting that federal agents were selling liquor in Norfolk, Virginia; Elizabeth City, North Carolina; and in a speakeasy masquerading as the "Bridge-Whist Card Club" at 14 East Forty-fourth Street in the heart of Manhattan.

All this was an amusing way to make a point, but La Guardia hastened to remind Americans that there were sinister effects of the easy-to-scoff-at-and-blithely-defy law. Because of the flouting of an unwise prohibition of alcoholic beverages, "The importation of liquor into this country is of such magnitude, it comes in such enormous quantities, involving the use of steamers, involving enormous banking operations, involving hundreds of millions of dollars, that it could not carry on without the knowledge if not the contrivance of the authorities entrusted with the enforcement of the law."

He painted a picture of a murderous police officer who spends half of his time hijacking and the other half of his time enforcing the Prohibition law. "Politicians are ducking," he said in disgust, "candidates are hedging, the Anti-Saloon League is prospering. People are being poisoned, bootleggers are being enriched, and government officials are being corrupted."

All this was true.

"Prohibition," wisecracked humorist Will Rogers, "is better than no liquor at all."

And so La Guardia's protestations beat on like the boats in F. Scott Fitzgerald's last line in his 1925 novel about a bootlegger, *The Great Gatsby,* "against the current."

※

The Roaring Twenties. Fitzgerald was the self-appointed literary chronicler of "an age of miracles." Of art. And satire.

In many ways Fiorello La Guardia was out of step with the times. Two titles appended themselves to his name. He found himself "America's congressman at large" and "America's most liberal congressman." In a burst of literary aspiration he wrote a short story titled "Tony Goes to Congress." The hero was "Tony Scarbucco," himself not so thinly disguised. But he did not take it beyond a second draft. Instead, he directed his fondness for writing to starting up an Italian American magazine, *Americola.* To finance it he took another mortgage on his house on University Avenue. He was publisher, editor, staff, and chief contributor. Finding hardly any subscribers and no advertisers, he quickly folded it, then sold the house in the Bronx and moved into an apartment at 109th Street and Lenox Avenue. Now nobody could ever again accuse him of being a carpetbagger. Or so he thought.

By then the United States had a new president.

Warren G. Harding's vice president, Calvin Coolidge, had been catapulted into the White House on August 2, 1923, following Harding's unexpected death in San Francisco during what Harding had termed "a voyage of understanding" through the West, including Alaska. The cause was attributed to food poisoning from improperly chilled crabs. Some people suspected that he had committed suicide to escape the shame and ignominy of corruption disclosures that involved his friends and cronies. The worst was a nefarious deal involving federal oil reserves that became known as the Teapot Dome scandal.

Coolidge declared "The business of America is business," and business generally went on as before. Soon everyone was joyfully talking about "Coolidge prosperity." Few Americans paid much attention to the activities of their "most liberal" congressman, except to find him an amusing figure from New York City, where, almost everybody conceded, he would easily win reelection in 1924. There was a frisson of speculation that La Guardia would be on the ticket of the Progressive Party for vice president, but it passed. The pending question in the summer of 1924 was whether the New York Republicans would choose Fiorello as their candidate in the Twentieth C.D., or "read him out of the party" in favor of a "regular."

At the Star Casino in Harlem on June 15, 1924, he made his "annual report to his constituents." The man whom biographer Lowell Limpus was fond of calling a "stormy petrel" took on the "irregular" question in typical La Guardia fashion. He told the crowd of La Guardia enthusiasts, "As to my choice between loyalty to my party and loyalty to my country, I am loyal to my country first."

When the approving tumult subsided, he continued:

If a man does that which he knows is not right, he loses his soul; but if by doing right, he becomes "irregular" and loses a nomination, he really has not lost much.

This is 1924. The world is progressing. Times are changing.

What *is* "party regularity"? It is never urged until a party asks an individual to do something he believes is wrong.

I would rather be right than regular!

On August 10, 1924, La Guardia "burned his bridges" to the Republicans by endorsing Senator Robert La Follette for president and announcing that he would run for reelection on a new "Third Party ticket." Part of his statement given to the press read:

> The new party is here—and here to stay! The forces now united under the emblem of the Liberty Bell, and known as the Progressive Party, though they may differ in theory, have one great common object—which is the economic reformation of this Republic.
>
> Some of us have been laboring within the old parties, hoping we could reform them, or at least gain sufficient strength in either of them, to make it the party of the *people*—the party of workers and producers. It was a long, hard, tedious, discouraging fight.

The next day he received a letter from Norman Thomas, leader of the Socialist Party and its candidate for governor of New York. Thomas welcomed La Guardia's statement of the night before and hoped that La Guardia would one day become part of "a new Labor Party."

La Guardia replied, "I only did what was right. I do hope we can get together real soon for a talk!"

The Star Casino speech and Thomas's embrace were too much for the GOP. The party backed La Guardia's Twentieth C.D. predecessor, Isaac Siegel. The Democrats went again with Henry Frank. The La Guardia forces opened headquarters in a vacant store at 108th and Madison. It was run by Marie Fisher. The Progressive presidential standard-bearer, La Follette, expressed a hope that La Guardia would be able to make speeches for the party outside of New York; but the most liberal congressman in America found himself fighting for his political life.

It was Senator La Follette who had to leap in to speak for La Guardia. He told a crowd in Madison Square Garden on September 18, "There is not a better legislator, nor a more progressive one than La Guardia, in the whole country. It is an honor to commend him to you. Do all you can to send

La Guardia back to Congress. Not only the people of New York, but the people of the country, need him there."

Attacks came from all flanks. Frank renewed the carpet-bagger charge. Republicans said La Guardia was a turncoat who "crawled in at one end of the political tent, and came out at the other end a La Follette man. He has had his finger in every pie and party." In the Ku Klux Klan publication *Fellowship* he was a "member of the Sons of Italy" boasting of "his friendship for the Jewish immigrant." The article went on, "He seems to think more of keeping the bars down for the Jews and Italians, than to keep America for Americans."

Enter: Vito Marcantonio. Enlisting eight hundred other young Italians from the tenements of both Little Italys, he made them swear their allegiance to La Guardia. He even came up with a name for the group: the Ghibonnes. Roughly translated from Italian, it meant "swashbucklers." In short order there were eighteen hundred of them, and not only laborers from the tenements but also war veterans, fresh college graduates, young lawyers, and other professionals.

A pair of songwriting La Guardia stalwarts wrote a campaign ditty:

Fiorello H. La Guardia,
   We're with you—
   And we'll be with you to the end.

Fiorello H. La Guardia,
   Harlem needs a man like you in Congress:
   You voted for the Soldiers' bonus,
   Helped the Immigrants,
   And fought in Congress for us!

Fiorello H. La Guardia,
   With a record like yours,
   Harlem needs you!

The Ghibonnes would be part of every La Guardia campaign thereafter.

But the Irish and the Jews were not forgotten, nor sitting on the sidelines. One day Marie Fisher gleefully handed reporters copies of a telegram from one of the most popular

Irishmen in the country. Sent from Maine, it expressed the sender's regret at not being able to attend a La Guardia rally that night:

> WILL GET TOGETHER WITH YOU WHEN RETURN. BEST WISHES FOR A BIG VICTORY. (SIGNED) GENE TUNNEY

Jewish voters would not forget La Guardia because of an event in early October at New York County Supreme Court. Having heard that Charles Lipschitz, of 8 East 108th Street, had not been allowed to register to vote because he produced no proof of citizenship, La Guardia stormed into court demanding a show-cause order to compel the election board to reconvene.

"Mr. Charles Lipschitz is an American citizen," La Guardia fumed, "and has been living at the same address for over five years, and on four previous occasions has voted from that address. He happens to be a Progressive, and the board refused to enroll him because he did not have his citizenship papers with him. The law explicitly provides that a citizen who has previously voted need not exhibit his citizenship papers."

Lipschitz was allowed to register and vote. On election day, presumably, his was added to the 10,756 cast for La Guardia. Frank was second with 7,141. Siegel got 7,099.

Nationally, La Guardia was the "sole monument to the Progressive cause in the East." La Follette carried only his home state of Wisconsin. Republicans saw Calvin Coolidge elected as president in his own right in a landslide. No one saw why the good times should not go on.

Among the congratulatory letters received at La Guardia headquarters was one from his brother Richard. Married with children and acting principal of the School of Letters in the New Jersey State Prison at Trenton, he wrote:

> Dear Brother:
>
> Mary and the children join me in extending to you our most sincere congratulations on your victorious result. While none of us are personally in favor of the party to which you are now a member of, we realize, however, the special handicap you had in succeeding as well as you did.

Among the sons of Achille and Irene La Guardia, Fiorello was not the only one who followed his own conscience.

When Fiorello La Guardia filed a financial statement for the campaign, it showed that he'd spent $3,828.98, of which $3,764.25 came in contributions of $5.00 and $10.00. The rest had been given by the Amalgamated Clothing Workers of America.

Still a fighter for decent wages for workers, Congressman La Guardia returned to the House to introduce a bill for the relief of "wage slaves" of organized baseball, and a requirement that baseball clubs that "sold" players to other teams be taxed 90 percent of the proceeds.

He also proposed a measure to ban political contributions from out-of-state donors.

And not forgetting his battles with City Comptroller Craig, he tried to have the office made a nonelected post.

All these proposals died on the legislative vines.

Returning to the issue of Prohibition, he demanded larger appropriations to enforce the law. It was a doomed measure, he knew, but he reveled in embarrassing drys while offering them "every chance to attempt to enforce this impossible law." When seized liquor was given back to a rich violator of the law in New York City, La Guardia sought a House resolution requiring the secretary of the Treasury to submit an explanation.

He told the House, "I want to determine whether there is to be one sort of enforcement for the rich and another for the poor, and whether it is necessary for an agent to carry a *Social Register* along with the statutes of the United States in enforcing the law."

Such statements were avidly jotted down in the notebooks of congressional reporters in the House press gallery and sent to newspapers across the country by wire associations teletypes. That the representative of New York's Twentieth C.D. was famous nationally was evidenced by the tourists who asked Capitol guides to point out "Congressman La Guardia." If they were lucky, he was the on House floor—a short, stout figure with black hair (a few strands of gray were noticeable up close) moving restlessly, listening intently, and usually munching peanuts.

La Guardia was among the best-known members of the House, and possibly *the* most. In preparing to write a biographical book on him that was published in 1937, author Jay Franklin and researcher Joseph C. Bailey tabulated La Guardia stories in the *Times* during seven years in the House. They found that he "rose steadily," from only 25 mentions in 1922 to 54 in 1924, 60 in 1926, and 150 in 1928. In a chapter titled "The Making of a Progressive," Franklin divided the La Guardia congressional years into three "episodes." They were his emergence as a national gadfly with progressive tendencies during the period 1923–1929; his campaign against Jimmy Walker for the mayorship of New York in 1929; and his vindication as a political prophet in the years that followed the stock market crash.

Many observers came to look on La Guardia as an "act" and his political career nothing but "showmanship." Biographer Lowell Limpus chose to describe him "winning a reputation by his brilliance in debate" in the House. His fame was a combination of both.

On the floor of the House, in press interviews, and in regular "radio talks" on station WRNY he presented his opinions on a dazzling array of topics, from Prohibition (a frequent subject) to assailing the use of American troops in China and Nicaragua, federal control of electric power, an overreaching federal judiciary, autonomy for Puerto Rico, and an end to federal injunctions in labor disputes.

The latter interest would result in La Guardia joining forces with Senator George W. Norris of Nebraska to pass the Norris–La Guardia Act (1932). The law outlawed the "yellow dog contract" by which employers kept workers from joining outside labor unions, put restrictions on antilabor injunctions, and guaranteed jury trials in cases where it was charged a contempt of court had been committed outside the courtroom.

La Guardia self-promotion would extend to writing a column for the *New York Daily Graphic* titled "I'm Telling You

Confidentially." In it he issued a "manifesto" urging the reduction of gas and electricity rates, water conservation, better liability laws, old-age pensions, state parks, government involvement in eradicating preventable diseases, and a demand that judges stop interpreting statutes and "take the law as Congress passes it."

A frequent target in all La Guardia forums was Secretary of the Treasury Andrew Mellon. La Guardia said Mellon was not as good a financial administrator as "the average New York housewife."

When Mayor James J. Walker backed construction of a posh restaurant in Central Park (the Central Park Casino), La Guardia rose in high dudgeon to declare, "Just think of a public park, paid for and supported by the people and maintained for their use and comfort, being transformed into a *giradino* of a high-priced exclusive rendezvous for the frivolous."

Astute analysts of city politics and reports on the government beat eagerly anticipated a day, presumably not long in the offing, when the town would witness a grand electoral fistfight between the "Little Flower" and the dapper, debonair, mayor-about-town, blithely-wisecracking Broadway first-nighter affectionately dubbed "Gentleman Jimmy," and known by the types who would patronize the Central Park Casino as "Beau James."

Had F. Scott Fitzgerald's 1925 bootlegger, the Great Gatsby, been real, he could well have run across Assemblyman James J. Walker in any number of Manhattan speakeasies. Fitzgerald's description of Jay Gatsby fit Walker like a glove. He wrote that if "personality is an unbroken series of successful gestures, then there was something gorgeous about him."

A year and a half older than La Guardia, James John Walker was the second son of an Irish immigrant, William Walker, who became a successful builder and lumberyard owner. Jimmy's mother's father was a saloonkeeper. In 1886

William settled his family in a house on St. Luke's Place, the best neighborhood in Greenwich Village, then went into politics. Elected alderman for the North Ward, he served four terms and graduated to state assemblyman. Meanwhile, his second son picked up a schoolyard nickname, "Jimmy Talker." Destiny, it seemed, had marked James for the law and following his father's footsteps into politics.

But Jimmy had set his heart on being a songwriter. In that endeavor he produced one success in 1905, "Will You Love Me in December as You Did in May?" Its music was by one of the country's most famous popular composers, Ernest R. Ball, who gave Irish Americans three enduring valentines to Erin in "Mother Machree" (1910), "A Little Bit of Heaven" (1914), and the biggest of all in 1913, "When Irish Eyes Are Smiling."

Ironically, the question posed in the title and lyrics of Walker's only hit song would be on the mind of Gentleman Jim in the election year of 1933, when he found himself the smiling but battered symbol of modern New York's worst political scandal.

Until then Jimmy would warm the hearts of the average New Yorker, in the words of Robert Moses, as "the extrovert, the spontaneous eccentric, the sidewalk favorite, the beloved clown." After the music stopped and the party was over, Moses continued, "Jimmy had a curious, almost winsome humility. Perhaps his significance lies in being what all sophisticated, urban, frivolous folk admired in the jazz age."

No starker contrast existed between a pair of New York politicians in the 1920s than in Beau James, with all his Irish blarney, and the Little Flower, with all the Italian explosive heat that prompted one La Guardia critic to liken him to the volcano Stromboli.

＊

One place Jimmy Walker would never be found was the bottom of a coal mine. But in 1925 it's where La Guardia went, guided by John L. Lewis, president of the striking miners' union. After seeing the working conditions, Fiorello emerged blackened with coal dust and vowed, "Asbestos will not hold the statements I shall make on the floor of the House."

Neither would one expect Walker to climb into a U.S. Navy submarine to observe the rescue operations for the sunken sub *S-4,* sent to the bottom after a collision with a ship and then mired in the mud of the seabed with its doomed sailors signaling feebly for a rescue that proved impossible. La Guardia spent thirty-six hours in the sub *S-8.* When he was attacked in the House and press for exploiting a tragedy, he retorted, "If going to the spot and talking with the men who know their business [about submarines and their place in the fleet] was a wrong thing for a member to do, then I plead guilty." He went on to support a submarine fleet while calling for improved conditions at sea and ashore, and for government insurance for dependents of men "who lose their lives in the line of duty."

And New York mayor Walker was not heard in 1928 giving an assessment of the "Coolidge good times" and warning, "Whatever may be said about 'prosperity' today, and personally I believe that a great deal of that 'prosperity' is simply stock-ticker prosperity, the fact remains that we have considerable unemployment."

In his *New York Daily Graphic* column La Guardia scoffed at "financial giants" of Wall Street and offered his own "financial genius" in the persons of "Mrs. Marie Esposito, or Mrs. Rebecca Epstein, or Mrs. Maggie Flynn." They were "keeping house in a city tenement, raising six children on a weekly pay envelope containing $30, trying to send the children to school warmly clad and properly clad, paying exorbitant gas and electric bills, and endeavoring to provide meat at least once a day for a family."

"*That's* financial genius," he said, "of the highest order."

Succinctly reviewing the Fiorello La Guardia of the second half of the 1920s, biographer Thomas Kessner wrote, "The causes continued, fueled by a tireless energy and a bottomless indignation." He stood in "perpetual dissent against the prevailing sense of the majority, against the bluff, the live-for-today-and-hang-the future spirit."

The nation was still giddily parroting songster Richard Whiting's 1921 jazzy musical query "Ain't We Got Fun?"

In an introduction to a collection of the popular songs of the 1920s and 1930s Richard Rodgers, composer of scores for great Broadway musicals while La Guardia was mayor, and long after La Guardia's death, recalled that the Twenties "sang of carefree nights and the frenetic days that rushed headlong into the nightmare and fantasy of the Thirties." But hardly anyone asking "Ain't we got fun?" as La Guardia's ranting in Congress made him into a "star" to be ogled by Capitol Hill tourists foresaw that only a few years later millions of Americans would feel right in tune with the 1932 pop song "Brother, Can You Spare a Dime?"

Predicting for himself the doom of living "in a hopeless minority for most of my legislative days," Fiorello La Guardia could only lament that there was no party division in Congress "on matters involving more than a million dollars." The Republican Party, he said, was the "kept woman of big business."

When President Calvin Coolidge handed out a slip of paper to the press in 1928 that said he did not "choose to run" for reelection, Republicans and a majority of voters did not miss a beat in their dance of prosperous contentment in electing Republican Herbert Clark Hoover, who immediately announced business as usual.

"We in America," said Hoover as he campaigned against the Democrat Al Smith in 1928, "are nearer the final triumph over poverty than ever before in the history of any land."

Given a chance to "go forward with the policies of the last eight years," he said, "we shall with the help of God be in sight of the day when poverty will be banished from the nation."

Al Smith had been given the title "the happy warrior" by New York's governor Franklin D. Roosevelt. But La Guardia knew that in 1928 an Irish Roman Catholic from the Lower East Side of New York stood no chance of winning.

Running that year as a Republican, with the party's grudging endorsement and personal reservations about doing so, La Guardia was reelected by twelve hundred votes. "Desirous as I am of cooperating with you," he wrote to Sam Koenig, "I must reserve the right to carry on the fight." Koenig wrote back that La Guardia took everything too seriously.

Happy to have him returned to the House, the press gallery voted him "the most effective, interesting, and picturesque member." The editor of *The Nation* magazine, Oswald Garrison Villard, opined that La Guardia was the most valuable member of the entire Congress, as well as "the most fearless, the most truth-telling."

Fiorello groused to congressional observer Ray Tucker, "It's damned discouraging trying to be a reformer in the wealthiest land in the world."

"In the morning, in the evening," happy and content Americans everywhere, it seemed, were singing, "ain't we got fun?"

Part of that fun for followers of the activities of Congress was waiting to see what La Guardia might do next. On Thursday, February 28, 1929, the House press corps gathered in the gallery in hopeful expectation of fireworks. The legislative day dragged on, with routine business interrupted here and there by La Guardia, but nothing worth devoting newsprint to. He seemed a trifle cranky about a conference report on naval appropriations. When the House took up a Senate bill to impose five years in prison and a $10,000 fine for possession of intoxicating liquor (it was known as the 5 and 10 bill), La Guardia got a laugh. He warned that if he managed to get the floor, he would send forth his "best guns and heavy artillery." The bill passed 284 to 90.

Early in the evening after a long session, Representative John J. Boylan of New York was recognized. "Mr. Speaker," he began, "I desire to make a very important announcement to the House, and with the permission of the Speaker I will make it." Ears perked up and all eyes in the House fixed on Boylan. "And that is that our distinguished colleague from New York, Representative La Guardia, was married today." A burst of applause cut him off. When it subsided, he added, "I move, sir, that the felicitations of the House be extended to the happy couple."

Reporters joined in the applause, but most of them were noting that only Fiorello H. La Guardia would get married and then rush back to work in the House.

Seeking the bride, they looked toward the gallery reserved for guests of House members.

Beaming with pride and blushing a little from all the attention sat Marie Fisher.

10

How forty-seven-year-old Fiorello La Guardia decided he should marry thirty-three-year-old Marie Fisher after she had been his private secretary for fifteen years was explained in what is probably a fanciful account in Lowell Limpus and Burr Leyson's 1938 book *This Man La Guardia*. At the end of a long, busy day at the office La Guardia said to Marie, "Good Lord. I've kept you here until almost midnight. You go home right now."

He watched as she donned her coat and hat, Limpus wrote, "and suddenly he started as from a galvanic shock. Congressman La Guardia was really SEEING his secretary for the first time as woman rather than machine."

"Good night, Major," said Marie.

"Muh-REE!"

He ran after her in a panic.

"Yes, Major? What is it?"

"Marie, you're FIRED! I mean it. How can I court a girl that works for me?"

The scene may not have happened that way, but Limpus was correct in writing that La Guardia would not mix personal feelings with business. The more plausible scenario in which he asked Marie to be his wife was presented by biographer Thomas Kessner. La Guardia was not one to suddenly fall head over heels for a woman he'd known so long. He was comfortable with her and knew she was devoted to him. Marie had been hoping to be Mrs. La Guardia for a long time.

The wonder was that he hadn't recognized the situation and asked her to marry him sooner.

The honeymoon was put off until the end of the congressional session. They lived in a small apartment in Washington and in a tenement walk-up at 109th and Madison on weekends in New York. Thursday nights were reserved for themselves as "music nights," either listening to it on the radio and records, or going out to concerts. Marie's sister Elsie said of her new brother-in-law, "The only time he was really reserved and quiet was with music."

On Saturday evenings in New York friends and political allies came over for Italian food. "Hustling from stove to table, creating a hollandaise sauce and conducting a conversational crusade basting the stuffed capon and lambasting stuffed politicians," wrote a frequent guest, Ray Tucker of the *World Telegram,* "La Guardia directs and dominates with the artistry of a maestro, the tempo of good food, good cheer, good fellowship, and stimulating argument."

There was a lot going on in the nation's capital and New York to talk about in 1929. High on the list of topics was whether La Guardia should again toss his hat into the electoral ring and try to unseat Mayor Jimmy Walker. The potential candidate said he was not only ready, but that he was feeling so fit that he was ready to take on anyone, even heavyweight boxer Max Schmeling. But would the Republicans of New York want him in the ring against Walker as their candidate?

One GOP leader, Ogden Mills, who liked La Guardia's "capacity for indignation," saw him as "the only possible antidote to the smiling complacency and indifference" that prevailed in Jimmy Walker's New York. A nervous and hesitant party convention gave La Guardia its mayoral nomination, but the *New Yorker* noted that in choosing a "maverick" the "respectables of Republicanism then asked themselves whether this Italian-American Congressman was not even more of a clown."

The Progressives also had doubts about La Guardia, so rather than take a chance on him, they picked the unequivocal

Socialist who once invited La Guardia to help him organize a Labor Party, Norman Thomas. This assured a three-man race: Thomas the Socialist; La Guardia the reluctantly chosen Republican; and the Democrat/Tammany man and sitting mayor, James J. Walker, whom philanthropist August Hecksher had praised for "brilliant effort in the service of the City of New York."

More than a few people who read Hecksher's rhetorical bouquet in the papers did so with a rueful smile. Since becoming mayor, Walker had gone away on vacation 7 times for a total of 143 days. He never arrived for work before noon, and usually well past. After all, how could anyone expect him to get up early in the morning when he'd been out on the town all night? Slender as a reed and wearing clothes that he designed himself (and changed five times a day), he now was not only the "Jimmy Talker" of his school days but also the headline writers' "Jimmy the Jester," "Our Jazz Mayor," "Playboy of City Hall," "Beau James," and "Night Mayor of New York."

He was also the Jimmy-the-married-man with a girl on the side, and everyone knew it. Her name was Betty Compton. A showgirl. He'd spotted her in the musical *Oh, Kay!* And if his wife, Allie, knew about her and didn't seem to care that a man in his forties was squiring around a girl half his age, it was okay with the people Walker was supposed to be governing.

On the day that six hundred prominent citizens met to beg him to run for reelection, Walker asked, "Who could say no?"

Before too long, he would find himself in deep, hot political water because he proved to be a mayor who had rarely let "no" cross his lips.

By coincidence, on the very day that Walker let it be known that he would be running for a second term, the chubby, poorly tailored, often scruffy-looking, no one's-idea-of-a-dapper-man-about-town whose favorite words in the political dictionary were "no" and "wait a darn minute," faced down hesitant Republicans who thought Congresswoman Ruth Platt would be a better mayoral candidate. If that's whom the GOP wanted, La Guardia said, that would be fine with him.

But if they figured that he would run as an independent, guaranteeing a Republican loss, and then hold him responsible, they would have to think again.

"I am refusing to be the goat," he said. "You think that you will then blame it all on La Guardia. Well, you can't."

He'd take a vacation in Bermuda and sit out the entire election, then be back next year to run for governor while reminding defeated Republicans that they might have had him in City Hall . . . if he hadn't been refused the nomination.

It would be Platt or La Guardia, he said. "You choose."

They picked him.

The next day he opened campaign headquarters in the Cadillac Hotel at Forty-second Street and Broadway, but without Marie to run it. She was now Mrs. La Guardia, and her role as adviser and political problem solver was reserved for conversations between them at home.

To those who said the odds were against him beating Walker, La Guardia replied, "There is one thing I know how to do and that is how to beat Tammany Hall."

Vito Marcantonio again mobilized the Ghibonnes, but now their marching song was:

Seven times he's won elections,
Seven times he's reached the top.
He's proud he's an American
And he's proud he is a wop!

Who do you want for mayor, they asked as they roamed the streets for Fiorello—the wop, or the guy who dresses like an English fop?

La Guardia's themes were familiar ones aimed at Tammany: graft; corruption; pillaging the public coffers; contracts to cronies, crooks, tinhorns, and chiselers. And all of this going on either with the mayor's knowledge or without it, which was just as bad.

Walker asked, "Can anyone expect me to keep my good nature in this campaign? I refuse to go any further than the gutter. I will not go down in a sewer."

During the campaign, the Central Park Casino opened. So many of the rich and connected wanted to attend that the debut was held on two nights. The mayor toasted the occasion with champagne. Betty Compton had a beer. The illegal drinks for the festive crowd were kept in coolers in cars in the parking lot, then brought in as required. After the orchestra played "Will You Love Me in December?" the grateful lyricist tipped the leader $100. On his way out Walker gave the hat check girl double that amount.

Noting that Mayor Walker went to the Casino three nights a week, La Guardia said, "So great is the interest in its success that a certain high official in the city government when he calls at the Casino asks what the income was on the previous day. The Casino is not only a whoopee joint but also a source of great revenue for important Tammany officials."

Maybe so, but no one seemed to fault Walker. On October 25 he attended ceremonies marking the start of work on the Triborough Bridge. The *Times* noted the mayor "was sighted afar and from that moment . . . the audience stood and cheered him."

The span linking Manhattan, the Bronx, and Queens was but one symbol of a city on the go, and also on the rise. At Fifth Avenue and Thirty-fourth Street the old Waldorf-Astoria Hotel was being torn down to make room for "the tallest skyscraper in the world," to be named the Empire State Building. The city's most posh hotel was being relocated to Park Avenue between Forty-ninth and Fiftieth Streets. Eight blocks north and three east of the Empire State, automaker Walter Chrysler's builders had secret blueprints for adding a needlelike spire to the top of the "Chrysler Building" that they expected would trump the Empire State's claim to "highest building" (a scheme that was thwarted when the Empire State added a sixteen-story tower that would serve as a mooring mast for dirigibles). And blocks of tenements, brownstone town houses, small restaurants, and shops between Fifth and Sixth Avenues from Forty-eighth to Fifty-first Streets were being gobbled up by John D. Rockefeller to turn the area into a business and cultural center named after himself.

The boom in skyscrapers would be unmatched in New York City history until the 1960s, but in 1929 the sight of rising shafts and crossbeams of structural steel had everyone looking up with amazement and pride. Plans for Mr. Rockefeller's "Center" contained a sixty-five floor "RCA Building" that would contain twenty-eight studios of the National Broadcasting Company and be called "Radio City." Opposite it, on the corner of Sixth and Fiftieth, theater builder Samuel L. "Roxy" Rothafel would surpass his "Roxy Theater" with the "Radio City Music Hall."

These and seemingly countless other architectural gems would dot the city of the mayors who succeeded whoever took office at City Hall on January 1, 1930. In New York and across the United States in the last year of the Roaring Twenties and the first year of the administration of President Hoover, there were not many Americans who did not believe that in theirs and their country's future, not even the sky was the limit.

Down on Wall Street, smiles a mile wide celebrated the "Hoover bull market." It was a new era, wrote historian Frederick Lewis Allen in *Only Yesterday: An Informal History of the 1920s.* "Prosperity was coming into full and perfect flower."

Obviously, when Hoover foresaw the end of poverty, he knew what he was saying.

"While supersalesmen of automobiles and radios and a hundred other gadgets were loading the ultimate consumer with new and shining wares," Lewis continued, "supersalesmen of securities were selling them shares of investment trusts which held stock in holding companies which in turn controlled holding companies—and so on *ad infinitum.*"

But on the day before Jimmy Walker was hailed by a crowd anticipating a great bridge across the upper East River, the stock market wobbled. And on Tuesday, October 29, 1929, it collapsed. "Wall Street," cracked the show business newspaper *Variety,* "lays an egg."

Two days later, Fiorello La Guardia wound up his campaign by issuing a statement to the press that summarized a race for mayor that he said had been "fought on the proposition that this community is entitled to honesty, efficiency, and competency in the administration of its affairs."

Instead, he said, years of absolute Tammany rule had resulted in graft, corruption, waste, and neglect. "I have charged the Walker-Tammany administration with specific acts of favoritism, racketeering, inefficiency, and waste—with a total disregard of the taxpayers' interests," he declared. "I have sustained every charge. Tammany cannot deny them."

New Yorkers yawned. Of 1.2 million voters, La Guardia got 368,000.

America's most liberal congressman returned to his seat in the House and took up the old Progressive banners and renewed his fight against Prohibition. Two years later, he would be reelected. As Franklin D. Roosevelt reaped the whirlwind of America's blaming Hoover for the economic depression that followed the 1929 stock market crash, Congressmen La Guardia ran once more from the Twentieth C.D. as a Republican, but with support from his labor-union friends, Progressives, the leaders of the black community, and prominent Puerto Rican politicians—even popular boxing star "Kid Chocolate." However, the nature of the Twentieth C.D. had been changing. In 1930 the turnout at the polls had been 18,000. In 1932 the tally was 31,000. Most of them were Democrats at heart, and when they voted for Roosevelt for president, they went right down the FDR slate to give La Guardia's Democratic opponent, James Lanzetta, the victory by 1,200 votes.

"It's no use," said La Guardia despondently, "they got me at last."

Marie and friends spoke of the next time.

"I'm too old to start over," he said. "I'm going to get a little place in the country and settle down and raise chickens."

But as he returned to Washington in 1932 as a lame duck with a few weeks left as a member of the House, chickens were coming home to roost at City Hall and for its rulers in the Tammany Wigwam.

11

⚬⧸⌒

At this point in the story of Fiorello H. La Guardia arises one of those "iffy" questions that are so tantalizing in considering history:

If there had been no Arnold Rothstein, would La Guardia have been mayor of New York?

Who was Rothstein?

His lawyer said of him, "Arnold Rothstein dwells in doorways. He's a gray rat, waiting for the cheese."

Attorney William J. Fallon's client had been a gambler. In 1919 he had bribed members of the Chicago White Sox baseball team in a "fix" of the World Series, in what became known as the "Black Sox" scandal. In a biography of Fallon, *The Great Mouthpiece,* published in 1931, New York journalist Gene Fowler portrayed Rothstein as a "tremendous gambler" with "an arterial system that, instead of blood, held a solution of arsenic in ice water. His usurer's soul and the availability of his bankroll placed him in the king-row of the criminal checkerboard."

When Fiorello and Jimmy were contesting for City Hall in 1929, Arnold was a year dead. He had been "bulleted," to use Gene Fowler's colorful verb. In November 1928 Rothstein had been shot in the groin as he partook of a high-stakes floating card game at the Park Central Hotel. He died in Polyclinic Hospital, refusing to name his executioner.

"Whether his passing was a loss to mankind and a gain to either branch of the Hereafter, or vice versa," said Fowler in his Fallon biography, "is a problem too weighty to handle in hot weather and hard times."

But the influence of the man the newspapers had headlined as "The Master Mind of the Criminal Empire" did not go to the grave with him. His assassination by a gunman whom the police files listed as "unknown" became a weapon in La Guardia's fusillades aimed at Walker's administration in 1929. Again and again La Guardia asked why the cops still hadn't solved the sensational rubout. He also charged that a Walker crony, City Magistrate Albert H. Vitale, had borrowed $19,600 from Rothstein. How could a judge have been on good terms with America's most notorious gambler and still be wearing a robe?

The sensational accusation was dismissed by Walker and Tammany Hall as La Guardia's attempt at a smear because Vitale was working to line up Italians for Walker in 1929.

All of this presented a problem to the Democratic governor of New York.

<hr />

Planning to run for president in 1932, Franklin D. Roosevelt was in no position to seem to be looking the other way in a possible scandal involving New York City Democrats and a Police Department that was still nagged by memories of the scandalous activities that had been exposed by the Lexow Committee investigations in the 1890s. That awful mess had certified Tammany's record of skulduggery and had put FDR's cousin Theodore on the road of "reform" that eventually took him to the mansion in the nation's capital that FDR hoped to soon occupy.

In part as a result of La Guardia making issues of the unsolved Rothstein case and the Vitale situation in the 1929 election, FDR was able to present himself to the country west of the Hudson as a reformer in the TR tradition by going along with the creation by Republicans in the legislature of a special committee for "investigation of the departments of the government of the City of New York." Its chairman was Senator Samuel H. Hofstadter.

In accepting the bill that authorized the committee, Roosevelt had done an about-face. He had vetoed an earlier, similar measure. "If logically pursued," he'd explained when he was running for reelection as governor, "it would compel future governors at one time or another to meddle in the affairs of every county and city in the state."

His change of mind resulted from demands by citizens, including Rabbi Stephen S. Wise on behalf of the City Affairs Committee, and other good-government groups (known by the folks at Tammany Hall as "goo-goos"), for such an investigation. With the legislative committee now authorized, Chairman Hofstadter asked a respected retired judge, Samuel Seabury, to come on board as the committee's counsel.

Mayor Walker received the news calmly. "No one welcomes such an investigation," he said, "more than myself."

He then invited any New Yorker with information on graft to tell him about it personally.

La Guardia asked rhetorically, "How does he get away with it?"

Judge Seabury defined the nature of the committee's task. "There are two paramount questions," he said. "What are the conditions in the magistrates' courts? Is justice being done?"

The choice of Seabury was fine with FDR. Seabury had a reputation as an "independent Democrat" who had lost a bid for the governorship in 1916 and blamed it on Tammany Hall and in part to the lack of backing from FDR. Because Seabury was not a man who could be bossed, he was just the one to demonstrate that the governor who would be president was not in the pocket of a political machine.

Looking every inch one of the people whom La Guardia scorned for boasting that their ancestors came over on the *Mayflower,* Seabury was a ruddy-faced, tall, and portly figure with white hair who wore pince-nez, carried a walking stick, and had his suits tailored in London. The *Literary Digest* would say of the referee in the investigation into the courts, "Judge Seabury is perhaps the most thoroughly patrician figure in our public life today—at a period when any hint of aristocracy is supposed to be fatal."

Roosevelt knew Seabury personally through their association with a group of distinguished Americans with families whose pedigrees stretched to the Pilgrims and other early English settlers. These "bluebloods" (as La Guardia saw them) had organized the Anglo-American Records Foundation. Its purpose was collecting documentation on their ancestry. FDR was one of the directors. Seabury became president, and with very good reason.

The Seaburys went back to John and Priscilla Alden of *Mayflower* fame. The granddaughter of two-thirds of America's first love triangle (the other third being the hapless Miles Standish, who foolishly sent John to present his case to Priscilla) was Elizabeth Alden. She married the original Samuel Seabury. Later, a third Samuel Seabury became the first Episcopal bishop in America.

When FDR welcomed the bishop's great-great-grandson to investigate Mayor James J. Walker's city, he launched a chain of events in which a Seabury and a Walker would confront one another in legal contest, but not for the first time. The present Judge Seabury had battled Mayor Walker's parent, William, over a plan that William had proposed for a park. It was, not coincidentally, across St. Luke's Place from the Walker house.

Being in the construction trade, William also would do the work of building the park. He also was an ex-alderman and current commissioner of public buildings, a Tammany job. His problem lay in the fact that the land was a cemetery, St. John's Burying Ground. It belonged to Trinity Church. Samuel's law firm, Morgan and Seabury, was retained as counsel by the Trinity Church Corporation to resist the scheme.

Seabury's problem was the city's "right of public domain." The situation was resolved in a compromise. Walker would get his park. The city would move the residents of the graveyard, along with their headstones. Transported to resumed eternal rest in a cemetery at 155th Street and Broadway were two of Seabury's distant kin.

Now Judge Samuel Seabury had a writ from Governor Roosevelt to dig around to see if there were skeletons in the chambers of authority in the city whose popular, effervescent mayor was William Walker's son.

⚜

The "Seabury hearings," as they would become known in newspaper headlines, opened in October 1930. They began with Seabury and his staff of lawyers in possession of affidavits and interviews gathered from more than a thousand individuals that filled more than fifteen thousand pages of transcript. When many of the witnesses who were on public payrolls balked at talking openly, Governor Roosevelt snapped, "Pleading immunity by public officials in regard to public acts will cease."

An anonymous wiseacre-songsmith quickly offered:

Tammany Hall's a patriotic outfit.
Tammany Hall's a great society,
Fourth of July they always wave the flag, boys,
But they never, never wave immunity!

New Yorkers hadn't heard such examples of malfeasance, misfeasance, nonfeasance, graft-taking, bribery, intimidation, payoffs, covering up of lawlessness, and overall corruption in thirty years. Presently the shocked citizenry found itself laughing out loud at the brazenness of some of the people who testified. They were especially amused by a bit of repartee between the judge and New York County sheriff Thomas M. Farley. Seabury desired to know how Farley acquired nearly $400,000 within six years on a yearly salary of $8,500. Farley said he saved it.

SEABURY: Where did you keep these moneys that you had saved?
FARLEY: In a safe-deposit box at home in the house.

Seabury asked where in the house.
In a safe, said the sheriff.

SEABURY: In a little box in the safe?
FARLEY: A big safe.
SEABURY: But in a little box in a big safe?
FARLEY: In a big box in a big safe.

Was "this big box that was safely kept in the big safe a tin box or wooden box?"

"A tin box."

Seabury asked about the source of $83,000 in 1930, excluding Farley's salary. Did it come from "the same source that the other money came from?"

It did, said Farley.

SEABURY: Same safe deposit vault?
FARLEY: Yes.
SEABURY: Same tin box, is that right?
FARLEY: That is right.
SEABURY: Kind of a magic box?
FARLEY: It was a wonderful box.

The chamber in the New York County courthouse resounded with laughter. Thirty years after Sheriff Farley's appearance before Judge Seabury, songwriters Sheldon Harnick and Jerry Bock had theater preview audiences in New Haven and Philadelphia, and then crowds in New York's Broadhurst Theater, rollicking in their seats as a chorus of "politicians" sang "A Little Tin Box" in the musical *Fiorello!*

As New Yorkers in 1930 chortled about little tin boxes, Farley was summoned to Albany by FDR and fired. But the mayor of New York faulted the focus of the investigation on "little things to the exclusion of big things done in this greatest city in the world."

Many in the city agreed with him, but that did not keep them from paying attention to the juicy parts. They could barely wait for the testimony of New York's best-known and classiest "madam," Miss Polly Adler, whose business card was a sketch of a parrot above her telephone number: LExington 2-1099.

In her memoir *A House Is Not a Home* (1953), she recalled skipping out of town in the hope of avoiding a subpoena, and her reason for hiding out in Newark. "I had nothing to fear from Judge Seabury," she wrote. "This time the
heat was on the law-givers and law-enforcers, not the law-
breakers." Preferring not to testify was sound business practice. "If I accepted service of a subpoena a lot of people might
be dubious about my ability to keep clammed up and decide
to ensure my silence in ways I didn't care to dwell on."

Unable to avoid a summons, she appeared in the 60 Centre Street courtroom. The *New York World* eagerly anticipated telling its readers "who's who after the sun goes down."

Polly disappointed. She answered most of the questions
"No," or "I don't remember."

She told reporters that she thought Seabury treated her
with "meticulous politeness."

All of this was entertaining, but not exactly new. New
Yorkers expected an outbreak of corruption-investigating about
every twenty years. Besides, Seabury had pinned nothing on
the mayor that everyone didn't already know; that he was
generally disengaged with his job. But so what? He was an
extremely engaging character, and a delightful diversion from
the gloom and doom of the "Hoover and Republicans' Depression" that just kept going on and on and on.

Down in Washington and in an "I told you so" mood, Congressman La Guardia said to a reporter, "Several of the charges
which I made during the campaign and which Tammany and
some of the Republican intelligentsia termed mud-slinging
have already been sustained."

The Seabury investigation called some four thousand witnesses in private and in public, accumulating almost a hundred thousand transcript pages. Out of it came no indictments,
no trials, and no convictions. Seabury had been empowered
to *only* investigate and file a report. But twenty-six people
resigned or were dismissed from the courts, police department,
and office of the district attorney. Six men were convicted for
crimes that the hearings exposed. And the corruption-soaked

police Vice Squad was disbanded, to the relief of Polly Adler and her payoff checkbook.

As required, Seabury sent Governor Roosevelt a bill of particulars regarding Walker. The charges ranged from "indifference to elementary standards of office" to at no time making "the slightest attempt to correct existing conditions in the magistrates' courts," to "procrastination" and "persistent refusal to meet crises."

Concerning this scathing referral to Governor Roosevelt, Walker said at a dinner in his honor given by the Jewish Theatrical Guild in April 1931, "I come to you with no brief for myself. I come to you with no apology for my public life. . . . I am guilty of many shortcomings, but when the list is completed there will not be included selfish political ambition."

The audience of two thousand applauded, indicating that at least that many people who'd loved him in December still did in April. A few days later, he released a rebuttal to the Seabury report in which his answers were either vague or specious. On May 9 he led six thousand New York City cops up Fifth Avenue in the annual police parade. The men in blue and the mayor in his top hat did not know what to expect along the route. They found cheering onlookers, some of whom tossed flowers. Many shouted encouraging words.

In June, Walker turned fifty. On August 8, he boarded the German liner *Bremen* for a six-week tour of Europe. He returned on September 21, tanned, cheerful, and in good health.

A reporter asked, "Are you prepared to appear before the Hofstadter Committee at the call of Mr. Seabury?"

"That," said the mayor curtly, "is for Mr. Seabury to decide."

Fiorello La Guardia also was abroad in the summer of 1930. He and Marie had sailed on the SS *America,* bound for London. His official purpose was to be a delegate to the Inter-Parliamentary Union. Beginning on July 16, it was the organization's twenty-sixth conference and convened in the Royal

Gallery of Britain's Parliament Building for a week. For Fiorello and Marie the trip also was a delayed honeymoon that included a homeward-bound diversion through Ireland. They returned on the SS *Roosevelt,* named for Fiorello's political idol and favorite in the Progressive cause, Theodore.

While Walker awaited the pleasure of Judge Seabury, the congressman whom Walker had humiliated at the polls in 1929 was on Capitol Hill flailing at injustices he seemed to find at every turn, and doing his best to persuade his colleagues to vote for repeal of the Eighteenth Amendment. On December 14, 1930, in an article in the *New York Herald Tribune* ("Drys Can't Win in '32 against a Wet on Repeal Plank") he declared, "Whatever happens the end of Prohibition is near." Sensing that "Repeal" was gaining, he decided that shooting at a retreating foe was a waste of time and energy. He switched attention to "unemployment."

"There is a school of thought," he told the House, "which believes that unemployment is a condition to be taken advantage of, to drag down wages, and to lower labor conditions. This school is based on sordid selfishness and lack of vision." He proposed "a plan of rotation of employment." He labored for and saw enactment of the Norris–La Guardia labor union protection measure.

In January 31 he declared war on the Edward G. Robinson gangster movie *Little Caesar* as "most unfair and objectionable in many respects" to Italians. In a telegram to movie industry "morality czar" Will Hays, he conceded that "legislation cannot take greed from producers or compel ordinary common decency in consideration of people's feelings." But he vowed to make "a public appeal to the people of my city to remember these producers and be guided accordingly in the future." He did not form picket lines in front of theaters showing the hit film.

During the last two years of the Hoover administration, noted biographer Lowell Limpus, "the indefatigable New Yorker became a sort of congressional whirling dervish, spinning so rapidly from one issue to another that it was difficult even for his enemies to pin him down."

"A satisfactory victory," said La Guardia at his campaign head-quarters on the night of his reelection to Congress in 1930.

But the approach of his 1932 reelection campaign had found the persistent reformer in just about the most uncomfortable position of his career. With the hated Hoover in the White House he bore a Republican label. To be a member of the GOP was, he realized, a manifest handicap in the face of a gathering Democratic landslide.

As noted earlier, when voters in the Twentieth C.D. went to the polls, many of them were new to the district, and in greater numbers than before. They'd thrown him out and left him thinking his career in public service was over, and that the only thing to do was head for the countryside with Marie and start a chicken farm. Never mind that he knew nothing about poultry, except how to cook it using an Italian recipe.

All that changed on June 8, 1932, when Judge Seabury sent Governor Roosevelt the transcript of Mayor Walker's testimony and Seabury's devastating analysis of the evidence of the Walker administration's corruption. Because the Democratic majority of the Joint Legislative Committee refused to endorse his report, he sent it to FDR "not as formal charges but for your information so that you may determine what shall be done."

It arrived on the eve of the Democratic National Convention. FDR sought Walker's reply. The mayor deferred it until after the convention.

The governor/presidential nominee decided to give Mayor Walker a forum to answer the Seabury allegations. The judge at the hearing would be Franklin Delano Roosevelt. It opened in the Executive Chamber, Hall of Governors, the Capitol, Albany, New York, on the eleventh of August 1932. "Here was high drama," wrote Herbert Mitgang in *The Man Who Rode the Tiger,* a life of Judge Samuel Seabury subtitled "the Story of the Greatest Investigation of City Corruption in This Century [Twentieth]."

It was "enacted before an audience of millions, which followed the events in this room every day and evening on the radio and in the newspapers."

Jimmy Walker was quoted as quipping, "There are three things a man has to do alone: be born, die, and testify."

Roosevelt promised him a "fair deal" by questioning Walker himself. The proceedings went on for days, interrupted once so that Mayor Walker could attend the funeral of his brother William, who died on August 26. The date for resumption was September 1. At the funeral Jimmy told a friend, "I think Roosevelt is going to remove me."

The mayor consulted Al Smith. The "happy warrior" was blunt: "Jim, you're through. You must resign for the good of the party."

On the evening of September 1, 1932, FDR was informed by telephone from New York City that Mayor James J. Walker had sent an official message to the city clerk. It said, "I hereby resign as Mayor of the City of New York, the same to take effect immediately."

The post went to Surrogate John P. O'Brien. But temporarily, after a by-election. He would serve out the remainder of Walker's term; O'Brien had succeeded Joseph V. "Holy Joe" McKee, president of the Board of Aldermen, who had automatically become acting mayor following Walker's resignation. If O'Brien wished, he was free to seek the office in his own right in the regular mayoral election in November 1933.

Two months after this sudden turn of events, Fiorello La Guardia became the lame duck congressman for whom, if he wished, the door was now open to another chance to go into the history books as the first man with an Italian name in the office of mayor of New York City.

He lost no time in forgetting about raising chickens.

12

In the spring of 1933 Fiorello La Guardia's final congressional session ended, Franklin Delano Roosevelt became the first Democrat president of the United States since Woodrow Wilson, and Tammany Hall was as disgraced as Jimmy Walker. For the first time in Fiorello's adult life, he was not in office or actively running for one.

Because Marie was unable to have children, they decided to adopt a daughter. Five-year-old, dark-haired Jean was the child of the sister of Fiorello's late wife, Thea. Unable to afford to raise the little girl, the mother was delighted that Jean would be in the care of her former brother-in-law and his capable wife. The only condition of the adoption was that Jean be brought up Catholic. (As an adult Jean turned Episcopalian.) The La Guardias subsequently found a son. Three-year-old Eric was of Scandinavian parentage. Adopted through a city children's placement bureau, he had been temporarily with another family. Loving Jean and Eric as though they had been born to him and Marie, Mayor La Guardia would bristle at any reference to them in newspaper stories or La Guardia biographical sketches in magazines and reference books as "adopted."

Many years later Jean would recall numerous days of standing next to her father as he reviewed parades, going along when he dedicated schools, touring sewage plants, and attending all the occasions, ceremonies, and events that crowded his official calendar. The summers were passed in rented houses in cooler suburbs. Every Fourth of July meant

The La Guardia
family in 1933:
(left to right)
Marie, Jean,
Fiorello, and Eric.

listening to him read them the Declaration of Independence.
When Eric was old enough, he was sent to the ranch of his
father's friends in Texas because, said the man whose boyhood was in Arizona, "The change will do him good."

Regarding his brother Richard and sister Gemma, Fiorello's relationship had been at a distance. Gemma lived in
Budapest, married to a Jewish bank clerk. For many years
she and her famous brother were out of touch. Richard's work
had taken him to Trenton, New Jersey, as a social worker
connected to church work. He died of a heart attack in 1935.

Out of office in March 1933 and supporting the family as
a lawyer, Fiorello could only observe from the sidelines as the
people of the city rinsed their collective mouth of the bad
taste of yet another government scandal and resumed their
lives, leaving the picking up of the pieces to Jimmy Walker's
permanent successor, whoever that might be.

Joseph V. McKee had done well as acting mayor, but in
the by-election to pick the man to finish Walker's term, Tammany bosses shunned McKee in favor of party stalwart John
P. O'Brien as the candidate. The Republicans had put up
another party "regular," Lewis Pounds. O'Brien trounced him,
but La Guardia noted that while O'Brien got a little over
1 million votes and the GOP candidate about 500,000, a total
of 241,899 independent voters had written in McKee.

Everyone who knew the history of Walker's downfall agreed that if La Guardia had not raised "holy hell" about Gentleman Jimmy's administration there would not have been Judge Seabury's devastating investigation. The only person with the right to stand up and say "I told you so," declared the *Times,* was "former Congressman La Guardia." The praise was fine. It was being called "former" that rankled. In the La Guardia biography "past" was as unwelcome an adjective linked to his name as "politician." But it was a politician who pondered the McKee numbers garnered without McKee having been a candidate. He also noted that McKee would have had even more if tens of thousands of voters who picked up pencils to write in his name hadn't spoiled their ballots by misspelling his name, in many cases writing it in Yiddish.

Out of Fiorello's political lexicon and into his mind leaped a word that was one of his favorites: "FUSION."

The brain in which the enticing word rattled and ricocheted in the spring of 1933 was that of a reformer, but it was also the gray matter of a political strategist. And a devious one. Exhibiting "a real mastery of the delicate art," to borrow and endorse the analysis offered in the La Guardia biography by Lowell Limpus and Burr Leyson, La Guardia wanted to head an anti-Tammany Fusion ticket himself. Therefore, he put forth the name of Alfred E. Smith.

Confident that the ex-governor, former presidential aspirant, and Democrat "regular" would turn down the honor, former congressman La Guardia put out a statement on May 10 in which he promulgated an ideal Fusion ticket with Smith's name next to "Mayor." For president of the Board of Alderman he proposed another unlikely receptor, Socialist Norman Thomas. In the slot for surrogate was John P. O'Brien (a Democrat who was certain to decline). Ex-mayor Hylan (another nonstarter Democrat) was listed for borough president of Queens. For the post of comptroller (the city's chief moneyman) he "nominated" an up-and-coming Republican but an Al Smith protégé named Robert Moses.

Should the "happy warrior" decide not to leap into the fray, La Guardia said in an aside in the statement, Fiorello La Guardia would be "forced" to substitute.

The result among the regulars of the GOP was panic. In hopes of derailing La Guardia's clever scheme, they turned to the strongest Republican on their short list of potential mayoral contenders, the man whom La Guardia had proposed for comptroller.

Six years and seven days younger than La Guardia (born December 18, 1888), Robert (no middle name) Moses was born in New Haven, Connecticut. But at age twelve his family moved to New York City (20 East 46th Street). Just off Fifth Avenue, it was a neighborhood of German Jews. He had an older brother, Paul, and younger sister, Edna. The boys got their schooling at the Ethical Culture School, followed by the Dwight School, and the Mohegan Lake Academy prep school near Poughkeepsie. Robert's college was Yale. Postgraduate work was at England's Oxford University, where he wrote a thesis questioning the basis of the American system of elective politics, especially in cities. His answer to the deficiencies of popularly elected officials was to rest city government in the hands of college-trained urban experts.

Just such individuals could be found in the Bureau of Municipal Research. A sparkplug of governmental reform, it was described in Robert Caro's monumental biography of Moses, *The Power Broker,* as the spearhead of reform not only in New York but throughout the country. In 1913 Moses had enrolled in the Bureau's two-year-old Training School for Public Service.

If he hadn't, and *if* his path had not crossed La Guardia's, there is no telling what kind of New York City might exist today for historians of reform and students of urban renewal and city development and improvement to examine.

And what might have happened if Moses had not had a chance meeting one Sunday in 1914 with Frances Perkins? Caro relates the event: Moses crossing the Hudson on a ferryboat for a picnic in New Jersey, Perkins overhearing him as he gazed at the cluttered, ugly western edge of the island of Manhattan and asked a companion, "Couldn't this waterfront be the most beautiful thing in the world?"

Perkins remembered the Moses of that time "burning up with ideas" and walking around the city thinking of "some way that it could be better."

Circumstances that are too complex to relate here regarding Robert Moses' speedy rise in a reformers' circle that included Perkins, John Purroy Mitchel, Al Smith, and Franklin Roosevelt are related in detail in Caro's Pulitzer Prize–winning Moses biography. His ascent brought him in 1933 to the attention of FDR's successor in the governorship, Herbert H. Lehman. Impressed by work Moses had done for Roosevelt, the new governor put Moses in charge of the new State Emergency Public Works Commission. While serving in the Roosevelt administration, Moses had been instrumental in getting funding for construction of the Lincoln Tunnel and the Triborough Bridge. Then, with breathtaking suddenness, he found himself with what Caro termed "a chance to personally move the city—as its next mayor."

But he harbored no illusions about the challenge of running the country's biggest city, or about what he would offer voters. His would be a campaign rooted in the realities of what even the best governments could achieve.

"The official who promises 100 percent efficiency," he believed, "is taking the public for a ride."

And so, in the spring of 1933 events drew together a pair of honest, reforming, ambitious, and frank-talking realists in a wide-open arena in which the prize was the top office in City Hall. The lighthearted occupant who had been forced out of it was famous for asking, "Who would want to be president of the United States when you could be mayor of New York?"

It was the second most important, and second toughest, job in American government.

If . . . IF . . . everything went well, what occupant of the office would not think from time to time of using it to move up to the first?

Following publication of Fiorello La Guardia's roster of nominees for a Fusion ticket to complete the rout of the Tammany tiger, nervous leaders of the Republican Party saw through the La Guardia gambit of proffering Al Smith to head it. Obviously, the "happy warrior" would never accept the honor. And when he declined, La Guardia had let it be known, the Little Flower was there, the reluctant alternative. He was like Br'er Rabbit pleading not to be thrown in the briar patch. No! La Guardia just would not do. There had to be someone else.

Clearly, the best man for the job was Samuel Seabury. But the good judge let it be known that he was not interested.

If not Seabury, who? Several names floated up: merchant Nathan Straus Jr. (one Jew too many in government, in Straus's opinion [Governor Lehman was Jewish]); a broadcasting executive, Richard C. Patterson Jr. (his career was more important); a wealthy social worker who ran Al Smith's 1924 campaign, Raymond Ingersoll (rich, but not enough to help finance his candidacy); former mayor Hylan (not enthused by the idea); John D. Rockefeller (not with the building of Rockefeller Center to shepherd into fruition); and several others, each with a good reason not to be chosen.

One of the searchers for a stop–La Guardia candidate, Maurice P. Davidson, summed up the prevailing sentiment among alternatives. "They were afraid of it, of being licked."

Someone suggested Robert Moses. When he did not say "no," his name was laid before Seabury. The man who tamed the Tammany tiger recalled that Robert Moses was an Al Smith protégé. It was enough for the judge to turn thumbs-down.

The committee was back at square one, with an eager figure pacing in the wings whom no one wanted.

As the candidate-seekers wriggled on the horns of their dilemma, Seabury went down to the city where FDR was hammering together an administration that FDR saw as a "New Deal" for America. During a chat with one of Roosevelt's "brain trust" of advisers, Adolph Berle, Seabury asked, "What do they [FDR's advisers] think of the candidates for mayor?"

Berle replied that they looked favorably on La Guardia as a valued New Dealer.

That was sufficient for Seabury. But when he returned to New York, he learned that the Fusion committee planned to offer the mayoral nomination to Moses. The news was broken at lunch in the Bankers' Club. Seabury slammed a fist on the table so hard that dishes and glassware rattled. Only his voice was louder. "You sold out to Tammany Hall!" he boomed. "I'll denounce you and everybody else!"

The intimidated members of the committee reluctantly broke the bad news to Moses, and the good to a man whom one of their committee once called "half wop, half American, half Republican."

Moses gave La Guardia a resounding endorsement: "You have no strings on you. You are not engaged in an obscure struggle for the control of a rotten political machine. You are free to work for New York City. Go to it."

Like the melting-pot nature of the city, the Fusion effort was a patchwork quilt of differences. For the first time the top four slots on a ballot were an Italian, an Irishman, a Jew, and a white Anglo-Saxon Protestant. Backing the ticket were *Mayflower*-descended goo-goos led by Judge Seabury, Jews, Socialists, Republicans, dissident Democrats, Irish, Poles, Hungarians, dockhands, garment workers, shopgirls, schoolteachers, Greenwich Village intellectuals and Bohemians, people whose main issue was Repeal of Prohibition, and veteran streetwise political strategists and tacticians. The battlefields were all the neighborhoods. The headquarters was in the Paramount Theater building in Times Square. Five days before the balloting the campaign finale was a rally at Madison Square Garden, with an overflow of fifty thousand in surrounding streets.

The penultimate speaker was the man who had made La Guardia the top of the Fusion ticket. The rowdy audience quieted enough to hear Samuel Seabury tell them, "The hour is ripe for action. I ask you, by your votes, to strike the blow that will make the city free."

When La Guardia entered the arena at 10:25 P.M. to a rafters-rocking greeting from the largest and liveliest crowd in years, the band struck up "In the Halls of Montezuma," a tune that had been adopted as the campaign anthem. To the joyous throng before him and to an unknown number of listeners by radio, La Guardia said, "My friends, thousands of people came here tonight. Do you know what that means?"

The crowd roared, "Victory!"

But first the vote had to be turned out on November 7.

Then it had to be counted.

To assure that the greater number went for McKee, Tammany Hall sent out a small army of men wearing identical pearl-gray fedoras to polling places to "assist" voters. Some citizens later complained that the Democratic ruffians had exhibited blackjacks, brass knuckles, and lead pipes. Offsetting these "gangsters" were numerous Vito Marcantonio-led Ghibbones and a large cohort of well-muscled "Fusioneers."

"It was a day of violence, of Keystone Kops action," wrote biographer William Manners in *Patience and Fortitude* in 1976. From gangster Dutch Schultz down to the lowly pickpocket, "Tammany had willing helpers." But "Fusion set out early in the morning to prevent grand larceny at the polls." One of the Fusioneers was prizefighter Tony Canzoneri. But no one drew as much attention as an honesty enforcer or matched the fury and the indignation of Fiorello La Guardia. Barreling into a polling station on East 113th Street and discovering illegal Tammany representatives, he strode up to one, ripped off the astonished man's red Tammany badge, and said with a growl, "Get out. You're a thug." Glaring at others in the machine gang, he shouted, "You're all thugs! Get out of here and keep moving!"

When a Tammany police officer stepped in, it was La Guardia who was removed.

They were "a lot of punks," Fiorello said to a few Fusioneers as they left, "and I'm going to run them out of the city."

In the evening he waited for the count with Seabury in the judge's mansion on East Sixty-third Street. At ten o'clock, assured that his tally was running well ahead of his two opponents', he went downtown to the Fusion election night headquarters in the Astor Hotel on Times Square.

When word came in that the Fusion candidate for comptroller, Arthur Cunningham, was behind in four hundred precincts where he should have been leading, La Guardia smelled a Tammany rat, took Cunningham by the arm, and said, "Come on, Arthur, I'll get those precincts for you."

They sped to police headquarters, where the counts were reported and certified by the Board of Elections in a top-floor room. Bursting in, La Guardia ordered a police inspector to call for four hundred coppers in four hundred patrol wagons. "Roll 'em into the alley behind headquarters as fast as God will let you," he said. "As soon they get here, send one to each precinct in which the count for comptroller is being held up. Tell 'em to mount guard over that voting machine with drawn gun. By God, I'm going to count those votes for comptroller myself."

To the man whose own vote tally was yet to be completed, the awed inspector replied, "Yes, Mr. Mayor."

Confident that the expected Cunningham votes would be quickly reported, the man who was not officially elected returned to the Astor's grand ballroom knowing that on the stroke of midnight on New Year's Eve he would become the ninety-ninth mayor of New York.

When finally tabulated, the votes for him were 868,522. McKee was second, with 609,053. O'Brien garnered 586,672.

La Guardia boasted, "We licked both wings of Tammany."

Anyone who cared to look at the results from another angle could have pointed out that the total gotten by Tammany's two wings was more than Fusion's by 327,203, which was not exactly a "reform" triumph. The Fusion mayoral candidate got 40.37 percent of the vote. McKee got 28.31 percent and O'Brien 27.27 percent. The rest went to minor candidates. For two Fusion votes for mayor there had been five against him. And 1 million eligible voters hadn't bothered to turn out; not exactly a clarion call for change. The La Guardia tally in terms of all who were registered to vote came to 23.77 percent. The dispassionate analyst could also have speculated that if Fusion's candidate had been anyone else, either of the Tammany candidates probably would have won.

A pleased smile on the day after winning the 1933 mayoralty election. He'd told his campaign workers, "They didn't elect me for my good looks."

Victory was the man's, not the issue's. But because La Guardia believed that he was the embodiment of the issue, he could say with a straight face that "a cause, not a man," had won.

"They didn't elect me for my good looks," he told the Astor crowd. "They wanted things done and they knew damn well I'd do them."

Then to all those in the ballroom who had believed in, worked for, and loved him for the man he was and what he stood for, he said that none of them should expect a job. He would hire only the very best person for every job, even if that individual had voted against him.

"My first qualification for this great office," he said, "is my monumental ingratitude."

Part II

Animal Crackers

La Guardia was a dictator from the day he took office.

—Lowell Limpus and Burr Leyson,
This Man La Guardia, 1938

13

The first New Yorker to expect a benefit from Fiorello La Guardia's election as mayor was his wife. Looking down at a threadbare carpet in the parlor of their four-room apartment on East 109th Street on election night, she told her sister Elsie, "Now we can get a new rug."

As a reward for Marie's patience and fortitude during the long and brutal campaign, the mayor-elect treated her to a two-week Caribbean cruise. They were guests of Frank Tichenor, publisher of *New Outlook* magazine. Accepting such hospitality, La Guardia quickly found out, was a mistake. The host casually mentioned to reporters who had been invited along that he had given La Guardia a few names for police commissioner.

In the waning weeks of 1933 the question of who would be put in charge of the police was as frequently asked as it had been in 1895 when another Fusion mayor, William L. Strong, had to choose someone to clean out the corruption in the NYPD headquarters at 300 Mulberry Street. In 1933, headquarters was in a splendid domed structure on Centre Street at Broome and Grand Streets, and by most accounts, it was just as riddled with crooks and cops of easy virtue as in the Gay Nineties. Mayor Strong had brought in Theodore Roosevelt. Having made the police failure to solve the murder of Arnold Rothstein an issue during the Walker administration, La Guardia could not allow any suspicion that the police commissionership had been dumped into a politician's grab bag.

Embarrassed and irate, La Guardia shot off a cable to all New York newspaper editors in hopes of killing the report. "No justification for police commissioner story," he said. "I gave no statement. Said nothing concerning subject. Utterly groundless."

Finding the right man for 240 Centre Street would take the new mayor several months. His first choice was John F. O'Ryan. A Republican whose withdrawal from the list of possible Fusion mayoral candidates had removed one impediment to La Guardia's scheme to be mayor, O'Ryan had the distinction of having been the youngest divisional commander in the A.E.F. in the Great War. He'd been a fine soldier and a loyal Republican, hence his selection as police commissioner. But his service in the post would prove to be short. The mayor would find "the" commissioner in a man whose career as a cop had been stymied because he was seen by his bosses as too honest. His name was Lewis J. Valentine. He would loom large in La Guardia's twelve years at City Hall. But not at their beginning.

Filling other commissionerships went swiftly. La Guardia shattered precedent in the fire department by naming an actual fireman, Chief John T. McElligott. The mayor-elect asserted that McElligott would not be "a swivel chair commissioner," but one who personally knew how to put blazes out. To find the right health commissioner he asked the advice of the U.S. Public Health Service. The recommendation was John Rice of New Haven, Connecticut, a city that the federal service judged to have the best public health record in the nation. The head of the City Prison would be Austin H. McCormick, plucked from his desk as head of the Federal Penitentiary in Chillicothe, Ohio. Commissioner of Plant and Structures went to Frederick J. H. Kracke. The Republican leader of Brooklyn, he knew what he needed to know, but politics was more of a factor in his appointment than La Guardia cared to concede.

The most far-reaching decision made by the mayor-elect in terms of city commissioners was the appointment of Robert Moses to replace five borough commissioners in a new citywide post with the title of New York City parks commissioner. The amalgamation was demanded by Moses. "I was not interested in taking the city job," he recalled, "unless I had unified power over all the city's parks, and even then, only as part of the unified control of the whole metropolitan system of parks and parkway development."

Moses had been promulgated in New York politics by August Hecksher, a seventy-six-year-old millionaire philanthropist and recreation enthusiast who had financed a playground in the city. Hecksher's grandson, August III, would write a book about Robert Moses' new boss, *When La Guardia Was Mayor*, published in 1978, after the younger Hecksher had served for six years as administrator of parks and cultural affairs under Mayor John V. Lindsay in the 1960s.

Of the time when his predecessor, Moses, demanded creation of a city Parks Department, Hecksher wrote, "The city which La Guardia was now prepared to rule extended over 229 square miles, with a population larger than that of the country's fourteen smaller states together. Among cities it stood supreme." Taken as a whole it not only outstripped all others, but three of its separate boroughs stood at the time among the most eight populous of U.S. cities. "Brooklyn was larger than Philadelphia, Manhattan larger than Detroit, the Bronx larger than Los Angeles."

Yet behind the facade of "a pleasantly easy-going urban existence, of neighborhoods keeping an older scale and a traditional way of life, was a city grown rotten with corruption and bled white by a long period of public abuse" in which "every man had his price."

The result was a city on the precipice of bankruptcy—politically, morally, spiritually, and financially. La Guardia's challenge was to seize the moment and dramatize it as the beginning of change and the end of old abuses, but not in the manner and methods of changes taking place in other parts of the world. Contemporary La Guardia biographer Jay Franklin wrote in 1937, "It was a strange moment in history." Earlier in the year [1933], Adolf Hitler became chancellor of Germany and had followed his elevation by a general election that gave his Brown Shirt Revolution a mandate to create a "Third Reich" on a Nazi pattern. Italian general De Bono at the instigation of Fascist dictator Benito Mussolini was preparing an attack on the East African Abyssinian Empire in phase one of a new Roman Empire. In Spain, opponents of the Republic were looking approvingly toward Generalissimo Francisco Franco as a leader who might overthrow it. In the Far East, Japan was envisioning an Empire of the Rising Sun. In London the World Economic Conference searched for stability and a way out of the global Depression. In Washington, D.C., President Franklin D. Roosevelt thought the path back to prosperity in America was a New Deal, whatever that meant.

And in the City of New York, a small fraction of the enfranchised had cast their lot, and the city's future, with a rather funny-looking, energetic, once-defeated candidate for mayor, ex-aldermanic president, ex-congressman, World War hero, squeaky-voiced, short, messy-haired, multilingual, fifty-one-year-old, but only recently married, *Italian* whose given first name, translated into English, meant "Little Flower."

According to newspaper editorials and political columnists, Fiorello La Guardia had won a famous victory, so the best things for New Yorkers to do as they got ready for Christmas and Hanukkah was relax and wait to see what the new year and new mayor would bring.

The mood was summed up in a typical New Yorker's query: "Could it get any worse?"

And a familiar reply: "Don't ask!"

The New Year's Eve party given by the Honorable Samuel Seabury in his Upper East Side home offered the small group of guests a unique way to ring in 1934. At midnight, as the traditional crowd in Times Square went wild over the lowering of an illuminated ball atop the triangular *New York Times* building and the well-heeled were celebrating the end of Prohibition with champagne in posh hotels, state Supreme Court

Ending sixteen years of Tammany Hall domination of New York City politics on January 1, 1934, La Guardia was sworn in by Justice Philip McCook, observed by Judge Samuel Seabury (second from right), whose corruption investigations forced the resignation of Mayor James J. "Jimmy" Walker.

justice Philip McCook administered the oath of office to Fiorello Henry La Guardia.

Satisfied, Seabury said, "Now we have a mayor in the City of New York."

Bright and early on January 1, 1934, reporter Lowell Limpus joined a flock of City Hall journalists to observe the Little Flower dash up the front steps to take charge. Limpus wrote:

> He fought his way through a welcoming crowd which packed the central corridor and darted a hasty glance toward the office of the Aldermanic President which he had once occupied. This time, however, he turned to the left toward the Mayoralty suite at the west end of the building where [ex-mayor] John O'Brien was waiting to turn over the helm of the city government. The Major had reached the goal he had set for himself in 1920.

New York's City
Hall, 1934.

As soon as the ceremonies were over the new Mayor
bustled reporters, photographers and spectators out of the
private office, ensconced himself in the big chair, summoned
a platoon of stenographers and went to work.

Robert Moses observed the mayor "tossing letters at a pint-
sized secretary and shouting 'Say yes, say no, throw it away,
tell him to go to hell.'"

La Guardia ordered a larger wastebasket and removal of
a phone that other mayors had used to speak to commissioners. Henceforth, the mayor would address them "face-to-face."

There was no public ceremony, no celebration. La Guardia
told a reporter, "I have never heard of a receiver taking possession of a business with a brass band."

Instead, he swore in commissioners and gave each marching orders.

Swearing in Commissioner Robert Moses as a member
of the Triborough Bridge Authority in 1935. Moses
threatened to quit so often that La Guardia had a form
resignation letter made with a blank space for the date.

"I won't care whether the Law Department is the biggest in
the world," he told the new corporation counsel, Paul Windels.
"I want it to be the best."

Tax Commissioner Dominick Trotta heard, "There's something wrong in the tax department, but I don't know what it
is. See if you can find out."

He sped up to police headquarters to remind commanders
of "the Finest" that the force had not always deserved the
accolade. Crime and criminals would not be tolerated, he said,
in an area encompassing "the Hudson River on the west, the
Atlantic Ocean on the south, the Weschester County line on
the north, and the Nassau County line on the east."

"If not," he said, "get out!"

He appointed Lewis J. Valentine an inspector with the admonition "Be good or begone."

City Prison Commissioner McCormick was ordered to fire every deputy in the corrupt jail system and start from scratch.

At eleven o'clock the mayor rode up to the radio studios of the National Broadcasting Company for the first of what would be twelve years of mayoral talks over the airwaves (well before the first of FDR's famous "fireside chats"). He declared his government's Golden Rule: "Do after the election as you said you would before the election."

The broadcast ended with the "Oath of the young men of Athens":

"We will never bring disgrace to this our city by any act of dishonesty or cowardice.

"We will fight for our ideals and sacred things of the city both alone and with many.

"We will revere and obey the city's laws.

"We will strive unceasingly to quicken the public sense of civic duty.

"Thus in all these ways, we will transmit this city far greater and more beautiful than it was transmitted to us.

At City Hall again he told the Board of Aldermen they were an "assemblage of district errand boys" and demanded their support for his financial plan, then warned that he would push ahead whether he got "your cooperation or not."

"In this administration," he said, "I am the majority."

From the vantage point of twenty-four years later, Robert Moses said that La Guardia in his three terms, and notably in the first, presided over a strange collection of department heads and the deputies of a Fusion administration.

"Visiting City Hall," Moses said, "was like opening a box of animal crackers. You never could tell what kind of beast would come out of the Ark."

However La Guardia's advisers might be characterized, said Moses, "he was always their boss and never their victim."

14

ᐧᐧ∕ᐧ

How many ordinary New Yorkers paid serious attention, or took any notice at all, to the arrival of a new mayor no one can say. Of considerably more interest to many New Yorkers on January 1 might have been the victory of Columbia University's football team over Stanford University in the Rose Bowl game.

Residents who found sports and the antics of the political arena less fascinating than the offerings of the Times Square theater district had a wide range of selections. Eugene O'Neill had two plays running, *Ah, Wilderness!* and *Days Without End.* A good deal of sniggering was heard about a gritty new play called *Tobacco Road.* If drama was not the Broadway enthusiast's cup of tea, alternatives were the *Ziegfeld Follies* with Fanny Brice; *Roberta* with comedian Bob Hope; and *Let 'Em Eat Cake,* written by George S. Kaufman and Morrie Ryskind with a songbook by the Gershwin brothers in which a politician named Wintergreen surveyed the world scene and exclaimed, "Italy—Black Shirts! Germany—Brown Shirts!"

For the Music Box Theater Moss Hart had written the book and Irving Berlin the tunes for *As Thousands Cheer.* It needled Hoover, the U.S. Supreme Court, and nearly everything else. Musically, Marilyn Miller and Clifton Webb introduced "Easter Parade" and Ethel Waters sang "Heat Wave" and "Suppertime," a black woman's lament for a lynched husband. Waters also thrilled audiences with "Harlem on My Mind."

The title would soon provide the editorial writers and political cartoonists with a tempting opportunity to assign the words of the title to the new mayor.

But before Fiorello La Guardia's attention would be forced to turn uptown, he faced his first test as mayor in the matter of hailing taxis on the city's streets. On February 6, 1934, they suddenly became unavailable as the city's cabdrivers flipped up their "off duty" flags, drove into their garages, switched off the engines, and went on strike.

When owners of taxi fleets brought in replacements, strikers and sympathizers attacked the "scabs," seized the taxis, and set them on fire. Owners retaliated with hired strikebreakers. As battles broke out all over town, Police Commissioner O'Ryan wanted to send out the cops. The mayor who remembered how police power had been employed on the side of management in strikes in which the people's lawyer was a picketer vetoed the proposal. He then directed O'Ryan to order street patrol officers not to carry nightsticks.

The strike lasted a month and was settled through arbitration on March 6, but bitterness over the mayor's interference reigned in police ranks, and in the office of the commissioner.

In the meantime, the police faced two other instances of public disorder.

On February 16 at Madison Square Garden a rally to promulgate solidarity in the cause of world Socialism erupted into a free-for-all of fisticuffs between theoretical Socialists and advocates of the Soviet Union's style of communism. Moscow's admirers were feeling their oats following establishment of diplomatic relations by the United States with the USSR. Its first ambassador to Washington had been warmly welcomed by Bolsheviks of New York when he passed through the city on January 7 on his way to present his diplomatic credentials to the State Department. In restoring order at Madison Square Garden and surrounding streets the police were not hindered by orders from City Hall.

In La Guardia's mind, police breaking up a picket line was one thing and cops quelling rioting in Madison Square Garden was quite another.

A month and a day later, on St. Patrick's Day, hundreds of "the Finest" had to be pulled away from the annual police-led march up Fifth Avenue in a salute to the patron saint of Ireland and the NYPD. The cops had to deal with a very bad situation in Harlem. Panicky reports flowed downtown from uptown precincts that thousands of Negroes were rampaging through the streets in angry protest over the legal plight of "the Scottsboro Boys."

Two years previously (March 31, 1931), nine young black men had been arrested on a charge of rape involving two white girls. According to Ruby Bates and Victoria Price, they had been attacked in a gondola car of a Southern Rail Road freight train that was passing through the town of Scottsboro, Alabama. The young men (one was thirteen) vehemently denied the accusations, but were convicted and sentenced to death. A year later, an appeals court upheld the convictions. The belief among some Alabamans and northern liberals that the men were innocent resulted in a movement to "free the Scottsboro Boys." In November 1932 the U.S. Supreme Court declared a mistrial because the defendants' rights to counsel had been infringed. In March 1933 a judge ordered a change of venue for a retrial. It was this that triggered blacks in Harlem to flood into the streets on March 17, 1933.

In the mayoralty election in November the Fusion ticket had garnered 13.32 percent of the votes in "Negro Harlem" and 10.87 percent in "Spanish Negro Harlem." For this reason, and because Fiorello La Guardia's sympathies always tilted to the side of "the underdog," and having been made to feel that he was "a minority" all his life, he was not racist. His plans for the betterment of New York included dealing with the problems of its black citizens.

Should he feel the need for advice, he could turn to his friend Fannie Hurst. In a future article, "Harlem, Known and Unknown," she would write that the "osmosis" between "the seven million white-skinned New Yorkers and the five hundred thousand brown ones" was largely by way of domestic help, entertainers, slumming parties, social workers, headlines, courts, and the Police Department.

"Harlem, to the millions of whites who close it in on four sides," she continued, "is a badlands, where the chauffeur or the housemaid goes home to sleep, where the children have rickets, and no man is safe after dark. It is an incubator for vice, a lunatic fringe of savage music, a breeding ground for race riots."

Mayor La Guardia understood why the people of Harlem became incensed over the plight of the Scottsboro Boys. But rioting in the City of New York was impermissible. Consequently, Commissioner O'Ryan was allowed to deal with it as forcefully as O'Ryan and his uptown field commanders thought necessary.

But putting down a disturbance did not change anything. When Fannie Hurst got started on the conditions in Harlem as she talked to her friend Fiorello in the 1930s, she sounded like Jacob Riis lecturing Theodore Roosevelt in the 1890s. To go into the tenements of Harlem, she said, was to find underprivileged children crowded in dirty rooms packed with exploited rent-payers, furtive tenants prepared to fly by night, three-shift sleepers who occupy beds that have a new occupant every eight hours, prostitutes, pimps, hallway bathrooms, light housekeeping in rooms of minimum privacy, and the social hazards that go with a lack of privacy.

"The white mind seldom follows the Negro into his home," Hurst wrote. "He inhabits the New York scene as red-cap, porter, longshoreman, elevator man, waiter, cook, truck driver, soldier. Where he goes, what he does after the hours spent in the white man's world, is of little or no interest."

Until, that is, when trouble erupts, requiring police and getting into the headlines, as it did almost one year to the day after the Scottsboro Boys riot.

On March 19, 1935, a sixteen-year-old Puerto Rican boy, Lino Rivera, helped himself to a pen knife in a Kress five-and-dime store on West 125th Street. Two store guards grabbed him for shoplifting. A cop was called. The boy was taken to the rear of the store for questioning, then let go through the back door. A woman who observed the boy being led into the back room cried, "They're taking him to the basement to beat him up." A rumor quickly spread that a white cop had killed a black man. A crowd that had gathered went wild, invading the store and looting it. As more police arrived, a riot broke out. Fanning the flames were members of a militant black group, the Young Liberators, and the Young Communist League. By nightfall the disorder was widespread. Before order was restored and the story was refuted, 3 people were dead, 125 men arrested, and more than 100 people injured. More than 250 stores and shops that were "white-owned" had been looted.

Shocked by the violence and the cause of it, La Guardia appointed a "Commission on Conditions in Harlem." Chaired by Charles H. Roberts, the board formed six subcommittees, each of which was to look into "a special phase of community life." More than 150 witnesses appeared at a total of 25 hearings. Engaged to gather further data, Howard University sociologist E. Franklin Frazier assembled a staff of 30 assistants.

They produced "The Negro in Harlem: A Report on Social and Economic Conditions Responsible for the Outbreak of March 19, 1935." Its recommendations could have been mistaken for a Fiorello La Guardia manifesto of reform. The economic problems of Harlem could be addressed by more aggressive government action to prevent racial discrimination in municipal employment. The housing code must be enforced to combat overcrowding and overpricing. A building program was needed to provide low-cost apartments. Substandard health and education could be alleviated if Harlem got the same treatment as other areas of the city. If these problems were addressed, the crime rate would go down.

The report also dealt with why the rumor that sparked the rioting had been believed. It was accepted as truth, said the committee's investigators, because the Police Department had a reputation for brutality, racism, and overall indifference. The recommendation of the report was that a community board be established to review citizen complaints against the police.

Mayor La Guardia accepted the findings and recommendations as a guide to action, but not as a blueprint that he believed would commit him to a rigid policy. And he was not about to let anyone dictate to Fiorello La Guardia on the subject he felt he knew best: changing government for the better, and for the improvement of the lives of the people.

As to the Police Department, he'd already made a significant change at the top.

On September 24, 1934, Commissioner John F. O'Ryan had handed in his resignation and the mayor gladly accepted it. On the way out of office the "general," a title that the World War veteran liked and that newspapers were pleased to accord him, fired a salvo at the "major." He asserted that La Guardia had constantly overridden the rights of the general public and interfered "with the conduct and discipline of the Police Department." Still nettled by La Guardia's orders during the taxi strike, he charged that kid-gloves handling only encouraged "Communists and other vicious elements of the city to exploit these occasions for their own ends."

With O'Ryan gone, the commissioner whom La Guardia had appointed only because of a political debt was immediately replaced by a professional cop whom Fiorello knew he ought to have picked in the first place. At midnight on September 25, Lewis J. Valentine resigned from the force that he had joined as a patrolman on November 17, 1903, a month before La Guardia was sworn in as a consular officer in Fiume.

Wearing civilian clothes, at nine in the morning of the twenty-sixth Valentine reported with his wife, four daughters, three of his grandchildren, and his proud mother to City Hall to be sworn in as the police commissioner by a beaming mayor.

Handing him the commissioner's gold shield, La Guardia said, "It is not the badge that makes the office, it's the man."

Valentine had been born in Williamsburg, a part of Brooklyn known as "Irishtown," on March 19, 1882, making him eight months and twenty-two days older than the mayor. Becoming a New York cop in 1903 could have been the start of a career that offered ample opportunity to get rich by taking graft. That Valentine did not had impeded his rise through the ranks. If he had played by the Tammany corruption rules he could have become a divisional chief. At age fifty-two he knew he would have remained stalled until retirement had not mayor-elect La Guardia heard about "an honest cop somewhere in Brooklyn" and made him an inspector. And now commissioner.

When reporters flocked to Valentine's office to inquire what the new boss of "the Finest" intended to do, anticipating that "Lew" would be a continuing source for good stories, Valentine replied, "No publicity, no bluster . . . just enforcing the law and rigorously disciplining any members of the force who need it."

Lewis J. Valentine would be Fiorello La Guardia's police commissioner during the next eleven years, and in none of them would news-hungry men, and an occasional woman, on New York City's police beat suffer from a paucity of publicity-attracting events or lack of blustering by Valentine and his fortitude-preaching boss who had no patience for tinhorns and chiselers within the bounds of the five boroughs.

In the years ahead some reporters who hung out in rented space, known as the "shack," behind and across the street from police headquarters, would fashion successful careers as crime reporters and authors of books because of the crime-busting, racket-smashing, gangland-pestering duet of an Italian and an Irishman who hated crooks, cheats, and chiselers.

But uppermost on the mayor's agenda in his first year in office was the abysmal state of the city's fiscal underpinnings.

In the fall of 1932 the city's bankers had refused to provide new loans without guarantees that the city would make drastic cuts in its budget. Working with the moneymen, the governor (Lehman), and the state legislature, Mayor O'Brien obtained a commitment that saved the city from bankruptcy. Through a "bankers' agreement" the city would obtain operating expenses through 1937, in return for not raising real-estate taxes and carrying a minimum cash reserve of $50 million to be held in case of slow payment or nonpayment of taxes. The city also would cut costs by paring the size of the payroll.

Unfortunately, but typically, Tammany through O'Brien engaged in fiscal sleight of hand that left La Guardia with a budget out of balance by $30 million and $500 million in short-term obligations. The result was a low credit rating that kept the city from selling its long-term bonds and getting federal loans and grants. During the campaign, La Guardia pledged to abide by the bankers' agreement by tightening the city's belt, primarily by cutting back on the number of jobs. On his second day in office he asked the legislature to grant him the powers to do so. The "economy bill" would give him authority for two years to abolish, consolidate, and reorganize.

Governor Lehman denounced the request as a demand for "full dictatorial powers."

A compromise rested powers in the Board of Estimate to take many of the actions that were required, except in those agencies and departments directly under the mayor's control. The effect was to give La Guardia limited dictatorship. The city's credit rating improved.

It would continue to rise throughout his mayoralty.

Reviewing the La Guardia record as fiscal manager in *The La Guardia Years: Machine and Reform Politics in New York City* (1961), Charles Garrett, assistant professor of history at C. W. Post College of Long Island University, concluded, "Despite annual struggles with the budget, the La Guardia administration, in the final analysis, was always able to close the gap between expenditure and revenue. The city's credit rating was high." When La Guardia left office in 1945 New York City "had left the depression days of the early thirties far behind."

Without permanently straightening out the city's books, La Guardia could not tackle the greater problems that he wanted to solve, or at least reduce their severity.

He expressed his goals to a reporter in these words:

I want to build the healthiest city in the world, to wipe out tuberculosis and other diseases, to give people clean streets. It can be done. I want to improve hospitals and establish in New York the greatest medical center in the world.

Arguing for his budget at a meeting of the Board of Aldermen, 1934.

I want to improve the parks, to make New York beautiful, to give people something which will not only be of recreational value but also be esthetically stimulating.

I want to accomplish adequate housing for the wage earners.

I want to have some real markets which will decrease the cost of distribution and the price of food by at least 10 percent.

We must restore the supremacy of New York as a seaport. Everybody notices our skyscrapers but few ever think of the docks. Docks neglected, skyscrapers empty.

You know I am in the position of an artist or a sculptor. I can see New York as it should be and as it can be if we all work together. But now I am like the man who has a conception that he wishes to carve or paint, who has a model before him, but hasn't a chisel or brush.

Yet, after only six months in office, he listed "fifteen points of progress." They were:

1. Improved city credit.
2. Expanded city "relief" to provide clothes for 165,000 needy families and 140,000 more in 533 federal work projects.

3. Eliminated a $31 million budget deficit through business and utility taxes.
4. Centralized city purchasing, saving $1 million a year on coal alone.
5. Cut costs by reorganizing departments nonpolitically.
6. Expanded parks and opened 375 playgrounds.
7. Reorganized the Hospital Department (26 hospitals; $32 million a year budget)
8. Reorganized Health Department and built nine health centers and one research laboratory with federal loans.
9. Created a system of milk distribution, providing it to the poor at eight cents per quart at a time when milk prices were rising.
10. Developed plans to raise $4.5 million a month from current revenue to meet the cost of relief without borrowing.
11. Plans to improve and develop the waterfront for shipping by encouraging firms to locate in New York with a 20 percent reduction on pier rents.
12. Attacking racketeering in public markets and sale of ice.
13. Cut amounts paid to doctors under workmen's compensation.
14. Reduced the cost of city rentals by $500,000.
15. Planning for an expanded city water system to meet predicted needs in 1944.

Despite this formidable record, after a year of Fiorello La Guardia's ideas about how to make a Fusion government (one without a mandate from a majority of voters) work, the *New York Times* opined, "He has said some foolish things and done many wise ones, but has unfortunately too often given the impression of being a restless and undecided man, fond of toying with haphazard proposals that may be benevolent in intention but are dangerous or impossible in practice. He seems always to want to have in hand some socialistic plaything or other."

In fact, he *needed* to have his hand in *everything*.

15

To many New Yorkers he was "La Gardia," without the "u."

When a letter arrived at City Hall asking the proper way to say his name, he replied, "The name La Guardia is distinctly Italian and therefore should be pronounced La Gwardia, but I think what is most important is not *how* people will be calling me, but *what* people are calling me."

One journalist immediately chose the verb "energetic." Another wrote that he was "nonstop." Lowell Limpus's reporting often described a mayor who "bustled." In an account of the mayor's first week he wrote, "He had the nation's biggest city dizzy. Brigades of bewildered reporters were unable to keep up with his chameleon mind."

Variations of the word "storm" became well used. Two weeks after taking the oath of office he "came storming into the Municipal Building at nine o'clock in the morning and dashed [another popular active verb] from one office to another, while underlings frantically telephoned their missing superiors the Big Boss was on the rampage."

When he "stormed into Harlem Prison," he found a "trusty" preparing lunch without a supervising cook. The derelict chef was found and fired. Discovering two small boys being held in locked cells and each being kept for lack of $25,000 bail as material witnesses in a murder case, he ordered them transferred to the care of the Children's Society. Before he departed, he "almost took the quaking prison apart."

That night he reminded the city that the law empowered him to sit as a magistrate. With memories of appearing in

Night Court as "the people's lawyer," he marched into the West 100th Street police station, declared it a court, and took the bench. The first case was that of a man who had been arrested for running slot machines. Finding the "game is mechanical larceny" and that players did not get "a gambler's chance," he said, "Only a moron or imbecile could get a thrill out of watching these sure-thing devices take his money." Ordering the offender held for trial, he declared, "This will serve notice to owners, racketeers, and other riffraff who run this racket that they will enjoy no comfort."

A letter of complaint from a citizen about ill treatment he received at a Lower East Side "relief station" sent the mayor out to see for himself. He joined the long line of applicants. The scene that ensued was recorded by Lowell Limpus:

He found the personnel lounging about and the policeman on duty daydreaming. The latter's coat was unbuttoned and a carefree, lackadaisical air brooded over the place. Only one stenographer was interviewing the waiting applicants while a dozen others sat at idle typewriters. The little man in the big slouch hat waited—patient and unrecognized— until he had seen enough. Then he pushed through the crowd toward the head of the line until his way was barred by a brusque attendant.

"Where the hell do you think you're going?" barked the latter.

La Guardia went into action like a cyclone. He seized the man by the shoulders, whirled him about, and sent him spinning into the crowd. A second employee rushed forward and received the same treatment. By this time he had reached the rail and a cigar-smoking, derby-hatted individual came swooping down vengefully on the intruder.

He too received short shrift. The Mayor struck the cigar from his mouth with one swift blow and his hat with the another. "Take off your hat when you speak to a citizen," rasped His Honor, and vaulted the inner railing. Then, at last, he was recognized by the dumbfounded attendants and a sudden silence descended.

Invading the office of the director, La Guardia blew up when he found that gentleman missing. He ordered a secretary to telephone a summons to Welfare Commissioner William Hodson at once. Emerging from the private office, His Honor bawled out the policeman for his slovenliness and snatched up a high stool which he placed inside the railing. Perched on it, the Chief Executive took out his watch and barked, "Let me see how fast you can clear up this crowd of applicants." The bureau flew into action. Word spread through the adjoining offices that the Boss was on the job and the activity was epidemic.

The Mayor had arrived at 9:16 A.M. By 9:37 the entire crowd of applicants had been interviewed and hustled out. They lined up and gave a cheer for His Honor before they left.

When Welfare Commissioner Hodson arrived, La Guardia told him that if the absent director of the welfare station "doesn't have a good excuse, he's fired, and by good excuse I mean a doctor's certificate that he was ill this morning." Pointing to the cigar-smoker with the derby hat, he growled, "There's another s of a b that has no job."

Limpus felt that most of "these performances resulted from the dramatic reflexes of a highly emotional nature" while others were "due to an undeniable talent for the spectacular."

Such an opportunity arose at a luncheon for more than a hundred American aviators who had trained with him in Italy. The event was held at an airfield in Mineola, Long Island. La Guardia showed that he still had "the stuff" by taking up a plane.

For ground transportation he had a new car. This was justified because the one used by his predecessors, a Chrysler Imperial with thirty thousand miles on it, was declared unfit and unsafe for the streets. Previous mayors who were mindful that two mayors had been targets of assassins had detectives ride with them in the car as bodyguards. La Guardia saw a way to save money—and get publicity—by sending the cops back to regular duty. There was no need for bodyguards, the mayor explained, because he'd had the Fire Department install two compartments for pistols, one for himself and one for the driver, both of whom, he pointed out, had gun permits.

The car also was equipped with a folding desk so the mayor could "get work done" as he sped about the city. A police radio was added as well.

A second personal safeguard was using alternating routes to get to City Hall from his home. He, Marie, and the children now resided in a six-room apartment at 1274 Fifth Avenue in East Harlem. All previous flats had been in walk-up buildings. This one had an elevator, but it creaked as it carried him to and from the sixth floor. One of the rooms was converted to a study. Its window gave him a view of the northern end of Central Park.

Bookshelves lining one wall held biographies of public men, histories, volumes of the *Congressional Record* for his years in the House, books on the subjects of economics and government, and a real curiosity in the library of a big-city mayor—numerous back and current issues of the *Farmers' Bulletin.*

On taking office he'd vowed not to spend a lot of time attending banquets and making speeches. "Being mayor in the daytime is a man-size job," he said. "I shall cut out all public dinners, and even smokers. Most nights will see me in bed early, getting ready for the next day's work." It was a rare unkept La Guardia promise.

Although he never laid claim to Jimmy Walker's title "New York's Nighttime Mayor," he did not disappear after the sun went down. New York boasted that it was a city that never closed. The Irish writer-poet-playwright Brendan Behan said New York was a place "where the lights are always on." As its mayor, Fiorello found that being in bed by ten o'clock was a hard routine to keep.

Said the *Times,* "Perhaps never before did a mayor of New York begin his term with such an air of getting down to business and enforcing industry and honesty on the part of every city employee." The *World Telegram* ran the headline BREATH-TAKING ACTIVITY REPLACES TAMMANY SOMNOLENCE. Lines in the accompanying story read, "Aggressive, dynamic little Fiorello La Guardia has brought a new spirit in the conduct of municipal affairs."

La Guardia basked in the praise, but he bristled at the adjective "little."

No anecdote about La Guardia's lack of height illustrated his sensitivity more than one related by his commissioner of water, supply, gas, and electricity, Maurice Davidson. He had come to the mayor's office to discuss the appointment of an inspector in a "tough neighborhood." Davidson told La Guardia that the man he had in mind for the job was a "big, husky fellow." La Guardia suggested someone else.

"He won't do," said Davidson. "He's too small."

La Guardia leaped to his feet. With increasing volume he demanded, "What's the matter with the little guy? What's the matter with THE LITTLE GUY? WHAT'S . . . THE MATTER . . . WITH . . . THE LITTLE GUY?"

In telling this story Davidson noted that La Guardia "unconsciously put his hand inside his jacket in a manner made famous by a certain French general."

For La Guardia biographers' analyses of his personality as a manifestation of a feeling of inferiority, and a need to assert power, the temptation was to assign to Fiorello a "Napoleon complex." The first to draw the parallel were Lowell Limpus and Burr Leyson in the 1938 biography *This Man La Guardia*. They wrote, "La Guardia was a dictator from the day he took office."

In 1937 Jay Franklin asserted in *La Guardia* that Fiorello's early adversities produced both a man and a mask. "The mask is a stubby, plump little figure—five foot two in height with thinning black hair, active black eyes, quick gestures and a verbal fluency which is almost frightening and which so frequently becomes part of a current of uncensored thought as to lead him into difficulties. The mask has been much advertised as 'made in Italy,' a 'typical immigrant,' a 'scrappy, grotesque little ball of fire, a hard campaigner, and a natural-born showman.'"

Subsequent biographers followed suit in discerning a Napoleonic aura in the manner of the mayor. The following are examples:

Charles Garrett, *The La Guardia Years*, 1961:

> Success for La Guardia meant essentially power and recognition—the attention of others, applause, fame and glory—and

Opening day 1934 at Yankee Stadium.

these ends he sought chiefly through politics with all the avidity of a first class egotist. . . . [At] the root of La Guardia's egotism and quest for power and recognition lay a deep inferiority complex, the product apparently of several factors: the double social burden of being of Italian and Jewish descent, his short stature, possibly his limited formal education.

Arthur Mann, *La Guardia Comes to Power 1933,* 1965:

Some of La Guardia's associates thought, and still think, that in reaching out for power he was compensating for feelings of inferiority deriving from a hypersensitivity to his size, his lack of formal education, and his origins. To reduce the complexity of Fiorello's behavior to an inferiority complex is too pat and too simple. His wife, who knew him as well as anyone, dismissed the idea as preposterous. Yet it is a matter of historical record that the Little Flower *was* hypersensitive and, therefore, easily insulted and ferociously combative.

William Manners, *Patience and Fortitude,* 1976:

> The times called for belligerence, for belligerence usually
> went with action. . . . His hostility, aside from being an
> expression of his personality, stemmed from the realization
> that the odds were heavily loaded against him.

August Hecksher III with Phyllis Robinson, *When La Guardia
Was Mayor,* 1978:

> His diminutive stature had played a significant role in the
> creating a stance of belligerence. Like many small men he
> compensated for lack of heft by being prepared to take on
> all comers, on any issue.

Thomas Kessner, *Fiorello La Guardia and the Making of Modern New York,* 1989:

> There was something compulsive about La Guardia's bully-
> ing. For if part of him was ever untrusting, another needed
> to dominate. . . . Some speculated that this had something
> to do with La Guardia's physical size. . . . His resentments
> made him a tough, demanding boss, sparing with thanks
> and incapable of expressing gratitude. He approached his
> exceptional administration with the attitude of a reforma-
> tory supervisor, always sniffing for indiscretions, constantly
> reproving, unable to mind his own considerable business.

In 1906, when Fiorello decided to quit his consular post
and leave Italy, he said to his mother, "I am going back to
America to become a lawyer and make something of myself."

But personal ambition was not the aim of the following
twenty-six years. He wanted to make something of himself so
that he might have opportunities to right the wrongs he had
seen and felt. When Mayor La Guardia yelled "What's the
matter with the little guy?" he was expressing not only sensitivity to people of short physical stature but also all "the little people" who possessed no voice in shaping the course of
their lives.

Joining his resentments to a cause greater than himself,
he would use whatever power that success brought as he'd

used a chair to raise himself to equal footing with a bigger boy in a schoolyard fistfight. Being short had not restrained him in telling royalty that "majesty" could not obtain a "parade" of immigrants. Height did not keep him from taking to the skies to free Trieste and "make the world safe for democracy"; standing up for the powerless in the courts and on picket lines; battling Tammany Hall again and again; being heard in the Congress; and becoming mayor of the greatest city in the world—a city that, his shortness notwithstanding, he intended to turn into a place as close to Eden as patience and fortitude allowed.

If getting there required being a combination Napoleon, Machiavelli, and old-fashioned American demagogue, so be it. As he'd said to a friend after making a speech in 1919, "I can outdemagogue the best of demagogues."

To an aide the next year he bragged, "I invented the low blow."

While at work in his office he sat at a big walnut desk. It was a low one, to accommodate his diminutive figure. (Forty years later the desk was used by Mayor Ed Koch, an over-six-feet-tall chief executive who had wooden blocks put beneath the desk to elevate it to a comfortable height.) Rather than use a phone to summon people to the office, La Guardia had half a dozen buzzers to push, each with a commissioner's name attached.

In an "animal cracker" government no one doubted that the ringmaster was La Guardia. A close observer of his treatment of the men he'd appointed thought that the mayor "put on a great deal of his brutalities to test people out. If they could stand up against him it was all right, but if they couldn't they were in bad luck."

The nearly omniscient Lowell Limpus wrote, "He proceeded to browbeat his subordinates in the same fashion in which he had always bulldozed his little office force. That meant shrieking, screaming and cursing at them—frequently when others were present. It was no rarity for the Chief Executive to hurl his pen on the floor and launch into a bitter tirade against the head of some great city department."

One day after several explosions directed at several of his commissioners he upbraided an errant secretary by shouting at her, "You're so dumb I should make you a commissioner or something."

A favorite method of shaming a commissioner who had misstepped was presentation of the "boner award." The prize was a real bone—a shiny sheep shank kept in a desk drawer in a box trimmed with ribbons. At a moment deemed appropriate during a meeting of commissioners the box came out and was presented. Fire Commissioner McElligott received it for burning himself with a Roman candle while preaching to the press and the public of the hazards of Fourth of July fireworks.

Appreciating that most of his commissioners harbored jealousy against one or all of the others, La Guardia turned the human frailty to his advantage. He appeared to enjoy observing the struggles for his attention. "If he did not promote the interoffice feuds which sprang up," noted Limpus, "he certainly did nothing to check them. Before many months elapsed, most of the members of his personal entourage were bitterly antagonistic to each other. Angry subordinates continually poured complaints against colleagues and superiors into the Mayor's ear."

The La Guardia personal style of targeted vindictiveness was not confined between the walls of his office. On May 11, 1934, it reached into the press room, known then and still known as "Room 9." Because the mayor was feuding with Aldermanic president Bernard S. Deutsch, La Guardia refused to take part in a Deutsch inspection of the Williams bridge Reservoir. Not content with that snub, he let it be known in Room 9 that reporters also should boycott the event. When one of them attended, his boss got a call from La Guardia demanding that the reporter be fired.

Asked by another denizen of Room 9 if he had really asked a managing editor to do so, La Guardia snapped, "Damn right, I did. He wrote lies about me."

The puzzled questioner said sarcastically, "Isn't *that* a fitting performance for the man who always fought for the underdog, to use the prestige of the second most powerful office in this country to get the job of a forty-dollar-a-week reporter? Won't that be something for your children to boast about?"

"Good God," exclaimed the mayor, "I never thought about it that way."

It took years for Room 9 to forgive him (some of the reporters never did), and for a time La Guardia quit holding news conferences. Unlike his political idol, Theodore Roosevelt, he did not encourage closeness with reporters, although he "got along famously" with photographers who were delighted with him for providing a seemingly endless stream of shots decades before the "photo opportunity" became a daily staple of executive branch governance.

Cameramen and reporters found that the mayor who had pledged to be in bed by ten at night was available to them for news not just during the day. The mayor materialized at crime scenes, fires, and even at especially bad traffic accidents. How he knew of these occurrences and managed to arrive so quickly was a mystery, until a reporter discovered that the mayor's new car was equipped with a Police Department radio.

On a lovely evening of La Guardia's first summer as mayor he surprised press and public by showing up with Mrs. La Guardia at the Central Park Mall to preside at a dance contest. But to his and Marie's horror, a crowd of several thousand admirers hoping to get a close look at their mayor surged toward the platform that had been built for the contest. Police ropes broke and the throng poured onto the elevated wooden structure. Their weight collapsed it and sent everyone tumbling in panic.

Bounding from his car, La Guardia told a cop to look out for Marie's safety, then bored through the crowd and began snapping orders to cops. "Get on the phone for help." "Call out the reserves." "Break up the crowd from the outside edges." Climbing onto the shaky platform, he grabbed the microphone. "Be calm, please, ladies and gentlemen. Disperse calmly. We don't want anyone getting hurt. The contest has been canceled. Please make your way home."

Order was presently restored, but the mayor of New York, said one observer, "looked like a wreck." Sweat and dirt stained his face, hands, and white suit.

But that wasn't all His Honor did that night. As he and Marie were leaving the park in their car, he spotted an elderly woman frantically waving at other cars and trying to get them to stop. He told his driver to halt. Rolling down the window, the mayor asked the woman what he could do for her. She answered in a torrent of Italian. The mother of a contestant in the dance contest, she'd lost her daughter and had no idea of where to look for her and how to get to her home in New Jersey.

La Guardia told her who he was and to get into the car, then ordered the driver to take them to the nearby Arsenal police station. It was jammed with shaken, worried, and terrified people. When La Guardia began ordering a harried lieutenant to help the woman, the officer peered at the short, dirty, and disheveled figure and demanded, "What do you expect me to do? Just who the hell do you think you are, giving orders?"

La Guardia smiled. "Personally, Lieutenant, I am a person of no importance . . . but the job I happen to hold is mayor of the City of New York—and damn you, Lieutenant, I want to see my police force function."

Recognized at last, he felt confident that the woman from New Jersey had been turned over to capable hands, returned to his car, settled beside Marie, and said to the driver, "You can take us home now."

Significantly, in upbraiding the lieutenant he had said "*my* police force."

16

"**M**idget Mussolini."

The title was given to La Guardia by *New York Sun* columnist George Ritchie, writing an article on the mayor for H. L. Mencken's *American Mercury*. "His Honor holds in his own hands most of the portfolios of government," said Ritchie. "A one man autocracy with no ifs or buts, now rules New York."

The *Sun* itself declared in an early editorial assessment of the state of the administration, "New York has never been nearer a one man government than today."

Critics who could not bring themselves to compare the mayor to the bald, granite-chinned Italian Fascist dictator chose an earlier figure. To them he was "Little Napoleon." Others saw the "Manhattan Messiah."

Pejorative adjectives abounded: abusive, autocratic, belligerent, brutal, caustic, churlish, crude, cruel, cynical, demanding, grudge-carrying, harsh, hotheaded, ill-tempered, mean, nasty, overbearing, pushy, tyrannical, unforgiving, and unrelenting.

His physical stature and temper were short, but his memory was very long. Case in point: organ grinders. These men were almost always Italian. With their hand-cranked, mechanical music boxes going and leashed monkeys soliciting coins with tin cups or tambourines, they had been plying city sidewalks for as long as anyone could remember. Most New Yorkers found them quaintly amusing, charming, and colorful. They were as much a part of the town's fabric as Coney

Island hot dogs, Nedick's orange-drink stands, Adams Hats and Arrow Shirts billboards, double-decker buses, the horse-drawn hansom cabs in Central Park, the Macy's Thanksgiving Day parade, the Easter Parade on Fifth Avenue, the Times Square pinball arcades, overcrowded subways, nickel fares, burlesque houses, tiny lead Statues of Liberty in souvenir stores, the stone lions in front of the big public library on Fifth Avenue, and periodic outbreaks of reformers dead set on ridding City Hall of any vestiges of the Tammany tiger's money-grubbing influence.

Yet Fiorello La Guardia, still smarting over the humiliation he felt as a "dago" in Arizona in being asked where his monkey was, declared personal all-out war on the city's organ grinders with the same fervor he'd shown in battling Tammany Hall. By mayoral fiat he declared organ grinders public nuisances and ordered police to run them off wherever encountered. He believed that these foreign-looking individuals with their mustaches and broken English called attention to the stereotype of the Italian as the dago, greaser, and guinea. With their funny hats and hurdy-gurdy music, they were just as offensive to Italian sensibilities as Edward G. Robinson had been as "Rico" on the movie screen in *Little Caesar.* (Never mind that Robinson was a Romanian; his name in the film ended in a vowel.)

"What induces him to think," asked the *New York Post,* "that New York can be ruled by Proclamation?"

Part of his animosity toward organ grinders was rooted in the sensibilities and tastes of the cornetist son of an army bandmaster. He felt that what the mechanical contraptions emitted could in no way be construed as music. It was merely noise, and in the City of New York there was already too much of that commodity. To quell the endless city din he dashed off an order to Commissioner Valentine to also instruct patrolmen to issue summonses for auto horn-blowing, loud radios, blaring loudspeakers outside stores, and even Christmas caroling. To mute the clip-clopping of milk delivery wagons' horses he persuaded the Borden Company to shod the animals' hooves with rubber coverings. Billboards went

Mayor La Guardia was the first government official to make regular radio reports to the people. This broadcast was an appeal for support during a squabble with the state legislature in 1934.

up with images of Father Knickerbocker raising a shushing finger to his lips and appealing in several languages for a little more peace and quiet.

As the clatter continued unabated, most literate New Yorkers saw him as a squat Don Quixote tilting with windmills. The *Brooklyn Eagle* asked in a headline, "Can One Spunky Little Mayor Show the World?" In addition to using the offensive "little," the editorial said that a La Guardia proposal for a Municipal Arts Committee was "a cockeyed idea." It continued in a very personal vein, using words that to La Guardia were anathema:

> The *little man* [emphasis added] with the dark double chin is a curious anomaly. He cares more about art than the crease in his pants.
>
> He had rather give the city a municipal art center than to get somehow, by ways *politicians* [emphasis added] know, the money it would cost his own pocket. He'd rather give the people of New York the opportunity to listen cheaply to a symphony by Beethoven than to hear in his honor "The Sidewalks of New York." He actually considers Wagner better music than "Will You Love Me in December as You Do in May." I guess the man is crazy.

To promulgate his tastes the mayor led an effort to provide city funds to underwrite free summer concerts at Lewisohn Stadium. In hopes of assuring that there would be a continuing supply of musicians, he saw to it that New York had a High School of Music and Art (opened in 1936, it was the first in the country). When he browbeat the Board of Aldermen and the Board of Estimate into approving the Municipal Arts Committee, he pronounced that its goal should be to "endeavor through art to increase the grace, happiness, and beauty of our municipal life."

Sixty years later, another music-loving Italian mayor, Rudolph Giuliani, would express the same wish in launching a campaign to improve the city's "quality of life" by ordering the police to evict from the streets an army of auto windshield-cleaning "squeegee men" with the same vigor La Guardia had encouraged Police Commissioner Valentine's force to chase away organ grinders. When "Rudy" set out to rid the city of sex shops and pornography stores, he was emulating La Guardia's campaign to rid shelves in corner stores of "raw" magazines featuring scantily clad and even naked women. A Guiliani war against "three-card monte" games that had proliferated on midtown sidewalks was an echo of La Guardia's drive against the "tinhorns and horse thieves" who ran sidewalk gambling rackets.

With characteristic vigor and appreciation of the political value of a good picture in the newspapers, La Guardia personally went on the attack against all kinds of gambling, but especially the corner-store "one-armed bandit" in the form of the slot machine. The kickoff of the campaign was his appearance at the police station house in which he'd sat as city magistrate, to deal with cases of people who operated the hated devices.

Men who happily dropped coins in the slot machines were "boobs." With dripping scorn he said of one, "Does he use his last two bucks to buy his kids food? This boob pays it over to some tinhorn bookie. Some boob."

The chief of all the city's tinhorn bookies was Frank Costello. Born Franceso Sergilia in Calabria, Italy, in 1893, he was brought to the United States as a child shortly after his birth. At an early age he was running with a street gang in East Harlem. In the 1920s he ran rum for the criminal outfit overseen by Arnold Rothstein. When "Mr. Big" was rubbed out, Costello inherited the gambling operations. In that capacity he was associated with the "boss of bosses" in the Mafia, Charles "Lucky" Luciano. The year before La Guardia became mayor "Uncle Frank," as he was known in the underworld, with his partner Phil Kastel raked in more than $37 million from "mom and pop store" slot machines, estimated at twenty-five thousand in the five boroughs.

Just as bad was "policy," a racket in which the "boobs" put their money on picking the day's "number," a figure derived through a formula based on the outcome of daily horse races at a particular New York track. This wagering was in addition to actual betting on the horses that went on in "bookie parlors" all over a city that never turned the lights out and in which the people had a yen for striking it rich in a horse's dash to the finish line, a roll of the dice, a turn of a card, a spin of a roulette wheel, and dropping the kids' milk money in a slot.

Burning in Fiorello La Guardia's memory were the faro bucking and other gambling he'd seen take the people of Prescott, including his mother, to the cleaners. Should a fake or a phony be caught in Arizona, justice was swift and often at the business end of a hangman's rope. While the mayor of New York could not dispense that kind of treatment to tinhorns, he had the power to make their lives so miserable that they would swiftly decamp.

To draw the attention of that portion of the populace who knew little or nothing about the gambling that pervaded the city he staged "a gambling fair." Amid the Art Deco splendors of the lobby of the new Radio City Music Hall, New Yorkers were encouraged to learn by playing, but without actually having to ante up money. The theme of the fair proclaimed, "You Can't Win." Thousands of the curious came in for a look and a lesson in how not to be a boob, but it's unlikely that those who tried the slots and other gambling paraphernalia were the kind of people who would have done so otherwise.

Mayor La Guardia was famous for wearing a variety of hats. Putting on a high silk one, as he did in 1935 for a ceremony at the Cathedral of St. John the Divine, was a rarity.

As many came to see the mayor as those with an interest in observing how the apparatuses of "evil" worked.

Obviously, if the public were to be rallied behind an all-out assault on gambling rackets, something more eye-catching than a display of equipment in the Radio City Music Hall grand lobby would be needed. Unfortunately, a federal judge had ruled that before any slot machine could be confiscated by the police, proof had to be in hand that it was actually used for gambling. La Guardia's retort to the judge as "Magistrate La Guardia" held court at the West 100th Street police station, with a seized slot machine in evidence, was, "Section 982 of the Penal Act is so clear that there can be no mistake as to its intent and meaning. The machine speaks for itself. It is not a vending machine. It is a gambling machine. A slot machine."

On the basis of that section of the Penal Act, La Guardia followed up the "fair" with a "show." It began with police raids

La Guardia said he hated slot machines because the "boobs" who played them robbed their children of milk money. Holding a hat and looking on as the mayor smashes the one-armed bandits is Police Commissioner Lewis J. Valentine.

and confiscations of slot machines. They were put on a barge on the Hudson River, then towed to the deep waters of Long Island Sound. There, in the company of Valentine, police, reporters, and photographers, the mayor grabbed a sledgehammer and began flailing away at piles of them.

"These machines," he said, pausing to catch his breath, "were controlled by the most vicious of criminal elements."

No more indelible popular image of Mayor Fiorello La Guardia exists in the memory of the people who were alive then, and in the history of the La Guardia years, than that of the tubby, shirtsleeved, sweaty, fiercely expressioned warrior against organized larceny swinging a sledgehammer in the midst of a small mountain of slot machines. When he was through and cameramen had scores of pictures, the battered devices were dumped into the sound.

Grabbing slots from stores and other places where the boobs could feed them was not enough, however. When the mayor learned that a cache of the devices could be found at the True Mint Company at 1860 Broadway, he sent Valentine's cops to raid the place. They found four hundred of the machines, along with records which proved that the slot machines were part of an overall operation run by the Mafia that included the policy racket, bookie parlors, crap games, floating card games, prostitution, loan-sharking, control of labor unions, garbage hauling, extortion, blackmail, and murder.

Uncle Frank's response was to have fifteen thousand of his machines altered to dispense candy. It was clever but futile. La Guardia and Valentine kept the pressure on until Costello gave up and shifted his inventory of slot machines to the friendlier climate of Governor Huey Long's state of Louisiana. There the slots were promoted as "charitable" games. But out of millions of dollars taken in, Uncle Frank's organization handed out only $600 to the needy.

While going after the slot machine racket, La Guardia's police force tackled the policy game—the daily numbers racket—with equal ferocity. In March 1935 Valentine reported to the mayor, and through him to the public, that 7,093 policy arrests had been made. In the Court of Special Sessions between February 1 and September 30, 1934, a total of 30.7 percent of those arrested were found guilty, but given suspended sentences. Only 3.6 percent went to jail. One-third were fined, but only one person got the maximum of $500. The statistics served to validate La Guardia's long-held distrust of judges and contempt for lawyers.

"Swinging-door justice" did not, however, blunt the mayor's zeal for going after tinhorns and chiselers who found profit in serving the base needs of New Yorkers whose fervor against the "rackets" did not—and never would—match his. In his last year in office he was still receiving "tips" about gambling operations. "Go on out now," he blared at Valentine and his force. "Snap into it. Clean them out!"

One can only wonder what La Guardia would think, and say, if he could come back to life, look around his city, and find that "policy" had become "the lottery," run not by crooks but by the State of New York, with "tickets" on sale everywhere. And sold in vending machines. And that any New Yorker who desired to put a bet on a horse running anywhere in the country could do so in city-owned Off-Track Betting rooms, complete with food, drinks, comfortable chairs, and color television screens showing the races.

He might also note that nothing had changed in the relationship of some of the people of New York and their Police Department. The mayor who had seen his own police distrusted in Harlem would find the cops of seventy years later viewed the same way. And he probably would not be surprised that the Police Department was regularly pilloried with accusations of "going too far" and engaging in "police brutality." Nor is it likely that he would be astonished that almost anything done by the police drew howls of complaint from "liberals" about trampling the "civil rights" of criminals.

As noted by biographer Thomas Kessner, La Guardia carried with him a rather simple view of old-fashioned justice. Kessner quoted La Guardia's remarks to a meeting of the Holy Name Society. "Out where I was raised," the mayor said, "we didn't have much of a Police Department. We had a sheriff and a few deputies. Our sheriff was quick on the trigger, if you know what I mean. If gangsters speak well of the Police Department it's a sign there's something wrong in the department."

This was an opinion shared by Brooklyn-born and raised Lewis J. Valentine. As soon as he was in office, he reinstituted the "Strong-Arm Squad" to deal with gangsters. He promised, "There will be promotions for the men who kick those gorillas around and bring them in."

The assembled plainclothesmen were told, "I want the gangster to tip his hat to a cop."

That this was not "pep talk" rhetoric was made plain on November 17, 1934. Part of that morning Valentine had spent at the bedside of a patrolman who lay dying after being shot by a criminal who had escaped. Returning to headquarters, the commissioner learned that his men had arrested a young man in connection with the murder of a garage employee, and that the man was at that moment standing in a lineup. Valentine went to observe. In the glare of lights stood the youth wearing a smart pearl-gray fedora and a Chesterfield overcoat with a velvet collar.

"Look at him," Valentine blared. "He's the best-dressed man in this room, yet he's never worked a day in his life. When you meet men like this, don't be afraid to muss 'em up. Men like him should be mussed up. Blood should be smeared all over that velvet collar. Instead, he looks as though he just came out of a barber shop. You men will be supported by me no matter what you do, if what you do is justified. Make it disagreeable for men like that. Drive them out of the city. Teach them to fear arrest. Make them fear you."

Entering his office, the commissioner found a group of waiting reporters, and that word of his speech in the lineup room had preceded him. Still angry because a cop had been shot and killed while on duty, he was just as blunt to the "boys from the press shack."

With jutting jaw he said, "The sooner we get rid of gangsters the better." He quickly added, "On the other hand, no police brutality of innocent citizens will be tolerated. The decent working people should be and will be protected, but it will be the crooks who are carried out in boxes, not the cops."

In understated prose in *This Man La Guardia* Lowell Limpus and Burr Leyson wrote, "Next day Commissioner Valentine awoke to find himself famous."

He arrived at 240 Centre Street and into a cyclone of outraged public opinion and heated denunciations from civil libertarians. Undaunted, he said to another pack of reporters, "What I said yesterday I repeat today."

Among a flood of disapproving letters to the mayor's office La Guardia found one from Felix Frankfurter. The eminent jurist said, "Valentine has outbrutalized all the brutal utterances of his predecessors." The mayor repeated his assertion that judges were soft on criminals. The people such as Frankfurter and others of like mind who got up in arms over the idea that a cop would "muss up" a criminal, he said, "would

When Commissioner Valentine ordered his cops to "muss up" criminals, La Guardia backed him up despite protests from civil libertarians. His order to Valentine was to run the bums, tinhorns, and chiselers out of town.

be the first to suffer and complain" if the police failed to protect them and their property.

The storm got worse. Learning of the arrest of gangster Dutch Schultz, Valentine said he would have been "happier" if Schultz had been brought to headquarters "in a box." On another occasion, when a gangster was shot and killed by the police, Valentine shrugged and said, "Just another dead criminal . . . a small loss."

In January 1935 La Guardia cited "numerous recent killings" of policeman by criminals. "This is not a time for coddling crooks," he said. "When the war is on you cannot stand by and expect that a police officer is going to be shot by a cowardly crook."

A week later, Valentine declared that with "barbarians and savages" walking the streets, "It's about time we gave honest people a break."

Shouts for Valentine to resign fell on deaf ears at City Hall. Some La Guardia historians deduced from this that after having lost one police commissioner who had blasted La Guardia for interfering with the department, La Guardia was not eager to see a second top cop go. But at no time in La Guardia's three terms did he exhibit a reluctance to fire a commissioner or accept a resignation. If he had felt that Valentine should leave, he would have said so, and Valentine would have been gone. Resignation was not contemplated for a moment at City Hall or at 240 Centre Street.

This did not mean that La Guardia had taken a hands-off policy regarding the police. The commissioner found himself on the receiving end of La Guardia tirades as often as anyone else. One day, in reply to a written report to the mayor on an investigation La Guardia had demanded, Valentine received the following:

> Fortunately the report is on the letterhead of the Police Department, written in great big black letters. Otherwise I would be at a loss to know whether such a report came from the boy scouts or from some student of a correspondence school on How To Be A Detective. It is the most idiotic, incomplete, stupid investigation that I have seen and I have seen a great many along the same line.
>
> It is this kind of conduct that brings scorn upon the whole department. A known crook is pointed out to the police and he is called in and says he is a good man and that is all there is to it.
>
> Hereafter you will be good enough to read the reports before submitting any such drivel and rot to the Mayor. I am too busy to read such stupid writings, but I am not too busy to go over to headquarters and take hold of the department if that is necessary.

It was not. Omnipresent observer and prolific chronicler of La Guardia and his top cop, Lowell Limpus, offered a book on Valentine, *Honest Cop* (1939), that presented a portrait of an engaged police commissioner who "knew exactly what he wanted to do from the moment he was sworn in." The Lewis J. Valentine on Limpus's pages was a serene figure at his big desk, surrounded by Dictaphones, secretaries, clerks, and telephones. "There is no doubt," the passage concluded, "that he ran the Police Department."

In fact, nothing Valentine had said about "mussing up" criminals differed from the rules laid down by a previous police commissioner, Edward Mulrooney. Addressing the Patrolmen's Benevolent Association in 1931 he'd said, "I do not want you to have any hesitancy if you come upon a man who is a criminal or racketeer and you have reason to believe he is armed. I want you to pull first and give it to him if he makes any attempt to get you. Don't be the last to draw."

It was the era of the gangster, both in movies loved by the public but deplored by La Guardia and on the streets of New York City. But Edward G. Robinson's "Rico" paled in comparison to the real McCoys. There was nothing celluloid about Lucky Luciano, Frank Costello, Dutch Schultz, Owney Madden, Terrible Johnny Torrio and his scar-faced protégé Al Capone, Louis "Lepke" Buchalter, Waxey Gordon, "Two-Gun" Crowley, Legs Diamond, Socks Lanza, Joe Adonis, "artichoke king" Ciro Terranova, and others.

In the 1920s and halfway through the 1930s there had been more actual shootouts in New York City than in all the gangster pictures combined. In 1928 five cops had been killed in gun battles and thirteen had barely escaped with their lives. In 1931 Patrolman Frederick Hirsch had been shot dead by Two-Gun Crowley in a West End Avenue apartment. Crowley then blasted away against several cops in an exchange that had seven hundred slugs flying. Five hit Crowley, but he was alive and fighting when two detectives broke in and collared him. The one who got hands on him first was John Broderick, a hard-knuckled veteran police reporters dubbed "Two-Fist Johnny" and "Broderick the Beater." Unfortunately, the legendary cop was caught up in the revelations of police graft dredged up by the Seabury investigation and demoted. He had been so tough that writer Joel Sayre in a

1936 profile of him in the *New Yorker* turned his name into a verb. "To Broderick or to give the Broderick" meant "to apply wild physical force."

Almost all of the big-time gangsters had been made possible, La Guardia pointed out, by Prohibition. But in December 1933 the Twenty-first Amendment was ratified, marking the end of America's fourteen-year-long nose-thumbing of the Eighteenth Amendment and bringing in the repeal that Congressman La Guardia had called for almost ceaselessly.

With no more illegal liquor to sell, bootleggers had plunged wholesale and headlong into all the rackets that Mayor La Guardia and his intrepid police commissioner sought to eradicate, or at least minimize.

～

On July 1, 1935, their crusade against the lords of the underworld won an ally. He was a thirty-three-year-old former U.S. attorney in the Southern District of New York with a stellar record in winning convictions in cases against corrupt officials and gangsters who bought their services. A lifelong and ardent Republican, he was Thomas E. Dewey. Born on March 24, 1902, in the small town of Owosso, Michigan, he earned his law degree at Columbia University and went on to a distinguished career as a member of two prestigious law firms. Activity in the Republican Party earned him the job of assistant U.S. attorney and the challenging task of prosecuting one of the city's most notorious hoodlums.

Waxey Gordon (real name, Irving Wexler) had been a protégé of Arnold Rothstein and as such had controlled almost all rum running along the New York and New Jersey coasts. He was an underworld magnate and lived like one. His illicit enterprises had made him a profit of $4.5 million in two years, on which he paid income tax of $2,010. He had accounts in two hundred banks, and his mob was said to have committed sixteen murders in three months.

In going after Waxey, Dewey and his associates interviewed more than a thousand witnesses and followed up more

Mayor La Guardia confers in 1937 with crime-busting district attorney Thomas E. Dewey. They made a formidable team in going after gangsters such as Lucky Luciano and Dutch Schultz, gambling boss Frank Costello, and American Nazi leader Fritz Kuhn.

than one hundred thousand telephone tips. The result of two years of investigation was the indictment of Waxey for tax evasion. The trial jurors were so persuaded by the evidence Dewey presented that they took only fifty-one minutes to find him guilty.

Judge Frank J. Coleman said, "It is my firm conviction that never in this court or any other has such fine work been done for the government."

Five days after Waxey's criminal career ended Prohibition expired, and so did Dewey's as a U.S. attorney. The country had a new president, Democrat Franklin D. Roosevelt. In keeping with tradition, FDR replaced all the Republicans in the federal attorney posts with Democrats. Dewey went back to private practice, but not for long. In 1935 New York's Democratic governor, Herbert Lehman, chose him to investigate governmental corruption and criminal gangs as a special prosecutor.

One newspaper hailed the choice with the headline "The Young David Is Sent in against the Gang Goliath." For Dewey the adjective "young" would be as persistently applied to him in newspaper stories as "short" was to Fiorello La Guardia. Even Lowell Limpus in his La Guardia biography could not resist calling Dewey "the youthful Special Prosecutor."

On July 29, 1935, at the New York County Courthouse just a few blocks from City Hall, Justice Philip McCook, who had sworn in Mayor La Guardia, administered the oath of office to Thomas E. Dewey and his staff. Denizens of New York's gangland gave the special prosecutor another description. They derided him as "the Boy Scout."

A delighted mayor welcomed Dewey's appointment by urging that the position be made a permanent bureau for crime suppression. A mayoral memo went to police headquarters telling the commissioner to cooperate in every way with Dewey. Valentine began by ordering a "grand census" of criminals. The lengthy list was sent to Dewey's offices on the fourteenth floor of the Woolworth Building, diagonally across Broadway from La Guardia's office.

Dewey lost no time in explaining his mandate. "This investigation will deal with vice only where it exists in organized form," he told reporters. "We are concerned with those predatory vultures who traffic on a wholesale scale in the bodies of women and mere girls for profit."

In words that thrilled and encouraged the mayor he continued:

> We are concerned with professional criminals who run large, crooked gambling places and lotteries at the expense of the public. Any criminal operation which pours money into the coffers of organized crime is a continuing menace to the safety of the community.
>
> There is today scarcely a business in New York which does not somehow pay its tribute to the underworld—a tribute levied by force and collected by fear. There is certainly not a family in the City of New York which does not pay its share of tribute to the underworld every day it lives and with every meal it eats. This huge unofficial sales tax is collected from the ultimate consumer in the price he pays for everything he buys. Every barrel of flour consumed in New York City pays it toll to racketeers, which goes right into

the price of every loaf of bread. Every chicken shipped into
the City of New York pays its tribute to the poultry racket,
out of the pockets of the public. There are few vegetable or
fish markets in the City of New York where merchants are
not forced by sluggings, destruction of goods, threats and
stink bombs to pay a heavy toll.

In outlining an all-fronts attack on organized crime the
new special prosecutor read from the gospel of La Guardia.
The mayor said Dewey was "an invaluable reinforcement."

Reporters and especially photographers relished seeing
the two crime fighters together as the Columbia doctor of law
and letters and the NYU nighttime law school graduate sat
at La Guardia's desk. Dewey was slim and no taller than
La Guardia, but meticulously tailored in a gray suit with vest,
hair parted in the middle, and with a neatly trimmed brush
mustache as he held a cigarette. The mayor, with hair parted
on the left side and a large cowlick at the back, was chubby
in a navy blue double-breasted suit with pudgy left hand
cradling a bent-stem pipe and the right resting on Dewey's
left arm. Dewey is the one who is listening.

While welcoming Dewey into the war against crime, Mayor
La Guardia had no intention of relinquishing the entire fight—
and certainly not all the limelight—to a special prosecutor or
anyone else. When it came to histrionics and theatricality,
Fiorello would yield the laurels to nobody. To prove this he
chose to go after a gangster who was particularly loathsome
to the amateur Italian chef of East Harlem.

The hoodlum's name was Ciro Terranova, and he controlled
the market in a commodity that was as essential to a fine
Italian meal as olive oil. Terranova was self-proclaimed "king
of the artichoke." Based in the Bronx Terminal Market, he
had a stranglehold on importation from the West Coast and
distribution in the city. None came in without Ciro's impri-
matur. None went out to grocers and produce stands without
Ciro being paid a tribute.

To enjoy artichokes was to further stuff Ciro's already
bloated pockets. To the mayor, who despised anyone whose
activities demeaned Italians, Terranova was a double abomi-

nation. He was an Italian gangster who cruelly exploited Italians.

The day on which Fiorello La Guardia chose to take down Ciro Terranova, December 20, 1935, happened to be the coldest of the year. At six in the morning, when La Guardia and his minions departed City Hall for the Bronx, the air temperature hovered around zero. At that hour of the morning traffic was light. The mayoral automobile and police patrol car escorts proceeded swiftly to the Terminal Market. Their arrival was timed to coincide with that of numerous police cars from nearby precincts. Two Bronx officers carried trumpets. The mayor left his car carrying a rolled-up mayoral proclamation.

The trumpets blared, but the morning was so frigid that the valves of one froze tight. The remaining horn sounded again and again. Workers in Terranova's warehouse and others dashed out to see what was going on. They gazed in astonishment as Mayor La Guardia climbed onto the tailgate of a truck and unrolled a large sheet of paper. In disbelief the workers and a sizable crowd of workers from other produce warehouses heard a proclamation outlawing "the sale, possession, and display" anywhere in the city of artichokes, effective the next day.

His authority to do so, he declared, was found in ancient law that empowered the mayor in an emergency to ban distribution of food. What was the emergency? Appreciating that there was none, and anticipating a rush to the courts by Terranova's lawyers to find an amenable judge to declare the proclamation illegal, La Guardia had sent the corporation counsel, Paul Windels, to Washington, D.C., to get an eager-to-accommodate Department of Agriculture to revoke the king of the artichoke's Union Pacific Produce Company's license to purvey food.

As Terranova's lucrative racket was shuttered by Valentine's cops, New York's editorial writers flew into a tizzy. "Where," demanded the *New York Post,* "does La Guardia get the idea that he had the right to keep merchants from selling artichokes?"

La Guardia, in high dudgeon and with deep satisfaction, answered, "I want it clearly understood that no bunch of racketeers, thugs, and punks are going to intimidate you [the people] as long as I am the mayor of the City of New York."

The *Herald Tribune* deplored the action, but verbally shrugged its shoulders with, "It is impossible not to conclude the world today is a bit mad."

With Terranova out of business, La Guardia arranged for other artichoke firms on the West Coast to distribute in the city. Within a few days, neighborhood markets were overflowing with the spiny vegetable. Prices dropped by 30 percent.

La Guardia's striking out at Terranova was viewed by most New Yorkers as a publicity stunt, which it surely was. But inevitably the racket-busting spotlight shone on Dewey. He had considerably more power than La Guardia and Valentine because of his unique authority to seat grand juries. He also operated in a veil of secrecy as he moved against loan sharks; gamblers; the baking, restaurant, trucking, and garment industry rackets; and gang-dominated prostitution.

In the latter enterprise the fastidious prosecutor with the hairbrush mustache and his team of investigators set their sights on the most famous resident of the new Waldorf-Astoria Hotel. He was registered under an assumed name, but everyone recognized that the dapper little man with a crescent face scar was the former Salvatore Lucania, now feared as Charles "Lucky" Luciano.

Mayor La Guardia had a standing order to the police: "Arrest him on sight."

Arresting Luciano was one thing; getting the evidence needed to convict him of crimes was another matter altogether.

Knowing that Luciano ran prostitution in the city, Dewey began his pursuit by sending out teams to raid the houses and apartments where Charlie's "girls" worked. The women then found themselves escorted covertly to the freight elevators of the Woolworth Building. Dewey and his staffers waited to question them. The names the women gave were as colorful as any found in the stories of Broadway "guys and dolls" immortalized by the newspaperman Damon Runyon. Dewey stenographers jotted Gas House Lil, Frisco Jean, Nigger Ruth, Polack Frances, Silver-Tongued Elsie, Sadie the Chink, Jennie the Factory, and the one who finally gave Dewey a break in his pursuit of proof against Charlie Lucky, a brassy hooker named Cokey Flo.

On the basis of her testimony and evidence gathered by investigators, Dewey succeeded in arresting Luciano and putting him on trial, not as America's crime kingpin, but for the lowly crime of prostitution. When the trial began on May 11, 1936, Dewey admitted, "Frankly, my witnesses are prostitutes, madams, heels, pimps, and ex-convicts. Many of them have been in jail. Others are about to go to jail." He added, "We can't get bishops to testify in a case involving prostitution. And this [criminal activity] was not run under arc lights in Madison Square Garden. We have to use the testimony of bad men to convict other bad men."

The judge was Philip McCook, the very man who had administered the oaths of office to Dewey and at midnight on January 1, 1934, to Fiorello La Guardia. On June 6, 1936, McCook spent two hours explaining the charges and the law to the Luciano jury. They had sat listening to the witnesses, to Cokey Flo's damning testimony, and the circumstantial evidence since May 11. When they finished their deliberations early in the morning of June 7, they'd decided that it was time for Lucky's good fortune to run out. Judge McCook averred that Luciano was incapable of rehabilitation and gave him a sentence of thirty to fifty years.

At police headquarters Commissioner Valentine promoted sixteen patrolmen who had assisted Dewey's men in collecting evidence and witnesses.

Mayor La Guardia joined the chorus of praise for Dewey, but added that Luciano could not have existed without help from corrupt men in government and law enforcement. Of those individuals he recommended that "at least six commit *hara-kiri*."

By autumn of 1937 special prosecutor Dewey and his stalwart deputies would compile an amazing record of convicting all but one of the individuals indicted (seventy-two of seventy-three). The result was the breaking of the big rackets in Manhattan and imprisonment of numerous gangsters. But the credit for awakening the public to the extent of organized crime that led to Dewey's appointment belonged to the indefatigable foe of tinhorns and chiselers who presided in City Hall. The little cornetist who blew his horn to arouse sleeping people to a fire in Tampa, Florida, in 1898, had sounded the alarm to arouse the decent citizens of New York City to an enemy lurking in the shadows like a spider whose web radiated to every corner of the city and touched each facet of the people's lives.

If La Guardia had not been mayor in 1935, could there have been a Thomas E. Dewey? Perhaps, but probably not. If there were no Dewey, would Lucky Luciano have been sent "up the river"? Possibly, but not very likely at that time.

For Lucky Luciano, the Little Flower would remain a puzzle. "I just couldn't understand that guy," he said in a self-serving and frequently questionable autobiography. "We offered to make him rich he wouldn't even listen. So I figured what the hell, let him keep City Hall, we got all the rest."

Having chalked up victories against the tinhorns, chiselers, and an array of characters who were a lot worse, the mayor turned a page on the calendar and started planning to run for reelection in 1937. George Ritchie of the *Sun* delved into the history of New York's mayors and offered a gloomy observation: "In the 271 years of its existence as a chartered community no chief executive elected on a Holier Than Thou platform has survived to enjoy a second four year term." Normally Democratic, he continued, "the Metropolis has a habit of swiftly soothing its outraged civic virtue, whipped to momentary heat by rambunctious reformers, and resuming its incorrigible ways, under the smooth functioning, if reprehensible tutelage of Tammany."

If La Guardia wanted another example in history of the fickleness of "the people" he had only to look up the biography of the man to whom he was often compared. Even the French had tired of their Napoleon and shuffled him off into exile.

Might it happen that the good people of New York would go to the polls in November 1937 and do the same with theirs?

17

After one year of Mayor La Guardia the *New York Times* had opined, "He has said some foolish things and done many wise ones, but has unfortunately too often given the impression of being a restless and undecided man, fond of toying with haphazard proposals that may be benevolent in intention but are dangerous or impossible in practice. He seems always to want to have in hand some socialistic plaything or other."

Was Fiorello a Socialist? Or was he a "municipal officer" who liked some ideas of the Socialists, but realized the way to attain them was by making the S in Socialism more palatable by shifting it to lower case? He had embraced the platform of the Progressives, then said he was a Republican and ran that way. But not a "regular" one. Having been elected as the Fusion candidate for mayor, he'd frequently run city government as though the rest of the men on the ticket did not exist. This "failure," as it was termed by critics, to cement a Fusion organization for the future indicated that in La Guardia "principle" took a backseat to expediency. Was he, after all, the very creature he said he despised: a *politician?*

Analyzing La Guardia as he stood on the brink of another election, contemporaneous biographer Jay Franklin wrote in 1937:

> The truth seems to be that Fiorello La Guardia is afflicted with that noble disease of the mind: an artistic temperament. His principles and policies are those of a Western Progressive; his personal methods are often those of a prima

211

donna, a virtuoso, a political Heifetz, and administrative Gershwin—tending to sacrifice everything to the demands of the particular audience, often creating future difficulties for himself and his political purposes by adopting the slogan: "The show must go on!" It is an amazingly versatile performance, but it would be helped by occasional intermission.

In the three years between Franklin's portrait of La Guardia and that of the *Times* the record of the mayor provided ample evidence to support the argument that La Guardia was a man of principle. But just as much proof could be found to show that he acted on the grounds that the end justified the means. True, he could be dictatorial, but he was trying to run a city government of 140,000 employees with an annual budget of $600 million. The only head of a bigger government was the president of the United States. But Franklin D. Roosevelt had won in a landslide that also gave him a Democratic majority in Congress. Fiorello H. La Guardia came to City Hall as a Fusion mayor having to deal with a legislative body (the Board of Aldermen) and a second body that controlled spending (the Board of Estimate) without a reliable majority to back him and his policies. The Little Napoleon could boss and browbeat his commissioners, but not other elected officials. Unlike FDR, noted one observer, he could not attempt to solve the city's complex and interwoven political, economic, and social problems with the "magic wand" of monetary largess of the Roosevelt administration.

How La Guardia balanced political expediency against principle was demonstrated in the adoption of a new city charter. If approved, it would streamline city government by eliminating the sixty-five member Board of Aldermen and creating a City Council with twenty-five seats, thereby limiting the influence of the five borough presidents. The new charter also established a City Planning Commission to direct all future growth in the city according to a master plan. How the mayor felt about it initially was phrased in typical La Guardia language: "What a mess!"

Recognizing that the new charter was the best that could be had at that time, he threw his weight behind it because, he said, it represented "very substantial gains for the citizens." When the document was placed before voters for ratification in the fall of 1936, it garnered nearly a million assents and six hundred thousand dissents. The only borough in which it failed was Richmond (Staten Island), where voters feared a loss of seats when city councilors replaced aldermen.

As the charter revision was debated during the summer of 1936, the mayor had removed himself from City Hall to conduct business in the somewhat cooler Bartow-Pell mansion in the Bronx. (Marie and the children were evacuated from sweltering East Harlem to a rented house in Westport, Connecticut.) A handsome mid-nineteenth-century stone building, the Bronx summer City Hall was one of several old estates that had come into care and keeping of the city's Parks Department. To keep in touch with City Hall a teletype machine was installed and a Police Department patrol wagon, labeled CITY HALL BUS, shuttled people back and forth.

While the mayor was settling into the Bartow-Pell mansion, the overseer of all the city's public spaces, Robert Moses, was directing the final stages of work in creating Orchard Beach in collaboration with the federal government's Works Progress Administration (WPA). The new amenity included a mile-long beach of white sand imported from Long Island shores, a handsome red-brick pavilion with facilities for six thousand bathers, extensive landscaped playgrounds, and athletic fields and parking for seven thousand cars.

For sweating residents of upper Manhattan the first of ten "million-dollar pools" planned for the city was opened at Hamilton Fish Park, with the mayor on hand to dedicate it on June 20. A week later he was in Harlem dedicating improvements to Thomas Jefferson Park that included an Olympic-size pool. In time for July Fourth it was the Astoria pool in Queens, and on July 31 McCarran Pool in Brooklyn. Each of these openings featured Moses's ceremonial hallmarks of flag-draped speakers' platform and white-gloved park attendants in military-style outfits.

Other Moses extravaganzas for the mayor to attend that summer included the June 29 groundbreaking for the New

York World's Fair, scheduled to open in 1939. The area chosen as the site was a former city dump in the Flushing section of Queens. "The scene was forlorn as hundreds of hungry men waited in line hoping for work," wrote August Hecksher III with Phyllis Robinson in a 1978 La Guardia biography. "It was difficult to conceive how the immense garbage dump could be transformed into the glittering pavilions of 1939. Yet Moses saw well beyond the Fair to the day when its site would become a verdant park in the keeping of his department." Although Moses was a visionary, he probably did not imagine that the grounds of the 1939 World's Fair would also be the site of another World's Fair in 1964–1965, and that it, too, would be a Robert Moses realization.

Twelve days after the earth was broken for the World's Fair, the next Moses event was the dedication of the Triborough Bridge, an occasion deemed so significant that President Roosevelt came down from his summer White House at Hyde Park, New York, to participate. As though needing to participate in the biggest public event in New York since the welcome-home given to aviator Charles Lindbergh in 1927, Mother Nature saw to it that the date would be memorable in the annals of weather by boosting the temperature to the highest degree in the Weather Bureau's records, 102.3 degrees. Moses wore a white linen suit.

Along with these improvements to the city in the summer of 1936 the mayor basked in the accomplishment of an Italian American who was one of his favorite baseball players. On May 24 Tony Lazzeri of the New York Yankees drove in eleven runs in one game, including two grand slam home runs to set an American League record as the Yankees beat the Philadelphia Athletics, 25–2. The Yankees went on to win the 1936 World Series by defeating the New York Giants 4 games to 2.

That summer La Guardia's city hailed the arrival of a new queen of the North Atlantic as the Cunard Line's *Queen Mary* completed her maiden voyage from Southampton, England. For New Yorkers who desired faster travel to Europe, Pan American Airways inaugurated Clipper service on June

Future mayor La Guardia and Governor (and future president) Franklin D. Roosevelt at the dedication of the Triborough Bridge. (AP/Wide World)

27. The four-engine, sumptuously appointed seaplane *Dixie Clipper* departed from nearby Port Washington, Long Island, and landed at Lisbon, Portugal, twenty-three hours and fifty-two minutes later. For the former World War I aviator the accomplishment fueled a desire to see the day when a New Yorker would be able to board an airliner without having to leave the city to find an airport.

One long-held La Guardia dream became a reality in 1936. The doors opened to admit students to the High School of Music and Art.

One bright autumn day that year he led a procession of fourteen city cars in a whirlwind inspection of movie theaters in Manhattan to see whether another of his projects involving city children was being implemented. Concerned about the quality and content of the pictures being viewed by children, he had instituted a regulation under which theaters had to keep kids from entering to see some films unless accompanied by an adult. He found to his dismay that many of the children got around the restriction by asking strangers to take them in. The La Guardia edict also required theaters to set aside a children's section and to have a matron in attendance. It was another idea that sounded good in theory but failed in practice.

He demonstrated his interest in children by congratulating five hundred graduates of the Central Needles Trades High School and telling them, "A first-class tailor is worth a great deal more to the community than a third-class lawyer." Another group of students entered a civics class to find that their teacher for the hour was the mayor of their city. Sixteen high school students with an interest in government service were hired as City Hall interns.

When children in Brooklyn were about to be denied the experience of seeing a circus because License Commissioner Paul Moss yielded to demands from adults that the Ringling Brothers Circus be denied permission to set up its big top and thereby disrupt their tranquillity, Mayor La Guardia ordered Moss to grant the permit. "The circus under canvas," said Fiorello, "is an American institution."

One place where the artistic, music-loving promulgator of the arts would not be seen was an opening of a Broadway show. While Jimmy Walker had never missed a premiere, La Guardia declined a pair of opening-night tickets for him and Marie from showman Billy Rose with, "We never attend first nights. They are for the *Social Register*ites. We will go along with the common people sometime later on."

Being at a show did not necessarily mean staying through it to the end. While attending a movie and stage show at Radio City Music Hall he learned of a nearby fire, bounded from his seat, and dashed to the scene. The blaze was in a restaurant. Not content to watch the firemen do their job, he went into the building. When he emerged, he told the worried supervising fire chief, "I gave the refrigeration system a personal going-over. I wanted to find out whether the building code had been violated." The mayor appeared at so many fires that he was issued a fireman's helmet and heavy rubber coat.

While he was mayor it seemed that he rushed to see an emergency of every kind, from one-alarm fires to roaring infernos, building collapses, water main breaks, and anything else, including shootings, reported over his police radio. A common shout from the professionals who were dealing with the event became, "Will someone get the mayor out of there?!"

"New York saw its stocky little Mayor in many places and poses," wrote Jay Franklin in 1937. "In one case he arrived on the scene almost as soon as the police themselves."

To get to an emergency when the mayoral auto was in for repairs he commandeered a police motorcycle with sidecar and sped off with the gleeful shout, "I am not a sissy!"

He once explained to a reporter that his approach to emergencies and how he handled the day-to-day business of running the city were the same. "I am like the boys in the trenches at zero hour," he said. "It is not time to hesitate or reflect. It is not time to consider one's self. I am going over the top because it is my duty. If I succumb it will be in a worthy cause."

To assure citizens of the other four boroughs that he cared about them, he occasionally set up a temporary City Hall in one of them. "This is a big city," he said. After he had spent a week in Brooklyn, the borough's newspaper, the *Brooklyn Eagle,* said in an editorial, "It makes us in Brooklyn feel, Mr. Mayor, that you consider our interests, that you are solicitous for our welfare, that we mean something more than a taxable asset to the government."

In the midst of all this governing he always came back to the root of all the problems he and the city faced. "It is a most discouraging feeling to be the head of the largest and richest city in the world," he said, "and find yourself helpless because you want to clean the city, and it would be so easy if you could eliminate the selfish greed of politicians."

His causes were many: housing, health, crime, open spaces, music for the masses, art, labor, civic pride, citizens' duties, the welfare of children, the conditions of streets, clean water, garbage collection and disposal, schools, electricity and gas rates, the subway system, keeping the five-cent fare, the price of meat and produce, noise, and—always—"the people."

He tackled these challenges one at a time and all at once, big and small.

Back from the summer City Hall in the Bronx in September 1936 he learned that the city's milk suppliers, Borden and Sheffield, wanted to raise the price of a quart of milk at city health stations from eight to nine cents. This was, roared the mayor, "an unfriendly act" that meant "war." He waged it by switching the city's milk buying to small, independent dairies. He also proposed that the city build its own milk pasteurization plant at the Bronx Terminal Market as a means of providing a "yardstick" for milk prices. The big suppliers surrendered and kept milk at eight cents.

When the Consolidated Edison Natural Gas Company was deemed to be gouging the city on the cost of streetlights, he threatened to construct a city-owned power plant for that purpose. The lights powered by Consolidated stayed on, but at a reduced rate. Believing that private consumers were also being overcharged, he again held out the prospect of city-supplied electricity. Consolidated quickly announced lower rates that saved the people in the city that kept the lights on all night $7 million a year on their electric bills.

In a city caught in the depths of the Great Depression, many of its people had more to worry about than paying a light bill. Thousands of them were unemployed and did not have the money to pay the rent in tenements in some of the worst slums in the country, primarily on the Lower East Side and in Harlem. The problem was urgent, but so vast that fixing it was beyond the means of the city the mayor repeatedly described as the richest in the world.

During the campaign that had put him into office, La Guardia had advocated clearing the slums and building model multiple dwellings under a municipal housing authority financed by grants and loans from the federal government. Consequently, just weeks after taking office, he turned for assistance to Washington, D.C., and the president who had been elected promising a New Deal. The feisty little mayor who went with Stetson hat in hand in search of money in the national capital bore good credentials. As Congressman La Guardia in the first year of FDR's administration he had been an ardent supporter of New Deal programs. On the occasion of the president's birthday he'd sent a telegram that was as much political as congratulatory.

It said in part:

YOU CAN COUNT ON NEW YORK CITY DOING ITS PART BY FOLLOWING YOUR SPLENDID LEADERSHIP IN THE GREAT BATTLE NOW BEING WAGED AGAINST DEPRESSION, POVERTY AND UNHAPPINESS.

Roosevelt proved grateful and receptive to the mayor's appeal for help. FDR's Secretary of the Interior, Harold L. Ickes, also a New Yorker, wired City Hall that if La Guardia established a New York City Housing Authority, the federal taps would be opened. The result was swift enactment by the state legislature of the Municipal Housing Authorities Law. Under its provision the city created the New York City Housing Authority. Organized in February 1934 (and still in existence seven decades later), its purpose was to "promote the public health and safety by providing for the elimination of unsanitary and dangerous housing conditions, to relieve congested areas," and to foster the "construction and supervision of dwellings" and "apartments at reasonable rentals."

The popular term became, and remained, "public housing." As a concept it would be eventually coupled with unemployment compensation, Social Security, disability payments, rent controls, government medical benefits, child care, food stamps, and a host of other "benefits" and "entitlements" that would be characterized as "the welfare state." With the enthusiastic cultivation by Fiorello H. La Guardia it was incubated and came to flower first in New York. The city and nation's experiment in government-subsidized housing was launched on December 3, 1935, and called "First Houses." Built on property that had been owned primarily by Vincent Astor between Avenue A and Second Avenue (the Lower East Side), they consisted of eight new and renovated buildings that provided 122 modern, centrally heated, fireproof apartments at an average rent of $6 a room per month. Each unit had a common laundry room. There were common recreation areas indoors and meeting rooms. For children there were both inside play areas and playgrounds. A beaming mayor surveyed the bright, airy residences and said for the benefit of press and for critics who viewed the project as a boondoggle, "This is boondoggling exhibit A."

Among the dignitaries as he spoke were Governor Lehman and President Roosevelt's wife (and by now La Guardia's good friend and ally), Eleanor. They were bundled in coats in freezing December air as La Guardia said, "A great constitutional lawyer two years ago told me it would be a cold day when the government builds houses. Well, he was right that time."

Under subsequent federal laws La Guardia would oversee the city's Housing Authority's building of the Red Hook and Kingsborough Houses in Brooklyn, the Vladeck and East River Houses in Manhattan, the Queensborough and South Jamaica Houses in Queens, the Clason Point Gardens in the Bronx, and the Edwin Markham Houses on Staten Island.

Thirty-seven years after Fiorello hailed the realization of public housing, Marie would unveil a bust of her late husband at the La Guardia Houses in lower Manhattan.

18

"The Little Flower was mastering New York City as no mayor since Peter Stuyvesant has mastered it," wrote Robert Caro in his monumental biography of La Guardia's commissioner of parks. "But the Little Flower wasn't mastering Robert Moses."

The relationship from the start was one of verbal fisticuffs that often came close to an actual exchange of blows. A frequent witness to them circling one another "like a couple of stiff-legged bulldogs" was Reuben A. Lazarus. The city's official representative in the state capital, he spent a lot of time preparing for his Albany trips by conferring with the mayor and finding himself at ringside for bouts of screaming and yelling between mayor and commissioner. After one of the battles with Moses, La Guardia said to Lazarus, "Someday I'm going to hit that son of a bitch and knock him through that door."

Addressing La Guardia, Moses called him "Major." Privately, the mayor was often "that dago son of a bitch," and alternatively "wop son of bitch" and "guinea son of a bitch."

Although the mutual tirades and one-sided explosions were common knowledge to anyone within earshot of the mayor's office, and to the boys in Room 9, the pugnacious nature of the relationship was not known by the citizens whom both had sworn to serve. But the public ignorance ended on July 23, 1936, when newspapers reported that La Guardia had called out Valentine's cops to stop Moses from demolishing an East River ferry landing to clear the land for construction of a portion of a new highway. The East River Drive was to stretch from the southern tip of Manhattan to the northern end, with a connection to the Triborough Bridge. The problem with removing the landing was that the people on the Queens side of the river wanted the ferry to continue in service. The issue was further complicated by plans for erecting a low-income housing project on the Queens waterfront. Housing Authority commissioner Langdon Post agreed that the ferry should stay to provide transportation to Manhattan for the project's residents. Politicians in Queens had won a sixty-day delay in demolition from the Plants and Structures commissioner, Frederick Kracke, so that Queens ferry users could figure out other ways to cross the river. The mayor had assented to the two-month postponement.

Impatient to get going, Moses ordered a wrecking crew, barges, and a crane to proceed with the tearing-down. La Guardia phoned Moses and asked him to cease and promised that he would have the delay period shortened. Moses refused.

Only a swarm of cops and the presence of police boats stopped the destruction. Ferry service continued under police protection.

Said a droll mayor to the press, "All is quiet on the eastern front."

Unknown to the press and an amused public, La Guardia had the authority over the land transferred to the Parks Department, giving Moses what he wanted. Eight days after the mayor sent out the police, the ferry house's fate was sealed.

August Hecksher III and Phyllis Robinson's accounts of La Guardia–Moses contretemps were concise. They wrote, "They almost never met without fighting." Moses had established "his own stance of haughty independence, at once basically affectionate and slightly condescending." La Guardia acted as if he were Emperor Napoleon.

But if there hadn't been a La Guardia, there probably could not have grown the aura of legendary urban builder (some said "destroyer") that attached itself to Robert Moses. They might fight like a pair of junkyard dogs, but together they fashioned the city that each had dreamed of building. One was a practical visionary who knew how to get things done; the other, a romantic who imagined a utopia of lovely scenery, friendly surroundings, trees, sun, fresh air, civility, art, happy people, laughing and healthy children at play, crime-free neighborhoods, and beautiful music wafting everywhere.

The magazine *Fortune* summed up the activities of the team of La Guardia and Moses in the year 1936 in four words: "the swimming pool year." Ten opened in ten weeks. But there had been many more ceremonies to inaugurate playgrounds. On some days Moses had La Guardia opening as many as fifteen. Among this blossoming of recreational spaces for children was an expanse of swings, seesaws, jungle gyms, and a baseball diamond at Williamsburg Bridge Plaza named for the Little Flower. The best thing about the "Fiorello La Guardia Playground," said Moses to his boss, "is its name."

By all accounts the transformation of the city recreational spaces in the first three years of the La Guardia administration was an urban miracle. When he came into office, playgrounds were a mess and the parks a disgrace. Consolidation of control of the parks from a disorganized five-borough system to a unified department with a boss named Moses had been the key to the successes. But little could have been achieved had federal funds not been available. For that influx of dollars, credit belonged to the mayor's tireless efforts in coaxing them out of the Roosevelt administration. The result was an increase in playgrounds from 119 dilapidated areas in 1934 to nearly 400 modern and fully equipped play spaces. While in 1934 the Parks Department had five eighteen-hole golf courses, by the end of the La Guardia years there would be ten. Park acreage would increase from 14,827 in 1934 to 18,325. More than 200 tennis courts were built, and Randall's Island in the East River (in the shadow of the new Triborough Bridge) was cleared of derelict abandoned hospital

With Babe Ruth at the opening of a playground in Queens on July 26, 1935. (AP/Wide World)

buildings and turned into a sports center with a 30,000-seat stadium. Opened in July 1936, it accommodated track meets, baseball, football, soccer, and rugby games and an occasional light opera production.

With La Guardia ensconced at City Hall, the parks commissioner established his office in the Arsenal Building in Central Park, but like the mayor, Moses was not content with staying put. With so much work to do he dashed around his domain to supervise an army of workers engaged in restoring, refurbishing, renovating, reclaiming, and building in eighteen hundred projects. Said the *New York Times,* "The time, the place, and the man met in Mayor La Guardia's appointment of Robert Moses as Park Commissioner."

Moses in the *Herald Tribune* was "Hercules of the Parks."

After a court ruled that state law permitted the parks commissioner "to raze or remove" buildings that "had been erected as incidental to park uses, such as restaurants, boat houses and similar structures," Moses went after a structure in Central Park that La Guardia had made a symbol of all that was wrong with the Walker administration. The ink was barely dry on the court order when Moses ordered wreckers to demolish Jimmy Walker's beloved Central Park Casino. It was gone in two months, replaced by a playground. The only remnants of the symbol of the Roaring Twenties were stained-glass windows. They were installed in a new Central Park police station on the Eighty-sixth Street Transverse Road.

As the year of the swimming pools neared an end, the Hercules of the Parks offered a tribute to the Napoleon of City Hall for La Guardia's fifty-fourth birthday. December 12, 1936 (the day after the birth date), he had decreed, would be the opening of the Henry Hudson Bridge. Part of a grand design to encircle Manhattan with new highways on the banks of its two rivers, the bridge linked the Henry Hudson Parkway to the Riverdale section of the Bronx. Parkway and bridge connected the West Side Highway (running along the Hudson below Seventy-second Street) to the Saw Mill River Parkway at the Westchester County line. Spanning the Harlem River, the single-arch two-level bridge was 142.5 feet above the water and 2,000 feet long. It cost more than $2 million. At least part of that price would be recouped, it was expected, by a ten-cent fee collected by uniformed takers in handsome Art Deco–design toll booths.

Unfortunately, the combined dedication and mayoral birthday party was dampened by a sudden rainstorm that forced everyone to run for the cover of a small administration building. The date also proved inopportune. It coincided with a news story that was more fascinating to New Yorkers, and to their mayor, than a bridge opening. While Moses could control a dedication, he was not able to defer a speech by England's King Edward VIII in which the monarch announced his abdication so he could marry "the woman I love," the American divorcee Wallis Warfield Simpson. La Guardia demanded that a radio be turned on so he could hear a broadcast of the historic speech.

The Henry Hudson Bridge was part of an overall Moses development plan known as the "West Side Improvement." It was the realization of the young urban dreamer whom Frances Perkins had encountered on a Hudson River ferry as Moses gazed toward the western edge of the island of Manhattan and asked rhetorically what it might become if properly improved. He saw an opportunity to reclaim space for the people with parkland bordering an unimpeded roadway that would unclog the city's east–west streets and north–south avenues. As commissioner of parks he spent $109 million of the people's money. In doing so, noted author Robert Caro, he had uprooted trees, obliterated a freshwater marsh, destroyed a unique residential area, and cost New Yorkers "their most majestic waterfront."

In hindsight that is fair criticism. But it is also true, as August Hecksher III and Phyllis Robinson wrote, that Moses "strikingly improved New York City's appearance and phenomenally increased the opportunities of its inhabitants for rest, relaxation and enjoyment."

In the Depression-racked mid-1930s those were laudable, amazing achievements.

While Moses was demolishing and building for the present and the future, Fiorello La Guardia was working for the economic improvement of the people of the city. The term for this undertaking was "relief." Beginning in the spring of 1933, FDR's New Deal entity called the Federal Emergency Relief Administration offered a grant of $1 of federal money for every $3 of state and local funds to assist the unemployed. In November of that year the government created the Civil Works Administration, a "make-work" project.

But in 1934, as La Guardia took the reins at City Hall, federal assistance was found to be insufficient to meet the needs of suffering New Yorkers. His answer to the problem was the Works Division of the Department of Public Welfare. Unhappy with its results, he put the Works Division and a Home Relief Bureau into a new Emergency Relief Bureau, with William Hodson (commissioner of public welfare) at the head of a six-man board of mayoral appointees. In March

1936 one out of five New Yorkers was on "relief," either working for assistance or receiving direct payments.

In addition to needing help in housing and the basics of
life, the people of the city were in desperate straits in the
area of personal and public health care. To attack this problem the La Guardia Department of Health divided the city
into thirty health districts, each with a health center. It also
opened health stations for babies. Using WPA funds, the city
added to a hospital system by opening Queens General Hospital, the Triborough Hospital for Tuberculosis, and a hospital for chronic diseases. Improvements were made at the city's
biggest hospital, Bellevue, on the East Side of Manhattan,
Kings County Hospital in Brooklyn, Lincoln Hospital in Harlem, and other municipal hospitals. This resulted in an increase in bed capacity from 8,000 to 20,500, but still that was
not enough. The Department of Hospitals found itself with
more patients than it could satisfactorily accommodate.

Part of the solution to the problem of providing good
health care to all who needed it, La Guardia believed, would
be a voluntary comprehensive insurance program for everyone in the city earning less than $5,000 a year. Some of the
cost would be assumed by employers, and the balance by employee contributions to a health plan. The enrollee could see
the doctor of his choice from an "open panel" of physicians
who would be paid according to a regulated fee system. Under
another scheme, participating doctors would collect a salary
from the city. Neither idea had much appeal to the majority
of New York's physicians.

What doctors thought of the scheme didn't matter. Such a
vast program in the 1930s was prohibitively expensive. Mayor
La Guardia would have to wait a decade to see the incorporation of the Health Insurance Plan of Greater New York (HIP),
and two more years before it was up and running (March
1947, six months before La Guardia's death). HIP was at that
time the most comprehensive medical insurance program in
the United States (110,000 enrolled). It was some twenty
years ahead of the federal Medicare program and sixty years

in advance of a national debate (still unresolved in 2001) about how to provide and pay for comprehensive health care for all Americans.

Although La Guardia was a pioneer in offering innovative solutions to problems that were unique to New York in the mid-1930s, when it came to educating the city's children, he faced a challenge that had plagued his predecessors all the way back to the small town whose mayor was Peter Stuyvesant. Peg Leg's solution had come in the form of the Latin School. Since then the cost of an educational system had grown to $18 million a year, managed by more members of a Board of Education, superintendents, and associate superintendents than there were students in the city's first public school. Almost all the officials of the school system when La Guardia came into office were political appointees.

The influence of other politicians was greatly reduced. Jobs were no longer gotten through political connections, but on merit. Graft was largely rooted out and the morale of teachers improved. La Guardia's chief contribution to an improving education system was in providing more schools and reducing the size of classes. By the fall of 1941 there would be ninety-two new school buildings and additions to many others. His administration also provided more classes for physically and mentally handicapped students; added to the Board of Child Guidance; and expanded the Bureau of Reference, Research, and Statistics. What he could not do was bring the independently constituted Board of Education directly under the mayor. It is an independence that has remained intact despite efforts by successive mayors to control it, including Mayor Giuliani, whose battles with the Board of Education as late as 2001 were titanic and controversial, as were disputes with the National Education Association (NEA).

A mayor coming under criticism from the national teachers' union was not new. At one point in the La Guardia years the NEA declared that La Guardia was "a danger to the cause of free education." The organization appointed a committee of educators to investigate. It reported that La Guardia interfered with the independence of the Board of Education to the point that he was "injurious" to the school system.

"No one on the NEA board," La Guardia snapped back, "has the mental capacity to grasp the magnitude of the school system of New York."

❧

From the perspective of New Yorkers seven decades after Fiorello La Guardia became mayor of the biggest city in the country in the midst of the worst economic depression in the nation's history, it is difficult to appreciate the magnitude of any of the problems he was called on to handle. Observing La Guardia in the fourth year of his mayoralty, Jay Franklin wrote, "The whole world is restless; there are strikes and massacres; wars and rumors of wars; signs and portents of deep and lasting changes in the system of civilization under which we all have been nurtured. Because Fiorello H. La Guardia has placed himself near to the vortex of this worldwide maelstrom, by becoming administrator of one of the great cosmopolitan centers of modern life, his career is significant beyond the ordinary. If we know what La Guardia means and what will become of him and his work, we can say with greater assurance what will happen to us all during the next generation."

Franklin saw La Guardia as a man who, though a "western American" because of his boyhood roots in Arizona and alignment with the Progressives of the West, was considered a "typical immigrant" because of his name and heritage, a man who was a "New Dealer" before there was a New Deal, and a figure who was "quite as much America's representative *in* New York City as he was New York's official ambassador to the people of the United States."

By now a familiar visitor and irrepressible supplicant for federal money at the White House, the mayor of New York had found in Franklin D. Roosevelt a friend and an ally. La Guardia called FDR the "Chief." Roosevelt called him "Fiorello."

The president found him as amusing as he was relentless in pleading the cause of New York.

"I listen to Fiorello," FDR said with a chuckle, "and then I give him what he wants."

In the autumn of 1936 FDR was running for reelection, and in that enterprise he wanted and needed Fiorello's support. Knowing that endorsing Roosevelt invited retaliation from the New York Republicans whose backing he would need in 1937, when he planned to seek his own reelection, the mayor gave it wholeheartedly.

"Some of us are burning our bridges ahead of us," he said, "and we do so with our eyes wide open."

After another summer in his Bronx retreat, the mayor was back in Manhattan in time for Labor Day, the traditional date in presidential election years for the launching of campaigns. Democrats had renominated Roosevelt and the Republicans had chosen Kansas governor Alfred M. Landon. As the nation's two major parties mobilized, La Guardia believed that 1936 could be the last year in which they dominated American politics. Envisioning a coalition of Progressives and the labor movement, he joined with labor leaders Sidney Hillman, David Dubinsky, and Jacob Potofsky in the formation of the American Labor Party in New York State. Its purpose was to back Roosevelt and give him a second line on the New York ballot. The party also would field its own candidate, Newbold Morris, in a special aldermanic president election. Looking ahead to the 1937 mayoralty race, La Guardia saw his name on the ALP line as insurance in case the Republicans denied him renomination.

In a previous Labor Day speech in Chicago one of his subjects had been a future political realignment. He said, "Political parties, as such, are on the wane. Perhaps in 1936 we shall see the last contest between the two great existing political parties, and in that campaign I venture to predict that there will be the greatest political *chassé* ever seen in the history of American politics." With the labor portion of the envisioned new coalition secured, La Guardia joined in a call by Progressive leaders for a conference to be held in September in Chicago to rally to Roosevelt under the ALP banner. Speaking at the meeting, he gave his definition of a Progressive as "one who will look facts squarely in the face, who will admit conditions as they are, who refuses to follow any fetish and seeks to bring his government abreast of the times."

With both feet planted firmly in the Roosevelt camp (to the horror of New York State Republicans), La Guardia went to see Roosevelt in late September at Hyde Park. He was now not just a supplicant seeking favors from the president, but a significant political ally, and Roosevelt knew it. FDR also appreciated that if he were to adhere to the unwritten rule that a president served only two terms, the leading contender for the presidency in 1940 was likely to be the present mayor of New York. La Guardia left Hyde Park to tell reporters what he'd said to the president: "It's a foregone conclusion that Mr. Roosevelt will carry the city."

One of the reporters mentioned an item in that day's *New York Times*. If Roosevelt won, La Guardia was in line for appointment to the Cabinet as secretary of war. True?

The mayor replied, "I've got a contract with the people of New York City that runs to December 31, 1937, with an option for renewal."

The reporters took that as La Guardia's declaration that as soon as the presidential contest was over he would be off and running for his own reelection a year hence. Meanwhile, he would campaign for the slate of candidates on the ALP line and push for voter ratification of the new city charter.

When FDR came to the city for one of several sallies into La Guardia territory, he spoke to a wildly enthusiastic rally at Brooklyn College. La Guardia had introduced him. Looking at the mayor, Roosevelt told the audience, "Every time La Guardia comes to Washington I tremble because it means he wants something, and he almost always gets it."

On November 1, after riding in an open car in a procession spearheaded by fifty cops on motorcycles, the president wound up his campaign at an ALP rally. La Guardia was with him on the platform, along with Governor Lehman and bushy-eyebrowed miners' union president John L. Lewis. The mayor thrilled the crowd by announcing that when he cast his vote for Roosevelt it would not be on the Republican-Fusion ballot line, but the ALP's.

The incipient party fared well on election day. Tallying six hundred thousand votes, it was assured of a permanent position on the state ballot, guaranteeing a place for La Guardia's name in 1937. But its aldermanic president candidate, Newbold Morris, lost to a Tammany man, William Brunner. The voters endorsed the new city charter and added New York City to the Roosevelt landslide in which Republican Alf Landon won in only two states, Maine and Vermont.

With the 1936 election behind him, La Guardia doffed his campaign hat and donned his mayoralty one for the last acts of the Board of Alderman, soon be replaced by a City Council. The board accepted his budget proposal intact, voted $12,000 to restore City Hall to its original glory, and approved a new traffic code that would deny city drivers a heretofore seemingly God-given right to make right turns on a red light. But when the aldermen passed a bill to require police to arrest people for jaywalking (another God-given right in the minds of city pedestrians), La Guardia vetoed it. "I prefer the happiness of our unorganized imperfection," said the mayor, "to the organized perfection of other countries [such as Nazi Germany]. Broadway is not Unter den Linden [Berlin's main boulevard]."

(This would not be the policy on jaywalking adopted in the 1990s by Mayor Rudolph Giuliani. He demanded a strict enforcement of jaywalking restrictions, only to find that New Yorkers still preferred unorganized imperfection. They blithely continued crossing streets midblock despite the threat of being ticketed by cops. Only the construction of barriers in some midtown spots kept them from exercising their God-given right to cross the street wherever and whenever they wished.)

The mayor's reference to Nazi Germany as a country not to be emulated demonstrated, in the view of biographer August Hecksher III, that La Guardia "saw events abroad in much the same black and white colors as those at home." He was the only mayor in America in the 1930s who had a "foreign policy." It was emphatically anti-Nazi and founded both on revulsion against all that was happening in Germany under Hitler's dictatorship and a realization that the Nazis and European Fascists, along with Soviet-style Communists, were making appeals for support among New York City's populations with strong nationalistic and ethnic loyalties.

In the city's Yorkville section the German American Bund had a large membership. Many windows had the Nazi flag displayed. In April 1934 a pro-Nazi rally in a Queens stadium had erupted into small skirmishes between American Nazis and protesters. Five weeks later, twenty thousand people attended a pro-Nazi rally at Madison Square Garden. As these manifestations of sympathy increased, the mayor became more and more vociferous and unrestrained in his denunciations of Hitler. They reached a peak in March 1937 in a speech he gave to the American Jewish Congress. He expressed the wish that the forthcoming World's Fair would have a Chamber of Horrors for "that brown-shirted fanatic who is now menacing the peace of the world."

The German ambassador in Washington immediately protested to the State Department. The secretary of state, Cordell Hull, apologized, then complained to FDR that La Guardia was interfering in the conduct of U.S. foreign policy and should get a presidential reprimand. FDR said, "I shall." He tapped two fingers on Hull's wrist. "Like that."

The next entry of La Guardia into Roosevelt's office was greeted with Roosevelt raising an arm in a Nazi salute and a "Heil Fiorello." La Guardia responded, "Heil Franklin."

Newspapers in Germany savaged La Guardia and informed their readers that the mayor had a Jewish mother and was therefore a "dirty Talmud Jew."

The mayor who had once said to a reporter that he never thought he had enough Jewish blood "to justify boasting about it" was not motivated in his assaults of Hitler and the Nazis by the fact that his mother was Jewish. He railed at events in Germany because he saw them as an affront to all of humanity and a growing threat to world peace. Like Lucky

Luciano and other thugs, Hitler needed to be knocked down and out. If it had been in the power of the mayor of New York City to order Commissioner Valentine to go to Berlin and arrest him, he would have. Since he could not, he berated the dictator and his Brown Shirts at every opportunity.

This was not the case, however, regarding Benito Mussolini. In Little Italy the Italian-language newspaper *Il Progresso* called for active support of the Italian war of conquest in the African country of Ethiopia. In 1935, when plans were announced for a concert to benefit the Red Cross at Madison Square Garden, La Guardia accepted an invitation. But *Il Progresso* said that the concert was organized "to show that every Italian who resides in the United States is ready to help Italy fight the brutal international coalition headed by England."

Demands arose that La Guardia cancel his plans to attend the concert. Socialist Norman Thomas insisted. "Oh, Norman," La Guardia exclaimed, "you mean I can't even go to *Aïda?*"

The *Post* was blunt in pointing out La Guardia's inconsistency in blasting the Nazis but holding his fire against the Italian Fascists. "The mayor has got to stop posing as a great liberal in this country," it said, "and backing Mussolini in Europe."

The mayor brushed aside the criticism and went to the concert. He was not "going to be pushed around by a handful of anti-Fascists and Norman Thomas." Introduced to the crowd at the concert, he got a huge ovation and stood to take a bow.

His political friends and allies cringed. "It was not," said Thomas, "one of his most heroic efforts." He added, "But it was pretty good politics."

La Guardia had said of himself, "I can outdemagogue the best of the demagogues." In the arena of New York ethnic and nationalistic politics, where Italians greatly outnumbered Germans, and the Jewish vote often was decisive, it was easy and safe to excoriate Nazis, but not smart to alienate Italians by putting Mussolini in the same light as Hitler.

Another safe target was the "Reds." Communist organizations proliferated and grew in membership in the city with astonishing speed. In 1936 the Communist Party, U.S.A., had met in New York and nominated New Yorker Earl Browder as its presidential candidate. Of the Communists who fell into step with picketers seeking improvements in the doling out of relief, the mayor had said in 1934, "I know your kind. You don't want relief. You want to incite unfortunate people to riot." He told Communist leader James Garver, "I won't stand for yellow-dog leaders inciting these people."

On February 15, 1936, the issue of Communists influencing and fomenting unruly acts during protest demonstrations had become personal. At the center of the incident involving a cutback by the federal government in the number of WPA workers in the city was none other than Vito Marcantonio. The mayor's fiery political protégé had won La Guardia's seat in Congress. He'd run as a Republican, but his opponents had accused him of being a Communist at heart and in action. Irate over the WPA cuts, Congressman Marcantonio took the lead in a parade of WPA workers from Madison Square Park to the downtown headquarters of the WPA administrator, Victor Ridder, in the Port Authority Building at Fifteenth Street and Eighth Avenue. Police from the East Twenty-second Street station halted the march and took the leaders, including Marcantonio, into "protective custody."

Ridder exclaimed, "This was a Communistic demonstration."

Marcantonio ignored Ridder and assailed Police Commissioner Valentine as an enemy of the people whom Marcantonio would like to meet "alone in a gymnasium."

Informed of this, Valentine cracked, "This is just another evidence of what happens when you elect a boy to a man's job. His is the immaturity and the arrogance of youth. It's the example of a publicity-seeking demagogue who would love to don a martyr's crown, even to the extent of creating a grave disorder in order to crash into the headlines."

A reporter who knew a story when he found one asked, "But how about the challenge, Commissioner? Will you really meet him in a gymnasium?"

In La Guardian style the police commissioner replied, "Why meet in a gymnasium? Why wouldn't it be a good show for Madison Square Garden, put on for the benefit of the police pension fund? I'll come in with any weapon he wants, and I'll meet him with a flit gun."

Police watching of protest demonstrations continued, with special attention to those in which "Reds" were suspected of participating. With the approval of City Hall, police surveillance of known Communists and their activities was assigned to "Red Squads."

The mayor expressed disappointment and chagrin with Marcantonio with a "Dear Vito" note expressing La Guardia's dismay at behavior "unbecoming and entirely uncalled for" and showing a "lack of restraint." "You will be good enough," the note said in half plea, half command, "to refrain from such conduct in the future." The effect of the chastisement was the same as Don Quixote's in windmill jousting. Vito's antics would vex his mentor for the rest of Fiorello's life, even while he continued to treat Vito like a son, albeit an often wayward one.

⁓

Not all of 1937's public events meant trouble of one kind or another for a mayor who looked forward to a reelection campaign. Traffic began flowing on a portion of the East River Drive that was integral to Robert Moses's grand design for a Manhattan-circumscribing system of highways. To bring people in from New Jersey and take them out again, the first two "tubes" of the Lincoln Tunnel were almost completed (they would be open for traffic in December). Longer-distance travelers could now take a completely elevated Hudson Line train through the Manhattanville area of the Upper West Side. Much to the delight of the former customs official in Fiume, Italy, ocean liners in regular service from Europe, the West Indies, and Bermuda were permitted to enter the harbor after their own ships' physician certified the good health of the passengers by radio. This eliminated the need for U.S. Health Service officials to go out to the ships and conduct examinations. Consolidated Edison agreed to sell the city all of its streetlights and bill the city for the electricity. And a nice verbal bouquet had been tossed the mayor's way by the renowned French architect Le Corbusier.

Surveying the city during a visit in 1936, he exclaimed, "Today it is possible for the city of modern times, the happy city, the radiant city, to be born." He was preaching the gospel that the mayor would make his text in his bid to remain in City Hall.

As the 1937 mayoral election neared, a perennial critic of La Guardia on the *Sun,* George L. Ritchie, who saw the mayor as a "a jack-in-the-box gone haywire," sat at his typewriter to say, "He likes the feel of the driver's seat. He wants to stay there."

It was a rare Ritchie remark that La Guardia could agree with.

19

"The greatest mayor the City of New York has ever had."

So proclaimed the manifesto of the American Labor Party. Putting its new clout where its mouth was, the party that could bring six hundred thousand labor voters to the polls to endorse "unsurpassed integrity and achievement" nominated Fiorello H. La Guardia for mayor.

In a radio broadcast the candidate had pledged "a 100 percent union city." But he went on the air feeling stung and outraged by a circular put out by the Republicans of the Fifteenth ("Silk Stocking") District. It charged him with not having provided sufficient police protection during riots and strikes.

Mayor La Guardia retorted, "I now state that economic issues cannot be settled with the policeman's nightstick. Any philosophy of government under our Constitution can be decided only through the mediums and channels provided in the Constitution, and cannot be suppressed by the use of force."

Early in 1937 he had appointed an impartial City Industrial Relations Board to aid in settling labor-management disputes. In three months it had done so 187 times.

"His policies and appointments," the circular leaflet claimed, "have favored the growth of the American Labor Party at the expense of the Republican Party."

The "irregular" Republican gave his answer in a speech to a meeting of GOP regulars two weeks before the election. He declared, "I was selected as the candidate for mayor not because of my political virtues, but because of my political vices. I pledge a nonpolitical administration, and I have only

one purpose: to rehabilitate, reorganize, and preserve the
city. One other thing I want to say, and this is the proper
place to say it. On January 1, when I take office, I go out of
politics for four years. One can't be a good fellow and be a
good mayor. One can't be a good mayor and be a politician.
My responsibility is to the City of New York, and not to the
rehabilitation of any political party."

By then La Guardia's name was on the ballot under three
parties: Fusion, ALP, and GOP. But obtaining the important
Republican nomination had been a close-run thing. The key
to it was Republican leader Kenneth Simpson. Wily but civi-
lized, and a practical political strategist, he had a mustache
that made him look a little like Thomas E. Dewey. Simpson's
hair was parted in the middle. A Yale graduate and a member of the university's secret Skull and Bones club, he was a
man with his name in the *Social Register.*

He was also a connoisseur of classical music, so the lapsed
cornetist and active seeker of the Republican nomination invited him and his wife to join Mr. and Mrs. La Guardia for
dinner at the appropriately fashionable Claremont Inn, followed by a concert at Lewisohn Stadium. No political talk was
exchanged, but Simpson appreciated the intent of the invitation and asked the mayor to top off the evening with a night-
cap at Simpson's house on East Ninety-first Street. As the
wives chatted in the parlor, the men settled into chairs in
Simpson's library. Because the host was a reformed drinker,
he sipped White Rock ginger ale while La Guardia had a
whiskey from the bar that Simpson maintained for guests who
had not eschewed liquor. La Guardia took his whiskey with
soda. Like boxers testing one another, they danced around the
purpose of their meeting until La Guardia broached the subject.

He said that he assumed he would have the GOP nomination. Simpson reacted with an arching of eyebrows. Considering the mayor's affection for Roosevelt's New Deal, he
ventured, there was no basis for making that assumption.
However, should La Guardia somehow attain the party's blessing, the persons on the ballot with him would have to be approved by the party's leaders. For City Council president it

would have to be Newbold Morris. The comptroller spot would go to Joseph McGoldrick, both "regulars." La Guardia snapped, "Unacceptable." His man for Council president was Adolph Berle. The comptroller had to be someone from Queens or Brooklyn. The otherwise delightful evening ended in impasse.

In the days that followed, however, practical politics emerged on both sides. The name La Guardia provoked a cry from one overly agitated Republican woman, Grace Lease. "I don't know whom we want for mayor," she declared, "but I know whom we don't want. That is the man in City Hall today. Sooner than support him, I am willing to tie up with Tammany Hall." She protested in vain. The GOP leaders accepted La Guardia at the top of the ticket. La Guardia agreed to Simpson's slate of Morris and McGoldrick. That left open the question of who was to be the GOP candidate for Manhattan district attorney.

There was only one man for the job, everyone agreed: Thomas E. Dewey.

In the crime-buster's autobiography, *Twenty against the Underworld,* Dewey wrote, "I accepted a draft from the Republican Party to run for District Attorney of New York County." He also accepted the nomination of the Fusion Party, offered by Judge Seabury. As to the man at the top of both tickets, he continued in words that come off the page sounding smug:

> Mayor La Guardia was running for re-election and he had also been eager to have me run. We had two or three sessions, but he was a curious fellow. He made it clear that it was a very good thing, and that I ought to do it, but he never came around and said, "Won't you do it?" He did not want to get himself in any position of feeling obligated. We were fairly good friends and we became better friends, even though he had a little green monster in him.

One minor obstacle had to be overcome. An anti–New Deal Democrat, Senator Royal Copeland, challenged La Guardia in a Republican primary, while also running in a Democratic primary. La Guardia did not even bother to set up a headquarters or to campaign. He decided that the best way to prove his credentials for reelection was by working at being mayor.

Copeland lost in both contests.

The Democrats chose Jeremiah T. Mahoney, law partner of Senator Robert F. Wagner. As such, he had the support of major New Deal figures and all the trappings of Tammany Hall, good and bad. His main theme against La Guardia was that he presided over a "city of strife, a haven for agitators." Picking up sentiments in some New Yorkers that La Guardia was a "Red" at heart, Mahoney made "communism" his main issue. To be certain that he was understood when he spoke, he took elocution lessons.

La Guardia's theme, offered in whatever language predominated in a particular crowd, was that there was "only one issue in this campaign." It was his record. "If you like my kind of administration, you can have four more years."

It was glib, but it papered over his situation. Ever-watchful and analytical Lowell Limpus saw La Guardia "driving a four-horse team—and none of his chargers were especially fond of the others." He held in his hands reins that linked Silk Stocking Republicans, Democratic New Dealers, union labor, and assorted liberals. The race for the man who once thought he might be a jockey was run with four "colors." He carried the banners of the Republican Party, the American Labor Party, the City Fusion Party, and the Progressive Party.

The outcome of the contest would be determined by the labor vote. Keenly aware of this, Tammany Hall organized the Trade Union Party. Unfortunately and embarrassingly, most seats at a Trade Union rally at Madison Square Garden were filled with American Labor Party stalwarts who unfurled La Guardia banners. To make matters worse, John L. Lewis came out for La Guardia, followed by ringing endorsements from the CIO (Congress of Industrial Organizations) and the New York State Federation of Labor.

Nor did the Democrats hear a word against La Guardia from Franklin D. Roosevelt. The president's chief adviser on New York City politics, Adolph Berle, advised FDR that there was "nothing in this for you." Roosevelt remained mum but amused.

Regarding Mahoney's assaults on how La Guardia was running the city, the mayor said that he would have to give Mahoney civics lessons. They took the form of a series of "reports" on the gains that had been made since January 1, 1934. To underscore the "record," he presided over several events, including the opening of the Lincoln Tunnel (accompanied by ex-GOP president Herbert Hoover), the laying of cornerstones for two schools and a courthouse, and a parade of new Sanitation Department trucks for Manhattan and Brooklyn. He pointed to the Triborough Bridge, Randall's Island, the West Side Highway, the East River Drive, the Henry Hudson Parkway and Bridge, and scores of playgrounds and swimming pools.

At a giant and raucous rally on October 30 at Madison Square Garden he brought up the "Red" charge and then introduced "fellow Communists" Newbold Morris and Thomas Dewey. With that (one of the most enthusiastic gatherings in city history to that date), campaigning was done. Said Dewey, "Well, it's all over."

La Guardia had one more ritual to perform. He had always considered the corner of 100th Street and Lexington Avenue his "lucky corner." Appearing at a rally there on the eve of the balloting, he wore his "lucky" overcoat, a dark-gray Chesterfield with a velvet collar. He spoke to eight thousand people, most of them friends and neighbors when he had lived nearby as their congressman. The next morning he was up early to vote and up late, visiting polling places to make sure that the counts were honestly cast and properly reported.

When they were tallied, he had won the biggest vote for mayor in the city's history. He had 1.3 million to Mahoney's 889,000.

Roosevelt tendered congratulations and invited him to a chat at FDR's Manhattan home.

In mid-December the mayor and the Manhattan district attorney-elect were invited to a Washington, D.C., tradition known as the Gridiron Club banquet. The president spoke, as did his pal Fiorello. Dewey did not. A feature of the gathering was a postdinner show put on by club members. Two of the characters portrayed on this occasion were La Guardia and Dewey. The impersonators alternately sang a ditty titled "Dreaming White House Dreams."

LA GUARDIA:

> I see the White House just at eight,
> The table where they dine in state,
> Spaghetti on the White House plate.
> Why do I dream those dreams?

DEWEY:

> I see the White House just at three,
> I see a large-sized company;
> I see them shaking hands with me.
> Why do I dream those dreams?

LA GUARDIA:

> The New Deal my approval got,
> But now I think it's not so hot.
> I could improve it quite a lot.
> Why do I dream those dreams?

DEWEY:

> I know I could improve it, too.
> Though I'm not telling what I'd do,
> But I can dream as well as you.
> Why do I dream those dreams?

The mayor who could play a cornet; cook *perfecto* spaghetti; drive out crooks, tinhorns and chiselers; send the bosses of Tammany and the Republican Party to distraction; open the playgrounds built by Robert Moses; sing along with *Aïda;* take shorthand in several languages; and do all manner of other things found himself receiving an honorary degree from Yale.

The citation read:

The mayor is an expert in nerves. He knows how to explode
them to the public advantage, how to control them. Coming
in contact not only with nervous politicians but also politicians who have nerve, he rides in a whirlwind and directs
the storm. He recognizes the familiar symptoms of every
variety of crank and extremist, and steers a safe course between Sylla and Charybdis, aided by his hereditary knowledge of the channel. He has taken democracy away from
the politicians and restored it to the people.

On January 1, 1938, he was again in Judge Samuel Seabury's parlor, hand raised, facing Justice Philip McCook, and
repeating the oath of office.

Part III

Patience and Fortitude

I had a hard and trying day.
—Fiorello La Guardia, 1938

20

The night mayor of New York, James J. Walker, once cracked, "New York will be a great place if they ever finish it."

In 1938 the journalist Heywood Broun wrote that in the United States there could be found "no such beauty as exists in New York City." And if natural wonders were to be brought forward for contemplation, he continued, "I must admit that I would much rather crane my neck at the Empire State Building than stoop to survey the bottom of the Grand Canyon. The making of towers is a more noble endeavor than digging ditches. The plain fact of the matter is that New York is much too good for New Yorkers."

Author Hulbert Footner in his 1937 book *New York: City of Cities* wrote of a dull winter afternoon when he and a friend stepped from the Astor Hotel in the heart of Times Square. The friend, who had lived in New York City for forty years, stopped short, gazed at the scene before him, and murmured, "My God, what a town!"

Footner continued, "New York gets you like that at unexpected moments. Your eye may skate idly over the town ninety-nine times and on the hundredth be arrested by its magnificence. There never was anything in the world like Times Square after dark. The signs twinkle, flash, run along the side of a building, black out, revolve, change color; little dramas are enacted in light against the sky. Every night is the same yet not the same."

Adjacent to the Astor Hotel stood the Paramount Theater. Occupying the ground floor of the thirty-five-story Paramount

Building, it was a lavishly decorated movie palace that between first-run Hollywood films presented stage shows featuring the country's most popular bands and orchestras. In 1938 the music was "swing." Its best-known exponent was Benny "The King of Swing" Goodman. When the scholarly-looking clarinet player and his orchestra opened at the Paramount in the winter of 1938, a line of enthusiasts, mostly high school kids who skipped a day of classes, started forming at six in the morning of the first day. At eight o'clock the ornate doors swung open to admit the legal occupancy limit of 3,634. Still clamoring to get in were upward of three thousand swing fans.

The name given to these youths and millions like them across the country by the press was "jitterbuggers." In the spring of the year in which Goodman filled the Paramount seats, the City of New York's Department of Parks picked Randall's Island as the site of a "Carnival of Swing." More than twenty-three thousand jitterbuggers heard twenty-five bands present five hours and forty-five minutes of swing music. The next day the *Times* reported that police and park officers had their hands full in protecting the players from "destruction by admiration."

Swing may not have been the music Fiorello La Guardia envisioned for his remade city, but he was immensely pleased later in the year when Benny Goodman showed that he could play more than swing. On November 5, 1938, Goodman joined with the Budapest String Quartet to entertain the mayor and an adult audience at Carnegie Hall to play Mozart.

At Christmas the mayor took a seat in the National Broadcasting Company's Studio 8H in Radio City for a concert by the NBC Symphony Orchestra, conducted for the first time by the great Italian maestro Arturo Toscanini. Programs given out in the world's largest radio studio were made of satin to eliminate the noise of the audience of one thousand turning the pages.

New York's musical mayor believed that the city had an obligation to provide its hardworking citizens and their families with free concerts. This "music for the people" program was a boon to out-of-work musicians. As bands and orchestras were formed to play in the parks of the five boroughs, unemployed men and women musicians who had been living precariously since the beginning of the Depression were now on "work relief" that paid them twenty-four dollars a week. Suddenly, New Yorkers who didn't have the price of admission to hear music in a theater could go to Central Park on a summer evening and join five thousand others to hear the famed Goldman Band, free. One night when the Goldman musicians were playing in Prospect Park in Brooklyn the audience gasped and giggled as the conductor's baton was passed to the mayor of New York. As he led the band in a rousing John Philip Sousa march, he must have recalled with bittersweet pride his father's hopes that his son would one day be a leader of a band, just like Sousa. A self-appointed music critic who observed the mayor conduct on that night reported "a workmanlike interpretation in the pianissimo patches." The audience loved it. When the march ended, they applauded and cheered. When he returned to his seat, the ovation continued, requiring him to stand and take repeated bows.

Aficionados of other arts also flocked to parks in the summer. In addition to an office of music, the Welfare Department had a drama program. The first performance by actors on work relief had been in Jefferson Park, in La Guardia's old East Harlem district. The play was *Uncle Tom's Cabin*. Five thousand people, mostly Italians, attended, including the mayor.

La Guardia could be wildly enthusiastic about providing music and drama for the city's residents, but he also could be the adamant censor concerning entertainment he deemed "dirty." As a result, the venerable New York places of entertainment in which women had for decades taken off some or all of their clothing on stages were declared indecent. Burlesque theaters, most of them in the Times Square area, were closed by police order.

The mayoral campaign to stamp out "indecent" literature continued unabated, and not with very much criticism. When

Valentine's cops seized a quantity of "obscene" books and tossed them into a police headquarters furnace, no one appeared to protest. Certainly nobody drew a comparison between burning sexy material to the incineration of books in Nazi Germany. The *Times* did venture its opinion that "we cannot very well abandon sex and we cannot prevent young people from thinking about it." Perhaps not, but the mayor's campaign against "indecent" magazines plowed onward. In 1940 he invited a group of publishers to his summer City Hall and told them in "reading your publications" he'd "discerned a trend where there is plain ugly nudity or direct sex appeal." The mayor's message was blunt: Cut it out. And do it now!

His purpose, said La Guardia again and again, was to give New York City a government with a soul. The goal was expressed in many ways. "We are trying to make people happy," he declared. Not just safe and contented. HAPPY! Once, before addressing a large meeting as he waited in the wings, he listened to a chorus sing the spiritual "I Have Heard of a City Called Heaven." In his speech he pledged, "We are going to make our city a real heaven."

Doing "the people's work" as he defined it, he rushed here and there and seemed to be everywhere at once. Biographer Thomas Kessner's portrait of Fiorello La Guardia following his reelection was a "daffy" figure "in communion" with New Yorkers, "leading the Fire Department band; inspecting underground tunnels in a sandhog uniform; stepping off the pitcher rubber in Yankee Stadium, cap photogenically askew, to fire a high, hard one at the catcher; biting into a hot dog with a circle of laughing children about him; looking endearingly quizzical in academic robes while accepting an honorary degree."

Between this darting around he was "Hizzoner," as newspaper headline writers dubbed him, working at his desk in City Hall. Having found the formal office too confining, he'd moved into the spacious Blue Room to issue commands and summon commissioners to account if they were not carried out to the letter. Or he might choose to punish a miscreant department head by giving him the silence treatment. On more than one occasion a commissioner was fired "absolutely and permanently." The hardy among them took it. Some— many, in fact—didn't.

Commissioner of Housing Langdon Post quit in "disgust." The corporation counsel, Paul Widels, stuck it out through the first term but declined to serve in the second. La Guardia's first police commissioner, as noted earlier, gave up the job because of the mayor's interference. How many times Lew Valentine might have considered resigning isn't known. According to Lowell Limpus's midstream biographies of the two men, and Valentine's memoir, *Night Stick,* he never did ponder giving up the job. When the time came to reappoint Valentine to the post of top cop, La Guardia did not hesitate.

⚯

While the Little Flower's activities had made him popular with the boys in Room 9 who counted on a great story every day, the police commissioner enjoyed no such affection from the reporters who hung their hats in the police shack behind 240 Centre Street. Trouble had started almost from Valentine's first day in office. The issue was police press passes. They permitted whoever had one in a pocket, pinned to a coat, or dangling down his coat from a chain necklace to "pass police and fire lines wherever formed." Reporters from time immemorial considered them not only a right under the First Amendment but also a sacred talisman. The new commissioner had ruled in 1934 that the police had the right to banish reporters and photographers from the scene of any disaster whenever the cops felt members of the press were "in danger."

Reporters and their editors screamed that journalists had a right to risk their lives if they wanted to, and that the commissioner should butt out. To defuse the situation the mayor set up a special committee on press cards. It consisted of former and present journalists and news photographers, plus the commissioner. Valentine alleged that the fifteen thousand press passes currently in the hands of reporters and others who'd never come close to a police or fire line often were used to gain favors, such as parking their cars in no-parking spaces.

The mayor approved a recommendation by the committee that the number of cards be cut back. Who got one would be determined by a press pass committee. This resulted in cancellation of about fourteen thousand cards. But those who received press passes continued to ignore police orders at fires and other news events to stay behind police lines. The issue remained unresolved in 1936, forcing the mayor to call a meeting that he chaired. Everyone agreed to try to work the problem out. No one managed to do so.

The issue still nettled reporters and police at the time of the 1937 election.

When it was clear that La Guardia had won, reporters rushed to find Valentine to pose a question that prompted Valentine to have a little fun at their expense. When a reporter asked if Valentine was going to resign, he replied, "Almost any day now. As a matter of fact, almost any minute." The reporters scrambled to file stories to that effect.

Failing to find any humor in Valentine's jest, La Guardia ordered the commissioner to issue an official statement denying that he'd said he was resigning. It was a blatant lie, and the reporters deeply resented it.

For Mayor La Guardia the matter was closed. He had other concerns about Valentine's department. Unhappy with the morale and efficiency of the force, he called in the commissioner and asked where the problem was. Valentine replied, "Too many old-timers. We need younger blood." La Guardia responded, "You're responsible for the reorganization and revitalization of the department." In the La Guardia language that Valentine had learned to translate it meant, "Get on with the job you were hired for. If you can't, I'll find someone who can and will."

Valentine directed sixty-six old-timers to be in his office on November 19, 1934. The fifty-four-year-old commissioner, who was close in age to many of the inspectors, deputy inspectors, captains, lieutenants, sergeants, and patrolmen, told them to put in their retirement papers. Then he read a letter from La Guardia that ended with, "You leave the city service with a badge of honor." The following week, forty-five veterans who were over sixty-three were also gone.

On December 22, other old-timers in terms of years of service rather than age found themselves removed from key jobs and replaced by "young blood." When the commissioner attended the graduation of 143 graduates of the police academy in the Sixty-ninth Regiment Armory at Twenty-sixth Street and Lexington Avenue, La Guardia was on the dais with him. He dispelled all speculation that Valentine would not continue as commissioner. He declared, "I believe that the men of the department know that the mayor has confidence in the police commissioner, and as long as he is police commissioner and that confidence is entertained, he will have the full support of the mayor in the management of the Police Department."

In La Guardia language he meant that Valentine's job was safe only as long as the mayor said it was safe. But it was sufficient for Valentine to take a strong hand with the boys in the press shack by announcing in a press conference on December 28 that the reporters had attended the last one with the police commissioner. He told them he'd been thinking about it a long time, then explained his reasoning:

> I consider it an unnecessary burden on the police commissioner. I don't think it's fair for the police commissioner to discuss with anybody unsolved cases and what the police are doing. I object to "newspaper promotions and rumor committees," and I've told you men so a number of times. The mentioning of a man's name in print very often injures instead of helps. Very often a man's name has been suggested here as a possible candidate for promotion. Probably those were people whom you liked and you may have desired to help, but there are times when a man's name has been stuck in a story, perhaps purposely, to injure him.
>
> I have been described as upset and annoyed at questions which have been put to me when I wasn't upset and

annoyed. My answers have been misrepresented. I have been misquoted and I do not like the misrepresentation of my words and attitude as frequently described in the papers.

You'll get the news you're entitled to as long as it does not interfere with the administration of justice.

When he finished, a reporter asked, "Commissioner, are you going down to the sixty-year [-old members of the force] to enforce retirements?"

"There you go, right there," Valentine exclaimed. "There's the rumor committee working again. My answer to that is, 'No comment.'"

Reporters with questions thereafter had to submit them in writing. This brought a stinging protest in the *Daily News*. Formerly a supporter of Valentine, the paper ran an article by a veteran newspaperman and author of journalism textbooks, Carl Warren. He wrote, "Police Commissioner Valentine, who doesn't see reporters anymore, stood pat on his 'press-be-damned' policy. Via the note-passing route, he expressed wholehearted satisfaction with his rule ending all talks with newsmen."

Valentine quickly learned the folly of having a fight with someone who could always get in the last word, as journalists invariably do. Reporters who once would have edited his remarks began quoting him verbatim. Then they noted a series of suicides of cops and former ones. They knew that "police suicide" was not unusual, but in reporting these they hinted at a connection to Valentine's shakeup of the force. When an inspector took his own life on July 29, one paper noted, "The wave of suicides which has swept the Police Department since Commissioner Lewis J. Valentine assumed command four years ago claimed Inspector Louis Rosenfeld as its seventy-first victim yesterday."

In the midst of this turmoil Lowell Limpus had been working on a book about Valentine. When it was done in April 1939, he told La Guardia about it. "Now a lot of people are telling me that he won't be in office by the time it's published," said Limpus. "I wish I knew."

La Guardia demanded, "What are you talking about?"

"There are reports that you two aren't getting along so well. There's supposed to be considerable friction between you and—"

"Listen! Get this straight—and you can put it in your book if you want to. I love Valentine like a brother. I trust him completely. If he keeps his nose clean, he can have his job as long as I hold mine. Of course, if he deliberately went wrong, I'd crucify him. However, I can't visualize now any circumstances under which Valentine would go wrong. He's proved himself too often. Yes, he'll be in office when your book is published, and a long time after, I hope."

Lewis J. Valentine not only remained in control at 240 Centre Street when Limpus's book was on sale in stores, but to almost the last day of La Guardia's administration. He would hand in his resignation and file his own retirement papers on September 15, 1945. Two years later, in publishing his autobiography, he preached the gospel of La Guardia, and his own, as he wrote, "Only when we have honest public officials, with devotion to duty and regard for civic pride and decency, can a police machine serve its citizenry. A good and efficient police department is a thing of transcendent importance; one that will function only for the greater security of person and property, for public morality, respect for the law."

Until September 15, 1945, there would be much to put that credo to the test in the city that never turned out all the lights; where the mayor in the black Stetson, or whatever chapeau he decided to wear, never appeared to take even a moment's rest; and where no one seemed to be in a great rush to finish building.

On the day La Guardia began his second term, the Triborough Bridge was completed, but the Bronx-linking Whitestone Bridge was still under construction, as were the Queens Midtown Tunnel and additional tubes of the Lincoln Tunnel. All bridges and highways were supervised by Robert Moses, in whose fertile imagination other projects were being nurtured. But being the master of roads was insufficient. He also lusted for the tunnels, then the province of the Tunnel Authority. Thwarted in that aim by La Guardia, Moses was not reticent in pointing out that his bridges and highways proceeded quickly to completion while work on the tunnels dragged on.

Moses's simmering resentment came to a head in April 1938 when the Civil Service Commission decreed that toll-takers on his bridges had to be taken from the civil service lists, including those carried on the rolls of prison guards. Moses told the mayor, "I absolutely must refuse." He informed La Guardia that he would take up the matter with the attorney for the Triborough bondholders who financed the bridges and the roads.

La Guardia retorted that the city was not being run by attorneys for bondholders. "You are a city official," he declared, "and you will take up matters with the corporation council."

Moses regarded the city's principal lawyer as an enemy. Unfortunately, La Guardia learned that the state legislature had passed a law that was recommended by Moses to give authorities such as the Triborough power to hire outside lawyers. The statute had the effect of making Moses an equal with the mayor in matters related to bridges and roads.

Next, La Guardia pressed for cuts in the capital budget for another Moses project, the Cross Island ("Belt") Parkway in Brooklyn and Queens. It was part of the Moses plan to build circumferential highways. Moses objected to the cuts. La Guardia eventually caved.

The persistently critical *Sun* crowed, "His recital of the fiscal conditions of the city, of its many needs, was useless against this supersalesman who dreads him not."

Their next battle was over a plan to build another connection between Manhattan and Brooklyn to ease the load on the Brooklyn, Williamsburg, and Manhattan Bridges. Moses wanted another span. Others preferred a tunnel. Moses dismissed the idea "simply because it doesn't make sense." The Municipal Art Commission objected that a bridge would ruin the beauty of the lower Manhattan waterfront and skyline and virtually destroy Battery Park at the tip of the island with breathtaking views of the Statue of Liberty. Members of the new City Council called for a meeting to discuss the alternatives on March 28, 1938. It ended without resolving the issue.

Fed up with arguing, La Guardia went to Washington to see President Roosevelt. Never a friend of Robert Moses, FDR favored the tunnel, on the advice of the War Department. Admirals viewed a bridge as a hazard to ships making their way to and from the nearby Brooklyn Navy Yard. The president ended further debate by stating that the federal money needed to build either project would not be available for a bridge.

Work on the tunnel began in 1940 with a loan of $57 million from the U.S. Reconstruction Finance Corporation. Later, in one of those ironic twists that speckle the pages of history, Moses got his way regarding the Tunnel Authority. A year after La Guardia left office it was merged with the Triborough Bridge Authority. Moses would get his new bridge to Brooklyn in the 1960s. But the long, graceful Verrazzano-Narrows Bridge at the mouth of New York Harbor was not based in Manhattan. It connected Brooklyn and Staten Island. Moses would note that it was built "seaward of the navy yard." By then one of the greatest shipbuilding facilities in history was a shell of its former heyday, when the United States was building battleships and other kinds of vessels for World War II.

21

As La Guardia and Moses worked to build a new city, usually together but occasionally at loggerheads, they were also contending with the effects of the new city charter. Effective at the start of 1938, it drastically revamped the city legislature by abolishing the Board of Aldermen and creating a City Council. Its president was Newbold Morris. Judge Seabury bestowed his blessing on Morris, calling him one of "brightest stars in the Fusion administration." He'd risen in the political firmament following an educational route taken by America's stellar cousins in government, Theodore and Franklin Roosevelt, by graduating from Harvard. Politics also was in Morris's blood. His grandfather, Ambrose C. Kingsland, had been New York's seventy-first mayor (1851 to 1853). Despite having been an alderman, Newbold Morris was seen by contemporaries as never quite at ease in the give-and-take of politics, perhaps because he was too diffident and self-effacing. August Hecksher III in his book on the La Guardia years found that the qualities that should have made Morris one of the most attractive figures, a lack of arrogance or sense of superiority, gave him an air of being vague and "somehow inconsequential."

The City Council consisted of twenty-six members. It was split in half politically. The Democrats had thirteen seats. The others were Republican, three; ALP, also with three; and seven independents. This was a new reality for Tammany, which had always wielded absolute control of the Board of Aldermen.

Surviving the remake of the city charter was the powerful Board of Estimate, controller of the purse strings and still consisting of a membership that included the five borough presidents. Under the continuing weighted system of voting, Fusion members claimed a majority, with La Guardia, Newbold Morris, and Comptroller McGoldrick having a total of twelve votes, backed up by three borough presidents. They included Stanley M. Isaacs of Manhattan, who had worked in the La Guardia campaign in 1933.

Another new entity formed under the new charter was the City Planning Commission. It was seen as a body of professionals whose purpose was to weigh the pros and cons of proposed building and the tearing down that usually accompanied it. The commission found itself between the rock named La Guardia and the hard place called Robert Moses. The mayor appointed the head of the commission. He chose Rexford G. Tugwell. Part of FDR's original "brain trust," he was flamboyant and opinionated. Although La Guardia picked him, the two strong-willed men were soon confronting each other. Tugwell thought the city was wasting resources in the vast La Guardia housing projects, new schools, and roads. His master plan was to make the city a "more convenient, more efficient, and a better and happier place" by imposing strict zoning intended to preserve neighborhoods from encroachments by business interests that found nothing wrong with a gas station at the corner of a street of graceful old brownstones, or towering, sun-blocking office buildings with no regard for their surroundings.

This set him at odds with Robert Moses. On one occasion, when Tugwell suggested to Moses that the city wasn't big enough for both of them, Moses answered, "In that case, I suggest you leave." Eventually Tugwell accepted an offer from FDR to be governor of Puerto Rico. Virtually doomed from the start, the Planning Commission languished.

Another entity brought into existence by the revised charter was the office of deputy mayor. La Guardia appointed Henry H. Curran. A failed mayoral candidate in 1922, he had been a magistrate. Happy in the court system, he asked

La Guardia, "Deputy mayor? What's that? I never heard of that one before." La Guardia was amazed. Curran had helped write the charter. He handed Curran a half dollar and said, "For heaven's sake go across the street and get a copy and find out. It costs fifty cents."

Curran took the post. La Guardia set him up in a City Hall office with a small staff and wished him well. In a government in which the mayor felt perfectly capable of running the show alone the post was superfluous, and both men knew it. Curran's chief function was seeing people La Guardia had no time for, or didn't want to see. Years later Curran admitted, "I never did find out what it was all about—the deputy mayor."

Robert Moses said the post was "halfway between a warrant officer loosely attached to a retired admiral and a dignified eunuch at the door of a squirming seraglio."

While doing his best to adjust to the new governmental profile at City Hall, or simply ignoring the parts of the charter that did not suit him, La Guardia was attacked in the City Council as a spendthrift and a taxer. To deal with the fiscal crisis he'd found when he became mayor in 1934 he had raised the property tax to its highest level in city history. At the same time, outlays that went to relief were escalating. The Council declared the city coffers in an unacceptable condition and blamed the situation on the mayor.

Another part of La Guardia's plan for raising funds had been the imposition of a 3 percent tax on utilities. Then the state stepped in to claim two-thirds of the money, thus depriving the city of $12 million. La Guardia blasted the state government. He railed to reporters, "The mayor cannot print money. He cannot revise the multiplication tables."

The basis of his complaint was Albany's power to impose its will on the city. New York mayors had been trying to loosen the state legislature's hold on city affairs for decades, especially in the taxing power. Again and again, they had vainly appealed to the potentates in the State Capitol to grant "home rule."

La Guardia joined the long line of predecessors by accusing the legislature and Governor Lehman of "bodily carrying off" the utility tax windfall. In a tart letter to the men in Albany he demanded that the state abandon its claim. If not, the state also would have to take over the city's relief program. Lehman answered just as sharply, accusing the mayor of being "inaccurate and erroneous." He asserted that La Guardia had failed to supervise collection of sales taxes.

La Guardia shot back with his favorite detested word. "I wrote a letter to a statesman," he said, "and I received the reply of a politician."

To underscore his anger with the governor he canceled attendance at a banquet in the state capital where he would have been seated beside Lehman. He then demanded a special session of the legislature on the issue of relief. To show how serious he was, he ordered a cut of 10 percent in home relief expenditures. The legislature was unmoved. This forced the City Council to find new taxes. When they passed, the mayor said, "Lehman taxes, not La Guardia taxes," then restored the relief cuts.

Hope for home rule then rested with a state constitutional convention in the summer of 1938. La Guardia appeared before it to appeal for city independence. He got some of what he wanted, but much of the relationship between Albany and the city was left for courts to decide as disputes arose.

At the same time La Guardia was tilting with Albany windmills he found himself in a skirmish with the New Deal in the person of the head of the Federal Housing Administration. A former La Guardia ally, Nathan Straus, put a hold on applications for funds until a comprehensive federal policy could be formulated. Straus called for a conference. La Guardia groused, "For ten years we have had nothing but conferences. The law is clear. The thing to do is get architects and engineers." Stop talking and get on with the building. If the federal government was to have yet another round of discussions, fine. But the New York City Housing Authority would not be at the table. When NYCHA chairman Langdon Post sent a telegram to the conference, La Guardia told Post that his resignation was accepted. He immediately turned to his secretary, Lester Stone, and swore him in as temporary

NYCHA chairman. Reminded that the job had to be filled by a vote of NYCHA board members, La Guardia made it clear that he expected no one to oppose him. Post eventually returned, but in another fuss between Washington and New York the chairman was out again when La Guardia fired him permanently.

The mayoral center of activity in the summer of 1938 was not the mansion in the Bronx, but an unfinished office in the under-construction New York City Building on the site of the developing World's Fair in Flushing, Queens. When La Guardia arrived he found that the air-conditioning system was not yet working, while outside the building marched a picket line of striking workers. Rather than pick a fight with a friend of labor who was not, after all, coming to join in the construction work, the men stood aside to let his car enter the site.

They would see him coming and going quite a lot that summer. He dashed off to the Red Hook section of Brooklyn to ceremonially operate a steam shovel to break ground for another housing development. He also attended the groundbreaking for a new criminal courts building at 100 Centre Street, on the traditional site of the city's prison, known since the 1800s (and ever after) as "the Tombs." He was also present for the start of a new building at Hunter College, on the Upper East Side.

On June 22 he cheered the victory of boxer Joe "The Brown Bomber" Louis over the fisticuffs pride of Germany, Max Schmeling, at Yankee Stadium. Two days later he frowned at a report by professors at Columbia University that the American Legion was a "Fascist organization." He found this revelation unappealing because he was a proud member of the organization of veterans of the Great War, and because he was scheduled to address the Legion's national convention in Los Angeles in September. The speech would be one event in a planned whirlwind trip to the West that would include a sentimental return to Prescott, Arizona.

In mid-July the ex-bomber pilot beamed with pride at Brooklyn's Floyd Bennett Field in welcoming the landing of a

silver-painted monoplane named *New York World's Fair 1939.*
Its pilot was the dashing young aviator Howard Hughes. He
had just completed a much-heralded around-the-world flight
in a record three days, nineteen hours, and twenty-eight sec-
onds. Hughes and crew were welcomed officially at City Hall
the next day, after which mayor and aviator rode up Broadway in an open car for a ticker-tape parade that was bigger
than that given in 1927 to Charles A. "Lucky Lindy" Lindbergh, accompanied by Jimmy Walker.

Less than a month after the Hughes parade, New Yorkers
were again lining the "Canyon of Heroes" to yell a welcome to
another flyer. Thirty-one-year-old Douglas Corrigan had
taken off for a solo flight to California but wound up at Bal-
donnel Airport in Dublin, Ireland, *sans* passport. Corrigan
explained that after he had taken off from Floyd Bennett
Field and headed West, his compass went awry and he lost
his way. Most people bought the error story, but others suspected that "Wrong Way" Corrigan had planned the "mistake." The parade in his honor could have been in Brooklyn
or Manhattan, but Corrigan was not a fool when it came to
publicity. He phoned La Guardia from the ship bringing him
home to say that he was accepting La Guardia's invitation
to Broadway. The mayor grinned and appeared to blush during the City Hall festivities when Wrong Way opined that
La Guardia deserved a higher office. La Guardia thanked
Corrigan for his "deliberate impetuosity" and "Pickwickian
impulsiveness." Then everyone adjourned to Yankee Stadium
for another reception. Being Irish, Corrigan was pleased to
be introduced to the crowd by the city's most famous rakish
and devil-may-care Irishman, James J. Walker.

On the matter of Corrigan's nomination of La Guardia for
higher office, Fiorello had a momentary dalliance with the
possibility of running for the U.S. Senate, but decided not
to. On his mind, it is safe to assume, was the question of
whether his good friend Franklin Roosevelt would adhere to
the presidential precedent set by George Washington and not
seek a third term. Should FDR choose to retire to Hyde Park,

most political pundits believed, Fiorello's hat would be in the
ring for the Democratic presidential nomination in 1940, and
that he would probably manage to capture it.

Meantime, he was mayor. In that capacity he had greeted
the summertime adjournment for vacation of the City Council with, "I don't know what I'll do without you."

⌖

On September 7 he left for the West with two watches in his
pocket, one set to New York time, the other turned three
hours earlier. There would be stops in other time zones on
the way to his date in Los Angeles with the American Legion.
At Shreveport, Louisiana, he was greeted by the governor as
a guest from "a little town in the northeastern part of the
country." He added that it was a little town because "it is so
much smaller than the man who guides its destiny." The
Louisiana weather was not so pleasant. As La Guardia, the
governor, and the mayor of Shreveport motored into the city
in an open car they were drenched with rain. The inclement
conditions required cancellation of air maneuvers in the former pilot's honor, which was a very great disappointment to
the major.

In Waco, Texas, the weather was fine. Keenly aware of
La Guardia's penchant for hats, his hosts gave him a som-
brero. Then, on to Arizona. At Phoenix he learned that D.A.
Dewey's prosecution of the most powerful Democratic politician and kingmaker in New York, James J. Hines, had ended
in a mistrial. Hines was charged with working on behalf of
gangland gamblers by "agreeing to influence and intimidate
judicial and other officers," and taking money to do so.

Said the economy-conscious, disgruntled mayor, "We spent
a hundred dollars a day to air-condition that courtroom, and
now there's a mistrial."

Hearing that Hitler had made a bellicose speech in which
he had declared that a German-speaking region of Czechoslo-
vakia known as the Sudetenland properly belonged to Germany, La Guardia said, "When an individual goes berserk [in

New York], we take him into custody and put him in a place where he can do no harm." Five days after La Guardia's return to New York from his swing through the West (September 24), the British prime minister, Neville Chamberlain, arrived in Munich, Germany, to accept proposals put forward by Mussolini but drafted by the German Foreign Ministry that surrendered the Sudetenland to Hitler. Chamberlain then flew back to England to proclaim that he had gained "peace in our time."

As the "Sudetenland question" percolated toward its disastrous climax, La Guardia was arriving by train in Prescott. Astride a cowpony and followed by the high school band, he rode into a wild reception and a greeting by Senator Henry Ashurst in which the former reporter for the local newspaper was introduced to the crowd as "the most constant, the most famous, and the most powerful friend Prescott will ever have—a hometown boy who has achieved worldwide renown." Fiorello recalled the "gaudy and spectacular" frontier town he'd known as a boy. A rock outcropping was dedicated to Achille La Guardia. "He was the sort of man," Fiorello told the crowd, "who loved to bring cheer and happiness to those around him." Then he grabbed a baton and led the school band in a rousing tune.

The next stop was San Francisco. He did not enter the city by the bay quietly. Assembled to meet him at the Ferry Building were New York City employees on their way to the Legion convention in Los Angeles. A band also was there. On La Guardia's signal everyone formed into a parade and marched to City Hall. Noting that San Francisco also was building an exposition that would run simultaneously with the New York World's Fair in 1939, he told the mayor that the U.S. was big enough for both fairs. In a speech to the Commonwealth Club his subject was the plight and the future of American cities.

In his own city, he learned, truckers had gone on strike. Conferring by telephone with Valentine, he directed that police protect the movement of essential goods. If he was needed, he said, he would head back as fast as possible. Assured that his presence was not required at that time, he moved on to Los Angeles and the American Legion convention. He spoke at the opening session and led a parade of a thousand Legionnaires from New York, almost all of whom had jobs with the city.

On September 21 he received news that his city had been hit by a terrible hurricane. The *Herald Tribune* would report, "The visitation was sudden, unprecedented, and unbelievable." History would record it as "the Great 1938 Hurricane." Across the devastated region much of the destruction was on Long Island. The death toll was 462. Ten people died in the city. Damage to city parks and parkways was severe and broad. For reasons known only to La Guardia but to the shock, puzzlement, dismay, and quite a bit of anger of some New Yorkers, their mayor did not rush home. Instead, he took a tour of Los Angeles sites, including a visit to Hollywood film studios. He did not return until three days later. When he did, he found no public criticism.

Immediately confronting the continuing truckers' strike, he donned his labor mediator hat and presented both sides with a compromise. When it was not immediately accepted by trucking firms, he organized a fleet of city trucks manned by strikers and placed it on standby in the park in front of City Hall. The trucking companies got the message and settled.

"With his usual flair," said the *Post,* "the mayor has ended the trucking strike."

He settled once more in the rather opulent Blue Room. Some of his detractors said he reigned there "like Mussolini." To another observer cited in August Hecksher III's book he was "like a swarthy Buddha reaching for one his six buzzers to call his office slaves."

Hecksher's portrait of the "picturesque aspects" of La Guardia's routines continued, "He could impart to the day's events an almost unfailing sense of high drama, even of sheer fun; but he was also capable of tremendously hard and concentrated work."

At other times he seemed to be everywhere except the Blue Room. But nothing propelled him out of his chair faster

"I am not a sissy!"

than a report of a fire. Donning helmet and yellow slicker, he rushed to the scene as though he were the fire commissioner. When he arrived he acted as if only he knew how to put the flames out. As squat as a fireplug, he waded through water, danced between coils of hose, barked orders, and blazed himself into the hearts of New Yorkers who delighted in gazing at the front pages of their morning newspapers with pictures of their wet and sooty mayor at yet another conflagration.

He was the most visible and ubiquitous mayor the city had ever known. Mayors who followed him into City Hall would do their best to emulate him, some more successfully than others, but none with the Fiorello H. La Guardia flair and natural panache. Subsequent mayors at fires and other disasters were often deemed to be playing for cameras, headlines, and sound bites on the evening TV news. Somehow, mysteriously, the image of a politician grabbing for cheap publicity did not stick to La Guardia, although that was frequently exactly the result he had in mind. As to fires, he said, "I hate the damn things. But what would the men think if I didn't have the guts to go where they went, especially if there was danger?"

Physical courage was not lacking. One day as he was leaving City Hall he was attacked from behind by a deranged man. Spinning around, he pounced on the man and subdued him. As police seized the attacker, La Guardia was offended that the assailant had not exhibited more courage. He glared at him and demanded, "Why did you hit me from behind?"

Brushing himself off, the mayor said to a group of admiring cops, "All in a day's work. I've had worse blows than that below the belt."

Not even the possibility of an explosion deterred him. When an abandoned suitcase at Penn Station was suspected of containing a bomb, the mayor refused to obey a bomb squad order to stand back. Told that the bag contained some old clothes and a ticking alarm clock, the mayor smiled with relief and walked away twirling his hat.

"This job has aged me," he admitted "Sometimes my bones ache." Then the wartime ex-aviator said, "A public official, you know, is very much like a plane; it needs sustained flight or it will go into a nosedive. The mayor is not going into a nosedive."

In the year 1938, with the World's Fair taking shape, aviation was much on his mind. But the type of planes he was contemplating were sleek, speedy, continent-spanning airliners.

22

On September 29, 1938, sixteen days after the mistrial in the Hines case and five days after La Guardia returned from his triumphal trip to the West, George Van Slyke of the *New York Sun* sat at a typewriter in Saratoga, New York, and wrote, "The convention broke into one of the wildest demonstrations ever witnessed in a political convention. It was not like the orthodox demonstration of such conventions with rival candidates trying to outdo each other. This was unanimous."

The conventioneers were New York state Republicans. At twelve minutes after noon they had chosen Thomas E. Dewey as their nominee for governor. In his acceptance speech the most famous district attorney in the nation said, "Crime is the product of remote causes, of social pressure, and political cynicism. There are economic, social, and political crimes. Politics has been made the biggest racket of them all. The word 'politics' has come into disrepect. Representative government must become the most honorable profession. For politics is the lifeblood of democracy." After praising the record of Republican governors such as Theodore Roosevelt and Charles Evans Hughes, he deplored the decline of the GOP to a point where the two-party system had ceased to operate in the state. The result was that any Democratic governor was the "goodwill advertising, the window-dressing for what is in part at least a corrupt machine."

The current Democrat governor was Herbert Lehman. Renominated at the party's convention the next day in Rochester, he accused Dewey of abandoning "the important work for which he was chosen by the people less than a year ago and for the consummation of which he accepted an obligation to the people." He reminded everyone that he was the governor who appointed Dewey as special prosecutor. That said, he declared Dewey "entirely inexperienced in either administrative or legislative activities" and that there was no indication "that he is familiar with either the fiscal or social problems of the government of a great state of thirteen million people."

The nominations of two men who had been on election tickets with Fiorello La Guardia left the mayor of approximately eight million New Yorkers on the spot. That each candidate considered his support vital was a measure of his own political strength. Personally, he felt no warmth for either Dewey or Lehman. Among other things that irked the mayor, the governor had tried to hijack city utilities taxes. Dewey had resisted a La Guardia appeal that he forgo a run for governor and stay in the D.A. job. Faced with a Hobson's choice, the mayor decided not to make one. Rather than alienate himself and his city from whoever won, he chose neutrality. The closest Lehman came to appearing to have La Guardia's blessing was being invited to ride beside the mayor in the funeral for the minority leader of the City Council, B. Charney Vladeck, who had become such a popular figure that half a million people turned out to see the cortege pass by.

After a campaign filled with mutual personal attacks, voters rendered their opinion that each man should remain where he was, Lehman in Albany and Dewey in the district attorney's offices adjacent to the criminal court building, chasing crooks. The result was relatively close. In a state that was usually overwhelmingly Democratic, Dewey lost by sixty-seven thousand votes.

Nationally, the New Deal forces took a whipping. Republicans doubled their seats in the House of Representatives and added eight members in the Senate. Defeated for the Senate was Robert M. La Follette Jr., the son and namesake of La Guardia's late hero in Progressive causes. By any measure, the liberals had been dealt a stunning blow, maybe a fatal one.

A worried but combative La Guardia told a press conference that the future demanded "a well-defined, clear, concise Progressive platform." But he did not venture that the man to lead the revival was himself, assuming that Franklin D. Roosevelt would decline seeking a third term.

Might Thomas E. Dewey have won the governorship if La Guardia had endorsed him? Perhaps. Some political observers believed he would have. But in losing, the crime fighter of New York was no longer confined to being merely a member of the audience at the Gridiron Club dinner of 1939. He shared the dais with FDR as a guest of honor and principal speaker. Not renowned as a man of humor, he so astonished the glittery gathering of Washington journalists and politicians that correspondent Jesse S. Cottrell wrote, "His address sparkled with wit and humor." In a speech to the New York County Republican Committee on December 18, 1938, Dewey was more somber. "The fight for decent, clean government," he said, "has just begun."

Whether he would be a candidate for governor in 1940, or go for the presidency, was the unanswered question of the hour. Whatever Dewey decided, he felt that he first had to take care of some unfinished business in the matter of the *People of New York v. James J. Hines*. On January 23, 1939, he proceeded with the selection of jurors whom he hoped would correct the grievous error of the mistrial in the first Hines trial.

After thirty-two days of evidence and testimony by forty-seven witnesses, Dewey gave his summation:

> It is not an easy task for a district attorney to go through a case like this once, to say nothing of twice; but there is a high duty that comes in our lives. We [prosecutors] have ours every day. We have to do it. If we did not do it, civilization and democracy would be in a very, very bad way.
>
> The important thing is that you [the jurors] declare to the people of New York, the police of New York, that they are free; that they will no longer be betrayed by a corrupt alliance between crime and politics; that the alliance is

going to be smashed by this jury and branded as something we won't stand for, because we want to keep the kind of system we have in this country and we don't want it polluted by a betrayer. We don't want protection of gangsters by political leaders.

You are good New Yorkers and you love your city. You want your city to be better and better and to remain and become cleaner. You want to remove cancers that grow at the heart of your government, wreck the morale of your police force, wreck the morale of your courts, and wreck the morale of any public official who has to come within the contaminating influence of a politician operating with gangster money as his background.

Let us decide what we want for ourselves and our community. Do we want to remove that cancer? Do we want to see that in the future it shan't happen again?

After seven hours of deliberation, the jury said at 7:14 P.M. on February 25, 1939, that James J. Hines was guilty as charged thirteen times. Hines appealed the convictions, lost, and on October 14, 1940, began serving his sentence at Sing Sing Prison. He was paroled in August 1944. He returned to the city he had sold out and died in 1957 at age eighty, having outlived La Guardia by ten years and seen Thomas E. Dewey elected governor three times and defeated twice as a candidate for president.

While Dewey was preparing for Hines's second trial, New Yorkers read in their newspapers on January 14, 1939, that hundreds of thousands of dollars had been pilfered from the fare boxes of the city's privately owned subway system. A quick calculation came up with the astounding fact that the theft amounted to twenty-five million *nickels*. With echoes of the Seabury investigation's "little tin box" chorus ringing in their ears, city "straphangers" could only laugh out loud at the admission by a subway worker that he kept some of his loot, changed from nickels to paper money, in a kitchen cabinet inside Jell-O boxes.

In 1939 the intricate system of underground and elevated trains was transporting to and from work, to nights on the town, and to wherever its passengers wanted to go in the city's five boroughs, about 2 billion passengers a year in a 281-mile network of tracks, switches, and stations. The daily count was about 5.5 million. A WPA-financed *Guide to New York City,* written by a host of previously unemployed writers, noted, "These intent and humorless hordes cover uptown and downtown platforms, choke narrow stairways, swamp change booths, wrestle with closing train doors. Nickels jingle, signal bells clang, turnstiles bang. Beneath the sidewalks of New York the subways have created a second city."

The subway riders and those on elevated sections (the "el") traveled to and fro on lines that were laid down by three companies: Interborough Rapid Transit (IRT), Brooklyn-Manhattan Transit (BMT), and the Eighth Avenue Independent (IND). The three represented a combined investment of $1.65 billion. Their income came from a fare that had been five cents for as long as anyone remembered. Occasional attempts to raise it to a dime repeatedly failed because in the City of New York the five-cent fare was as sacred as Lady Liberty in the harbor holding the torch of freedom. To propose a boost in the fare was as certain a death as touching the subway's third rail. Consequently, the three transit companies found themselves at a financial dead end. The result was a deterioration in service and safety. The obvious solution was acquisition of the three companies by the city and their consolidation. To work for this goal the legislature in 1921 had created a Transit Commission. Ten years of wrangling later, there was still no unification.

When La Guardia had become mayor in 1934, the consolidation was as stuck as passengers on a broken-down subway train stalled halfway between stations. A proposal by the mayor to abolish the Transit Commission and create a Board of Transportation under the Public Service Commission failed in the state legislature. La Guardia turned to his allies Adolph Berle and Judge Samuel Seabury to come up with a plan. They presented it to the Transit Commission in June 1936. It appeared to be a breakthrough, but the Commission rejected it in May 1937.

Checking the control of a new subway train in the spring of
1936. The La Guardia years saw the city take over and unify
three privately owned subway lines.

Frustrated and determined to have the city take over the
transit lines, La Guardia set up another committee, which included himself, City Council president Newbold Morris, Comptroller Joseph McGoldrick, and two transit commissioners to
negotiate purchase deals with the IRT and the BMT. For any
agreement to be valid an amendment to the state's constitution was needed. Fortuitously, the constitutional convention
was in session. The amendment passed, giving the city authority to float $315 million in bonds. The city acquired the BMT
subway, elevateds, trolley, and bus lines for $175 million and
the IRT for $151 million.

The agreement allowed the city to demolish some el structures, with costs to be assessed upon property owners whose
vistas would be enhanced by removal of the ugly steel sup-
ports and street traffic–impeding pediments. The IRT purchase would take effect in November 1939 and the BMT in
February 1940. After two decades of haggling, the city was
suddenly in the business of running the trains.

On December 20, 1939, with unrestrained glee and blazing acetylene torch in hand, wearing a construction worker's helmet and protective face mask, and accompanied by Comptroller McGoldrick, La Guardia cut through a beam to begin the tearing down of the Sixth Avenue El.

Having grabbed the reins of city transit, the inveterate champion of the rights of labor and the individual worker declared in March 1940 that the transit union's "closed shop" was a thing of the past. There was no way, he said, that the city would be in the business of collecting union dues. The great defender of the right of workers to stage strikes banned them in the New York transit system because transit workers were now "civil servants."

Enter Michael "Mike" Quill, president of the Transport Workers' Union. Balding, bulldog-faced, and with an Irish temper, he once denounced the American Labor Party as "Socialists, Communists, and refugees from the Republican and Democratic Parties." Now he accused the mayor of being "the bankers' puppet." His answer to La Guardia's ban on strikes was to get an authorization from union members to call one as he saw fit. To demonstrate union muscle he staged a workers' march to City Hall on March 13. La Guardia made a show of walking through the picket line, then announced that he would sit down with Mike Quill for a talk about their differences. Joining the conference was La Guardia's friend John L. Lewis. They agreed that the union shop matter should be referred to lawyers on both sides. In a second meeting (March 26) La Guardia said a closed shop and a strike by civil servants were unconstitutional. Then he let Quill's proposed contract go intact to the Transit Commission. Mike Quill claimed victory, but continued a threat of a strike. It didn't happen. Lewis got La Guardia to agree to refer the strike issue to the courts, should the union ever go out.

The *New York Times* correctly discerned "postponement and evasion."

While negotiations were under way throughout 1939 for the city's acquisition of the transit system, Robert Moses's

Bronx-Whitestone Bridge opened to automobile traffic, allowing drivers in both boroughs to pass for the first time from one to the other without going through Manhattan, or "the city," as non-Manhattan residents called it. Another splendid bridge, named after President George Washington and carrying traffic between Manhattan and New Jersey, was used by eight million vehicles. Cars, trucks, and buses also were flowing through the new Lincoln Tunnel. Following FDR's veto of Moses's bridge from lower Manhattan to Brooklyn, plans were being drawn for the Brooklyn–Battery Tunnel that Moses had so vehemently resisted.

In the borough that proudly advertised itself as "the second-largest city in the world," the inhabitants welcomed a new manager for their beloved Brooklyn Dodgers baseball team. He had been a gutsy utility infielder for the Yankees in 1928 and 1929, and despite being born in Massachusetts, came across like a native New Yorker. His name was Leo Durocher. He guided the Dodgers to a third-place finish in the '39 season. Enthusiastic fans had thronged to Ebbets Field by close to a million, allowing the team owner, Larry MacPhail, to retire part of the debt he'd accrued in the refurbishing of the stadium and trying to build a winning club so that Dodgers fans would not have to bellow "Wait till next year!"

Bronx baseball fans did not have to wait. The Yankees had beaten the Cincinnati Reds in the World Series four games to none.

On August 26 the Reds had shared the distinction with "the Bums" of being the first baseball teams to appear on television, in a doubleheader. The cameras belonged to experimental station W2XBS. While the Yankees were not televised, they saw "Iron Man" Lou Gehrig inducted into baseball's new Hall of Fame at Cooperstown, New York. His last game had been on May 2, when he broke his streak of 2,130 consecutive games. He was suffering from amyotrophic lateral sclerosis, a paralytic and fatal disease that was later named for him. In 1940 La Guardia appointed him a New York City parole commissioner, a position he held until his death in 1944.

New Yorkers who might or might not care about baseball had flocked to movies such as *Gone With the Wind, The Wizard of Oz, Mr. Smith Goes to Washington,* and director John Ford's *Stagecoach.* Those who had the money and the interest to go to a Broadway show had made hits of Lillian Hellman's *The Little Foxes;* William Saroyan's *The Time of Your Life,* staged by the Group Theater; Philip Barry's comedy *The Philadelphia Story,* starring a beautiful, willowy newcomer named Katharine Hepburn; and the George S. Kaufman–Moss Hart comedy *The Man Who Came to Dinner,* with ex-Yale drama professor Monty Woolley portraying the playwrights' version of their outrageous friend and radio commentator Alexander Woollcott. New Yorkers who preferred the real Woollcott could tune in his Sunday evening radio program on CBS, *The Town Crier.* People who preferred a musical could go to the *The Straw Hat Revue* and rollick at the stage antics of new faces Danny Kaye and Imogene Coca, sharing billing with singer Alfred Drake and dancer Jerome Robbins. November brought the Howard Lindsay and Russell Crouse dramatization of the best-selling book *Life with Father,* with Lindsay as the father. It's likely that no one in the audience predicted that the play would run for seven years.

New Yorkers who could afford to dine out had their choices of restaurants with fare that ran in price from low-scale Longchamps (all over town) to the high-end Stork Club (dinner: $2.50), Jack and Charlie's "21" (if you had to ask the price, you couldn't afford it), and the Rainbow Room atop the RCA Building (dinner: $3.50), along with the greatest view of the city next to the panorama available from the eighty-sixth floor deck of the Empire State Building. For Old English decor there was Keene's Chop House at 72 West 36th Street (dinner: $1.25). The Upper West Side residents who yearned for a sandwich had a new delicatessen to patronize at 2245 Broadway named Zabar's.

Connoisseurs of international fare could dine Italian at Moneta's in Little Italy and perhaps catch a glimpse of Mayor Fiorello La Guardia, Hungarian at Zimmerman's Budapest on Forty-eighth Street, Japanese at Miyako on West Fifty-eighth, Austrian at the Hapsburg House on East Fifty-fifth, Russian at Casino Russe on West Fifty-sixth, and German at Lüchow's on East Fourteenth and Hans Yaeger's at Lexington and Eighty-fifth in the heart of Yorkville, known as Germantown. Nearby stood Yorkville Casino, the main meeting place for German American organizations, located just off Lexington Avenue at 210 East 86th Street.

One block south and a block east of the Casino was "The German American Business League." Its purpose was the publication of directories of New York firms exhibiting sympathy for the Nazi government in Germany. In the same building at 178 East 85th Street were the offices of the pro-Nazi German American Bund; its newspaper, *Deutscher Weckruf Beobachter;* and the Bund's leader, German-born Fritz Kuhn. *The WPA Guide to New York* noted that the Nazis occasionally "paraded through Yorkville in their uniforms, which were of three kinds: black trousers, white shirts with swastika armbands, and black caps, for rank and file members; olive-drab military uniforms, for the guards; and regulation German uniforms for storm troops."

There were also anti-Nazi centers in Yorkville, including the German Workers' Club; the German General Book Store (with books banned by the Hitler regime); and New York Labor Temple, built by German workers early in the century. The anti-Nazi newspaper was *Deutsches Volksecho.* It had wide circulation. Of the six hundred thousand people of German heritage in New York, few were members of the Bund. Yet on February 20, 1939, a pro-Nazi meeting at Madison Square Garden had drawn twenty-two thousand American Nazis to hear Fritz Kuhn speak. (On March 25 an anti-Nazi march attracted twenty thousand people, many of them German Americans. Five days later, Hitler's own nephew, William, who lived in New York City, told the press his uncle was "a menace.")

In his Madison Square Garden speech Kuhn spoke of President "Rosenfeld" and the "Jew *lumpen* La Guardia." The Manhattan district attorney was "Jewey."

When La Guardia learned from Commissioner Valentine that the police had been told that Kuhn was planning to leave the country and return to Germany, La Guardia arranged to have Kuhn's passport held up. He then asked Dewey to investigate the Bund for possible "sales tax irregularities."

On May 2, 1939, Dewey's investigators descended on the Bund's Yorkville headquarters with subpoenas for the Bund's records and those of the Bund newspaper, along with material related to a Bund English-language magazine, *The Free American*. The next day the newspaper's headline read:

JEW YORK DEMOCRACY IN ACTION.

HOUSEBREAKING AND BATTERY.

DISTRICT ATTORNEY DEWEY STAGES A RAID.

TWELVE STRONG-ARM MEN SEIZE PAPERS AND PROPERTY AT BUND HEADQUARTERS WITHOUT A SEARCH WARRANT.

PRESIDENTIAL ASPIRANT ACTS IN DISREGARD OF ARTICLE IV OF THE BILL OF RIGHTS.

On May 18, Kuhn was to appear before a grand jury. He showed up, but refused to waive immunity and testify. The grand jury indicted him for embezzlement. He then fled the state, only to be captured in Pennsylvania on his way West. Returned to New York, he was brought to trial on November 9, 1939. Kuhn's lawyers accused D.A. Dewey of "personal animus" against Kuhn. Dewey replied that if he had it, he should be removed from office. He said that Fritz Kuhn was "a nuisance to the community and probably a threat to civil liberties and the proper preservation of the American system if he should become more important than he was," but that Kuhn was not on trial for his views. He was charged with theft of Bund funds. After a three-week trial, Kuhn was convicted on November 29. Six days later, he was given a sentence of two to five years in prison. Dewey thought so little of Kuhn that there is no reference to him in Dewey's account of his years as Manhattan's "Mr. District Attorney." Dewey was now so

famous nationally that a radio program of that title, with a
D.A. patterned on Dewey, was presented weekly on NBC.

Pleased that at least one Nazi had been nullified, and with
matters well in hand for the city's takeover of the transit system, La Guardia attended the opening on November 1, 1939,
of Rockefeller Center. It was twelve buildings covering twelve
acres in the heart of midtown, and its western facades would
benefit from the removal of the Sixth Avenue El. On the eastern side of the center, on Fifth Avenue, were the international
buildings. Showcases for foreign nations, they consisted of the
British Empire Building, La Maison Française, and Palazzo
d'Italia. Its facade had a glass panel with a motto in Italian:
Arte E Lavoro; Lavoro E Arte (Art Is Labor; Labor Is Art).
New York's first Italian mayor had no argument with the philosophy expressed.

The mayor considered Rockefeller Center, with its dedication to arts exemplified in its many frescoes and murals, theaters, a radio network offering a symphony conducted by
maestro Arturo Toscanini, lovely gardens, impressive statu-
ary, and a commitment to business, a jewel in the crown of
the greatest city in the country. Rockefeller Center served to
promote the city as the location of a World's Fair dedicated to
the goals of the Fair's mottos: "Interdependence of Man" and
"Building the World of Tomorrow."

In an effort to cement New York's position as the city that
was committed to both those concepts, the former pilot with
the Army Air Service had worried that New York City was
not keeping pace with the rapid development of aviation because it lacked an airport worthy of the richest city in America—the city that he was determined to forge into the envy of
the world.

This gap in city services had been crystallized for him
soon after he'd become mayor in 1934. Business had taken
him to Chicago. When he bought a ticket on American Airlines for his return trip, it read "Chicago to New York." But
the plane landed in Newark, New Jersey, the airline's only
New York–area terminus. As the other passengers left the
plane, the mayor of New York remained in his seat. Told by a

stewardess that he'd arrived at his destination, La Guardia pointed to his ticket and noted that it said his destination was New York. He would not get off the plane, he declared, except in New York City.

Faced with an implacable person who was no ordinary passenger, the airline agreed to fly him to an airfield in New York City. There were five. Flushing Airport in Queens was privately owned and used by amateur pilots. Its runways were not suitable for an airliner. Neither was a private field in northern Queens called Holmes Airport, a facility for small and medium-size craft and dirigibles. Miller Field was federal property on Staten Island. Municipal Downtown Skyport was for seaplanes. Floyd Bennett Field, in Brooklyn, had opened in 1931 and was dedicated by Mayor Walker in the name of an aviator who'd piloted Admiral Byrd across the North Pole in 1926. Covering 387 acres surrounded by fens bordering Jamaica Bay, it could land an airliner but had been a commercial failure because it was deemed too far from the city.

It was to Floyd Bennett Field that La Guardia was flown.

When the door of the silver-painted, twin-engine, American Airlines plane opened for the only passenger to get off, the stewardess found newspaper reporters and photographers waiting to scramble aboard to greet the mayor. How they knew that there would be a story and photo opportunity at Floyd Bennett Field remains a mystery, but it is not a far-fetched deduction that La Guardia had planned to make a fuss about landing in Newark and demand to be flown to New York, and had tipped off the press.

His purpose was to demonstrate the city's need of a first-class airport. Having done that, he set out to get it. He did so by barraging the Post Office Department (the chief user of airlines as a means of carrying long-distance mail) with the information that Floyd Bennett Field's often foggy climate was not suitable for regular, daily flights. A new airport was needed. The perfect spot for it was a small peninsula in northern Queens that was adjacent to land where the World's Fair was to be built. While the postal authorities showed no enthusiasm for the project, the ex-bomber pilot resorted to a man who had heard him make a speech in Italy, the then-assistant secretary of the Navy and now president of the United States.

On La Guardia's side was the fact that Franklin D. Roosevelt was an ardent proponent of commercial aviation. The mayor also knew that FDR would welcome a chance to show that men engaged by the WPA were capable of more than "pushing around dirt and raking leaves," as critics of the WPA liked to say. Roosevelt was enlisted in the cause of a grand airport for New York City that would be in operation for the second summer of the World's Fair.

Plans for the airport were labeled "North Beach Field." The work commenced under the always watchful eyes of the mayor. "It was his own baby," said Marie La Guardia pridefully. And it was indeed his. The site he'd chosen had been an airfield in the 1920s. Called Glenn Curtiss Airport (named for an aviation pioneer), it had been used as an airpark for sports fliers. Financed by federal funds ($27 million) and other sources, the project encompassed hundreds of acres of reclaimed wetlands, augmented by landfills. When completed, the airport would have ninety acres of new runways and fifty-three acres of apron. Five thousand men worked in three shifts six days a week. They built the longest runway in the world (six thousand feet), an administration building bigger than most of the country's railway terminals, and hangars that each could hold Madison Square Garden.

La Guardia showed up so frequently during construction that workers jokingly handed him their tools. When the work was done, the mayor informed his patron in Washington that New York had "the greatest, the best, the most-up-to-date, and the most perfect airport in the United States." It was, he boasted, "the airport of the New World."

Determined to fill its passenger terminal with the finest amenities, he campaigned to sign up concessionaires. To assist in this undertaking he brought in young David Rockefeller. Soon the passengers who would use the airport had a post office, restaurant, flower shop, jewelry store, haberdashery, bank, and drugstore. People who weren't going anywhere but liked to see planes taking off and landing could go to a roof-top "Sky Walk." The small fee they paid brought the city $100,000 in the first year.

By then "New York City Municipal Airport," popularly called North Beach Field, was handling 200 flights a day, making it the busiest airport in the world. The planes were those of American, United, Transcontinental, Western, and Pan American airways. The Pan Am planes were Clippers, accommodated at the airport's seaplane docks. When the mayor officially opened the airport on October 15, 1939, a total of 350,000 people were on hand for the ceremony. In a radio broadcast the night before, La Guardia said the airport was "unsurpassed and unrivaled in utility, capacity, safety, convenience, and beauty."

On the motion of Board of Estimate member James Lyon, the borough president of the Bronx and a frequent critic of La Guardia, the board voted unanimously to change "North Beach Field" to "La Guardia Airport."

People who flew into and out of it were able to look out the windows as the airliners banked above Flushing Meadows, Queens, and gaze down in wonderment at buildings, pools, parks, and promenades of "The World of Tomorrow" as envisioned by the designers of the New York World's Fair of 1939–1940.

"While other nations of the world are wondering what the spring will bring," said the dreamer and optimist at City Hall, "we will be dedicating a fair to the hope of the people of the world. The contrast may be striking to everyone. While other countries are in the twilight of an unhappy age, we are approaching the dawn of a new day."

23

In 1925 in *The Great Gatsby* F. Scott Fitzgerald wrote of "a valley of ashes—a fantastic farm where ashes grow like wheat into ridges and hills and grotesque gardens bounded on one side by a small foul river." He was describing New York City's main garbage dump, in the ironically named Flushing Meadows. The area had been named after the Flushing River. The original Dutch name of the settlement founded in 1643, Vlissingen, came from a small group of English Quaker refugees who had fled Britain to Holland, then immigrated to the New World. Over time Vlissingen became corrupted to Flushing. Following the British takeover of New Amsterdam (renamed New York), a resident named William Prince created America's first large botanical nursery. In the middle of the nineteenth century Flushing had been one of Manhattan's leading summer colonies. To convert the area into the site of the World's Fair the city had spent $27,648,721, including $4,000,000 for a sewage treatment plant, street grading, and a subway branch. The transformed space was called Flushing Meadows Park, casting it into the domain of Robert Moses. His demand was that after the fair had run its course, the park would be restored.

In 1939 the population of the Borough of Queens was estimated at 1,340,476, or 14 percent of the city's total residents. Germans were the largest group and Italians second. Flushing, Jamaica, and Corona each had a large population of blacks. A considerable portion of the borough in 1939 was taken up by farms. In one agricultural section worked by

Chinese immigrants most of the vegetables for the numerous Chinese restaurants in the city were grown. The desire to turn part of Queens into the location for a World's Fair had arisen for three reasons. The first was a sense of New York City history. On April 30, 1789, George Washington became the first president of the United States by taking the oath of office at the corner of Wall and Broad Streets. A World's Fair in New York City that would open on the 150th anniversary of his inauguration seemed a good idea. The second motivation was money. The Century of Progress Exposition held in Chicago in 1933–1934 had brought the "second city" a great deal of much-needed revenue. Third, Queens had plenty of room for a fair. With history, finances, and space in mind in 1935, "New York World's Fair 1939" was incorporated, with one hundred prominent New Yorkers as members. In May 1936 the corporation chose Grover Whalen as its president.

Mayor Walker's last police commissioner, Whalen had been so diligent in enforcing Prohibition laws in 1928 that his teams of speakeasy raiders were called "Whalen's Whackers." In 1929 he attempted to deal with criticism of police handling of the Arnold Rothstein rubout by creating an undercover squad of gangland investigators. In 1931 he dispensed with a special "confidential squad" headed by then inspector Lewis J. Valentine charged with rooting out the corrupt cops. Whalen broke up the unit with the statement, "I see no necessity for having a gumshoe staff attached to my office nor for having any wiretapping done inside the department." In 1930 he said about Communists, "These enemies of society are to be driven out of New York regardless of their constitutional rights." A "Red Squad" was formed. He standardized the cops' sidearm. The .38-caliber Smith & Wesson six-shot revolver became known as the "police special." It remained the basic NYPD weapon until the 1990s, when an outgunned department switched to the fourteen-slug Glock automatic. In the 1937 mayoral race Whalen was the Democrats' first choice to run against La Guardia, but had lost out to Jeremiah T. Mahoney. Whalen then devoted himself to being a prominent business leader. It was in a conference between Whalen and

Robert Moses that Flushing Meadows was selected as the site for the World's Fair.

The state legislature passed enabling legislation. Congress authorized President Roosevelt to invite foreign governments to participate. At La Guardia's insistence, but with no real objection from FDR and the State Department, an invitation was not extended to Germany. No bans, however, were slapped on Italy for its aggression in North Africa and Japan because of its designs for a Japanese "greater East Asia coprosperity sphere" in Asia, starting with the conquest of China.

Mayor La Guardia's private verbal war with Nazidom continued unabated. His anti-Hitler outbursts so enraged Germany's air force commander, Hermann Göring, that the former air ace of World War I and deputy to Hitler said that if La Guardia didn't shut his "arrogant" mouth the Luftwaffe would bomb New York from Governor's Island to Rockefeller Center. When the German consulate requested special police protection for a visiting official of Hitler's Foreign Ministry, to guard him against New York Jews, the mayor called in Valentine and ordered him to organize the special detail with his biggest Jewish cops. La Guardia may have recalled that when Theodore Roosevelt was police commissioner, TR had answered a similar request for guards to protect a notorious anti-Semitic lecturer by assigning Jewish officers to the duty.

As planning for the fair continued, the exposition taking shape in blueprints and architectural drawings rapidly expanded its dimensions to dwarf Chicago's earlier extravaganza. The financial planners estimated that the New York World's Fair's entrance turnstiles would turn at the rate of four times a second, amounting to sixty million revolutions in the first season, for a projected $1 billion in overall business for the city. When ready, the fair would cover nearly two square miles of ground and extend a mile and a quarter across at its widest point. The territory would be divided into zones: Government, Transportation, Communications, Food, Community Interests, and Amusement. The centerpiece would be "the Perisphere and Trylon." The former was planned as a mammoth globe containing an exhibit called "Democracity." This would be a diorama depicting a future idyllic city and countryside. Inside a space as large as Radio City Music Hall fairgoers would be transported on two "magic carpets" (revolving platforms) to gaze in wonder "as if from Olympian heights to pierce the fogs of ignorance, habit, and prejudice that envelop everyday thinking, and gaze down on the ideal community that man could build today were he to make full use of his tools, his resources and his knowledge."

Fiorello La Guardia did not write that description of his own vision of a new world, but he could have.

This enlightening experience in the Perisphere would last six minutes, after which the observers exited by way of a bridge (the "Helicon") connecting the huge globe to the Trylon. It was a three-sided, upward-tapering shaft reaching 750 feet in height. Cost to build: $1.7 million.

The Trylon and the Perisphere became the dominant symbols of the fair. They were sold in miniature as paperweights, ashtrays, keychain fobs, pins, postcards, hairpins, money clips, and anything else souvenir entrepreneurs could think of for fairgoers to take home. (As this passage was being written, a Trylon and Perisphere ashtray sat on the author's desk beside a word-processing computer, which is one of the few future marvels that the New York World's Fair of 1939–1940 did not anticipate.)

In memory of the sesquicentennial of Washington's first inauguration, a colossal image of George Washington stood in a semicircular Washington Square to dominate a mall between the Trylon and Perisphere and a Lagoon of Nations, with flags of members of the League of Nations flapping in breezes wafting off Flushing Bay. Portending an America that would take to the highways and make the United States the biggest buyer and maker of automobiles in the world was the second most popular area of the fair—the Transportation Zone. Within it the General Motors Corporation presented a picture of a country on wheels, speeding along superhighways without red lights from coast to coast. Its Highways and Horizons "Futurama" was "a world of tomorrow." GM's rival Ford offered

The Trylon and the
Perisphere, New
York World's Fair,
1939.

"The Road of Tomorrow," viewed from rising spiral ramps.
Available to ride in were Ford V-8s and Lincoln Zephyrs.

Surpassing the automotive shows in public approval was
the Amusement Zone. Since the introduction of the entertainment "midway" at the World's Columbian Exposition of 1893
in Chicago, no world's fair could open without a place for fun.
The 1893 Chicago fair had introduced the Ferris wheel. The
New York World's Fair of 1939–1940 offered a breathtaking
parachute jump. It gave the brave and the hardy the "experience of all the thrills of bailing out without any of the usual
hazards or discomforts" of actually parachuting. Eleven permanently opened chutes with two side-by-side seats were attached to wires. They were lifted to the top of the tower and

released to fall (held by the wires) and come to a stop with a bounce. The ride was so popular that when the World's Fair closed in 1940, it was moved to Coney Island, where the tower remains, a rusted derelict and a reminder of a more innocent time.

Another successful entertainment was found daily at the Fountain Lake Amphitheater. It had ten thousand seats for watching a spectacular "Aquacade" of swimmers and water ballets staged by one of New York's legendary showmen, Billy Rose. The star of this "girlie extravaganza," as the show was known by some, was swimming champion Eleanor Holm.

Every night of the fair at nine-thirty, fireworks lit up the sky above the Lagoon of Nations. It was followed at ten-thirty by pyrotechnics above Fountain Lake that were described as "the nearest approach to chaos that man can contrive for purposes of sheer entertainment."

No longer able to operate from an office in the New York City Building in the Government Zone, La Guardia shifted his summer City Hall to the nearby Arrowbrook Country Club and an office larger than the Blue Room. It was furnished by a "raging assortment of cretonned couches and ornate pieces in the Louis XV style." Sallying forth each day, he greeted celebrated visitors and ordinary, but startled, fairgoers. He accepted for display from England the genuine Magna Carta. When King George VI and Queen Elizabeth came to take in the show, he escorted them in an open car, then told reporters that the royals were "easier to entertain and live with for a day than many other great guests we've had." The king and the queen proceeded from the city to call on President and Mrs. Roosevelt at Hyde Park, where Eleanor fed them the most American of summertime food, hot dogs.

The only thing in the fair that sparked La Guardia's displeasure was a "nude miss" contest. Otherwise, he was as ubiquitous at Flushing Meadows as he was outside its gates.

At the official opening of the fair on April 30, 1939 (150 years to the day after George Washington's inaugural), FDR formally pronounced the fair "open." When La Guardia's turn to talk came, the mayor of New York said, "May I point to

Lower
Manhattan,
1939.

one exhibit that I hope all visitors will note, and that is the
City of New York itself."

Symbolized by the Manhattan skyscrapers visible in the west-
ern distance, New York in the summer of 1939 had a population that was more than Arizona, Colorado, Delaware, Idaho,
Maine, Montana, Nevada, New Hampshire, New Mexico,
North Dakota, Rhode Island, Utah, Vermont, Wyoming, and
the District of Columbia combined. There were more New
Yorkers in the world than Australians, Bulgarians, Peruvians,
Greeks, Swedes, and Moroccans combined. Newspaperman
Mark Hellinger would see it as a "naked city" with eight million stories to be told. But the most fascinating and compel-
ling of those stories by far was Fiorello La Guardia in all his
numerous incarnations, costumes, and hats.

Who but La Guardia would pick a fight with British philosopher Bertrand Russell?

The fracas was occasioned by the announcement on October 1, 1939, by the Board of Higher Education that Russell had been appointed to a professorship at City College to teach the philosophy of mathematics. The mayor had no quarrel with Russell's views on numbers. What irked him was that Russell had written in a book, *Marriage and Morals,* that adultery was not only permissible, but even desirable, and that Christianity through "its whole history" had been "a force tending toward mental disorders and unwholesome views of life."

Understandably, the leading Christian clerics of New York in all their manifestations took a dim view of Russell lecturing to New York students on any topic. Most vociferous was the Episcopal bishop of New York, William T. Manning. Bertrand Russell was, he said, "an ape of genius." He lashed out at Russell as a "recognized propagandist against religion and morality."

The mayor proposed deleting from the City College budget the appropriation of $8,000 to establish a "chair in philosophy" that was to fund Russell's appointment. The striking of the funds, La Guardia told the corporation council, was not subject to appeal. The City Council proved more susceptible to public opinion than mayoral dictates. Flooded with protest from voters, the Council on March 14, 1940, ordered the Board of Higher Education to revoke the Russell appointment. Three days later, at the St. Patrick's Day Parade, La Guardia grumbled to a fellow march reviewer, "Why is it we always select someone with a boil on his neck or a blister on his fanny?"

The City Council that had been battered by an influx of anti-Russell mail and phone calls was by now hearing from the other side just as vociferously. It was also being told by the Board of Higher Education that it had no power to prevent appointments. Council members wavered, and enough of them voted on March 19 to let the Board have its way. But it was a brief victory. A private citizen took the Board to court. The case was heard by Justice John E. McGheehan, a Roman

Catholic who once tried to ban a portrait of Martin Luther from a city mural depicting the history of religion. McGheehan found that Russell's deficiencies were not only in morality. Russell was not an American citizen. For that reason alone he was unfit for teaching at City College.

The controversy continued into the fall, with Russell in the meantime taking a position with the Barnes Foundation in Merion, Pennsylvania. He was there in October when the Board of Higher Education decided the game was not worth the candle. It voted fifteen to two to drop the matter. Ironically, Russell had felt at the start of the brouhaha that he should withdraw. In a letter to the *New York Times* after the dust settled, he wrote, "If I had considered only my own interests and inclinations, I should have retired at once. But it would have been cowardly and foolish." They were sentiments that Fiorello La Guardia, who had challenged authority all his life when giving up would have been easier, could readily understand.

At the height of the controversy, La Guardia's trusted and loyal aide and adviser Charles Culp Burlingham, whom La Guardia called CCB, had asked La Guardia, "Why should a man with your record in a free country do to CCNY what the Nazis have done to the universities of Heidelberg and Bonn? It is not like you."

An increasing number of La Guardia intimates and many people who could not claim the sometimes dubious privilege of friendship noticed, and commented, that the mayor had changed. He had always been a little Mussolini and the Napoleon of City Hall, but there had always been some limits. When he told a commissioner, "You're so stupid it's an art," he did so because he felt that the commissioner was not doing his job. It sounded personal, but it was not. Sooner or later, but generally sooner, all was forgiven. He once fired someone, but when the man wasn't at his desk the next day he phoned him and demanded to know why he wasn't working.

But in the months following the opening of the World's Fair the mayoral disposition to *act* the tyrant when it suited him appeared to have ceased being a useful technique. It seemed to many that the Little Flower felt he possessed the same rights of monarchs who'd believed their powers came from God, not from "the people."

The *New York Herald Tribune*'s Geoffrey Parsons wrote confidentially to Burlingham that it seemed incredible that La Guardia "could do the outrageous things that he has done to decent unoffending folk, subordinates, large and small."

With a sense of bewilderment, dismay, impatience, and sorrow the letter continued, "I am becoming a little weary of this latest model of reformer, who because he is money honest and his aims are high, feels under no obligation to live up to the ordinary standards of courtesy and fidelity to a promise."

Burlingham feared La Guardia was on the verge of a nervous breakdown. He spoke to La Guardia's physician, George Baehr, and found the doctor equally concerned. Baehr informed La Guardia of his and CCB's worries and suggested to La Guardia that he needed rest, preferably in a hospital. La Guardia shot off a note to CCB: "I feel I must write you because I am so worried that you are not taking care of yourself. Here you are when you should be resting, in so many activities and giving so much of yourself to each of them. . . . Take it easy for a while and be guided entirely by your friends."

Not content with this needling, La Guardia dispatched a jesting telegram:

DR GEORGE BAEHR ABSOLUTELY FORBIDS ME GOING ANY-
WHERE AT NIGHT STOP DOES NOT WANT ME TO SPEAK AT
DINNER TOMORROW NIGHT AT HARVARD CLUB STOP WHAT
SHALL I DO?

Other mayoral assistants just gave up. Press secretary James Kieran had a fight with his boss and quit. La Guardia's longtime confidential secretary Mitzi Somach threw in the towel and resigned a job that she'd taken for a dollar a year because she believed in La Guardia. The mayor only added to concerns about his stability by wisecracking, "It has lasted six years and we got a lot out of her during that period." No one laughed.

The mayor may have been troubled by what might have been diagnosed decades later as "depression" and treated with a mood-regulating pill such as Prozac. Equally possible was that he simply had so many things on his mind that he became even more short-tempered and impatient. There has always been more truth than self-flattery in the mantra of New York mayors that the office they occupy at the sufferance of "the people" is "the second toughest job in the country." In addition to the stresses and strains of the mayoralty in dealing with building a new airport, opening a World's Fair, tilting with Nazis at home and abroad, contending with a philosopher from England who advocated adultery and disdained Christianity, and consolidating the subway system, La Guardia could not ignore the political calendar.

Forty-five years before Fiorello La Guardia found himself in the third year of his second term as mayor, his political idol Theodore Roosevelt (then police commissioner) had blasted his newspapermen friends Jacob Riis and Lincoln Steffens for asking him if he was planning to run for president one day. TR exploded. "Don't you dare ask me that. Don't you put such ideas into my head," he blared. "Never, never, you must never either of you remind a man on a political job that he may be president. It almost always kills him politically. He loses his nerve; he can't do his work; he gives up the very traits that are making him a possibility."

In 1940 Fiorello La Guardia was hearing talk at every turn that the presidency could be in his future. As to his present employment, La Guardia confided to a friend that he had done so much that he'd hoped to do that being mayor was now to be a "glorified janitor." But what could he do except sit and wait for the present occupant of the White House to let him and the country know whether the tradition of two terms only established by George Washington still held sway?

The answer came not from FDR but Adolf Hitler.

On September 1, 1939, as the turnstiles whirled at the World's Fair (August 26 marked a one-day record of 306,480 admissions), Britain and France officially went to war with Germany. Then began a period of inactivity that was called "the phony war." But at dawn on April 9, 1940, the Nazis sprang to life with attacks on Denmark and Norway. A month later the storm troopers invaded the Low Countries. On June 10, it was France.

"The hand that held the dagger," said President Roosevelt on that date, "has struck it into the back of its neighbor."

With England standing alone, her fate and that of Western civilization hung in a balance that only the power of the United States could tip away from a Nazi victory.

Knowing "Franklin" well, and knowing what Fiorello La Guardia would do in the same circumstance, the mayor of New York understood that the Democratic candidate for president in 1940 would be FDR. He wrote to Burlingham, "Everything seems so trivial in the face of world conditions."

To Roosevelt near the end of June went this heartfelt message:

> You have now assumed the most difficult task and responsibility of greater importance to the future of our country than ever before confronted by any man or candidate in our entire history. You are now facing one of the hardest campaigns ever waged in our time and you require all the strength, courage and fortitude God can give you, which is the wish of your sincere friend, Fiorello.

Then the mayor cast aside all imploring that he take a rest. There was a city to run and a president to help win reelection.

24

With Europe at war on August 17, 1940, President Roosevelt traveled to Ogdensburg, New York, to meet with Canada's prime minister, Mackenzie King. Their subject was defending North America. The next day they signed the Ogdensburg Agreement, creating the Permanent Joint Board of Defense. Notification that FDR had named La Guardia as a member reached the mayor while he was uncharacteristically taking a day off to rest in bed in hopes of shaking off a cold. The news of his appointment got him up and on his way to Washington for briefings and then a trip to Ottawa to confer with his Canadian counterparts. He said the position meant "only a little extra work and overtime." In fact, he had already been planning for war by activating a moribund Disaster Control Board that had been organized in the wake of the 1938 hurricane. To head the revitalized coordinating committee he named Police Commissioner Valentine.

As president of the U.S. Conference of Mayors, a post to which he was elected for the fourth time, he urged other mayors to prepare their cities for the possibility of war by making plans to deal with public panic and to draft tactics for dealing with air raids.

At the same time, he was keeping his eyes on the second summer of the World's Fair and in touch with Robert Moses on the subject of restoring Flushing Meadow Park following the end of the fair, scheduled for October 27. The second season had opened on May 11, the day after German troops invaded Belgium, Luxembourg, and the Netherlands. While admission turnstiles continued to turn, Billy Rose went on presenting bathing beauties in water ballets, the brave at heart dropped from the top of the parachute jump, and the GM and Ford exhibitions looked to a glorious future motivated by the internal combustion engine, the theme of bright tomorrows suddenly had a hollow ring. A year after La Guardia's declaration of "a new day" it was obvious to anyone who looked at the events in Europe that the mayor's words had been premature. The New York World's Fair of 1939–1940 had turned out to be not a celebration of the birth of a fair new age but a farewell party. The two-decade era that started with the 1918 Armistice had been, despite numerous problems and woes, a time of innocence. Americans thought they could, as in the words of a hit song of 1919, "build a sweet little nest somewhere in the West and let the rest of the world go by."

In mid-September 1940 the mayor of New York was in the full flower of his campaign mode and irking Republicans by disdaining the GOP's presidential candidate, Wendell Willkie, and going full blast for a third term for FDR. Joining Progressive senator George Norris in forming Independents for Roosevelt, he declared that FDR "has made America the hope of the world." A favorite campaign line was "Hitler understands the language of Roosevelt."

October found the mayor of New York in Newark, Pittsburgh, Boston, Providence, Rochester, Cincinnati, Chicago, and Detroit. At the latter's City Hall a man at a reception in La Guardia's honor obviously did not share the crowd's enthusiasm. He shouted to La Guardia, "Are you still taking orders from Boss Flynn?" Lunging at the heckler, La Guardia grabbed the man's necktie and twisted it tightly. As the man gasped for air, someone pulled La Guardia off him. The mayor later dismissed the incident as "just a drunk." In fact, the heckler had never had a drink in his life. Incensed at being attacked and insulted, he sued La Guardia for both assault and slander. (In a calmer moment the man dropped both suits.)

For the October 21, 1940, *Life* magazine La Guardia wrote an article titled "Roosevelt Preferred." It concluded with "Remember this is not an election for a municipal alderman—this is not an election for mayor. Bear in mind that we are electing this year a President of the United States—to the most difficult job in the world. The people's candidate is Franklin D. Roosevelt."

At the end of October the mayor and Roosevelt were together in Brooklyn to break the ground for that end of the Brooklyn–Battery Tunnel. On the same day they stood at the Manhattan entrance for the under-construction Queens Midtown Tunnel. With workers looking on, La Guardia hailed FDR as a consistent friend of labor. The presidential candidate's visit ended with him and La Guardia at rallies in Brooklyn, Carnegie Hall, and Madison Square Garden.

On October 30, 1940, Roosevelt was in Boston. His subject was the war in Europe. He told the audience before him and the millions of parents listening on the radio and worrying that their sons' names would be drawn in the new Selective Service, "I have said this before, but I shall say it again and again and again: your boys are not going to be sent into any foreign wars."

By ten o'clock election night the news moving in a zipper of lights around the New York Times Building in the "square" named after it at the crossing of Broadway, Seventh Avenue, and Forty-second Street in New York informed the people who cared to look up that Roosevelt was heading for a historic landslide victory. Fifty million voters had gone to the polls. Fifty-five percent of them (27,243,466) decided that they didn't care about George Washington's no-third-term precedent. They wanted Franklin Delano Roosevelt for four more years.

On the night of December 31, 1940, Times Square was the scene of another noisy welcome to a new year offered by hundreds of thousands of New Yorkers and out-of-towners, most of whom made their way to and from the "Crossroads of the World" on a subway system that everyone still recognized as the IRT, BMT, and IND, even though the lines were now owned and operated by New York City Transit Authority (TA). Since the takeover, the men who operated the lines and belonged to the Transit Workers' Union had been working under the contract that had been a bone of contention between Mayor La Guardia and union president Mike Quill in the spring of 1940. The agreement was up for renewal. The negotiations centered on La Guardia's opposition to a closed shop. When talks on that issue and a wage increase broke down, Quill ordered his members out on strike.

"A tragic mistake," cried La Guardia as the trains stopped running, causing the worst transportation tieup since 1926. Digging in his heels, he declared, "I am not going to fail in my duty for the sake of mistaken popularity."

The strike dragged on for eleven days. Trains started rolling after both sides agreed to submit the issues to arbitration. As before, it was agreed that the courts would decide who was right. The *New York Sun* accused La Guardia of "humiliating retreat." In a reference to Prime Minister Neville Chamberlain, who had gone to see Hitler at Munich carrying an umbrella and came back with it and a worthless piece of paper in 1938, at the cost of Czechoslovak freedom, the *Sun* said that La Guardia was an appeaser who came back "from Munich without even an umbrella."

At one point during the strike La Guardia had proposed to FDR that the subway system be assigned to carry mail so that the federal government could step in to keep the trains going. It was a ludicrous suggestion that Roosevelt brushed off.

While stumping for FDR's reelection in the autumn of 1940, Fiorello La Guardia had expectations of being rewarded with the post of secretary of war. Rexford Tugwell remembered that La Guardia's "hopes were so high and his eagerness so apparent." The hopes were well founded. Roosevelt was planning to offer him the cabinet seat. La Guardia's friend Burlingham told the mayor not to take it, or any other job Roosevelt might offer. "You won't get anything by cuddling up to Franklin," warned CCB. "He doesn't give a damn for you. I'm perfectly sure of that, and he would chuck you out in a minute."

Nevertheless, certain that FDR would have a significant place for his friend Fiorello in the third-term cabinet, the second-term mayor let it be known to those closest to him that he would not seek another term. He began speculating on who might succeed him at City Hall. Burlingham did his best to persuade him that his work in New York was not finished. "No one knows what the situation will be in New York or the U.S.A. six months from now," he argued. "You may be needed in New York as much as FDR was and is in the U.S.A. Next to the presidency, the mayoralty is the most important office in the U.S.A.—certainly more important than any cabinet post, even the highest. So I beg you to keep your shirt on and give out no statements. The less talk, the more do."

La Guardia said to Rexford Tugwell, "I can't stay here with the world falling to pieces."

"Rex," as the mayor called him, understood La Guardia's desire—his need—to move on to other things, to break out of the mold. Tugwell later wrote, "The trappings and routines of power, after a while, are not the compensation that they were at first. Gradually, they become bindings and ties; finally they become something submitted to and undergone with apathy, even with resentment."

All of this was one explanation for the changes in La Guardia that had been the concern of Burlingham and Dr. Baehr. Fiorello just didn't want to be mayor anymore. Nor did Marie want him to run again. Unfortunately for them, FDR passed the word that the Little Flower's proper place was not at the cabinet table but at his desk in City Hall.

"In these days no one can say with any degree of certainty just what he will or will not do," said the disappointed mayor in April 1941. "I prefer not to run again for mayor of the City of New York." But, he hinted, should he be drafted to run . . .

The *Daily News,* which had fondly named the mayor "Butch," said it didn't "want Butch to get a cabinet job." The paper declared him "the greatest mayor New York City ever had" and "the ideal mayor for a time like this, when the war across the ocean is pulling the various racial groups' heartstrings every which way."

Others who wanted him to run noted that he had said "I *prefer not to*" rather than "I will NOT run again." The consensus of those making this observation was that he needed to be *asked* to run again. An urgent appeal that he do so came from the Citizens' Nonpartisan Movement to Draft La Guardia for Mayor. Among the members were Fiorello's old friend Fannie Hurst; the historian James MacGregor Burns; publisher Bennett Cerf; Irving Berlin; and attorney Jacob K. Javits, a young Progressive with a bright future in politics. How they felt was expressed by the distinguished cleric John Haynes Holmes. He asked: If FDR proved two good terms deserved a third, why was La Guardia being reticent?

La Guardia answered that a third term for himself would be all right, provided "we do not get in the habit of perpetuity in office."

Holmes exclaimed his delight with worshipful verbs [emphases added]:

> I *rejoice* in your joy in the job. I *admire* your ceaseless energy and inexhaustible vitality. I *adore* your early morning and late at night fidelity to your multitudinous duties. I *reverence* your integrity, your courage, your pride in the city, your confidence in its citizens. I *love* it when you race to a fire, like the unquenchable boy within you; I *love* it equally when you take your horn spectacles and lock yourself in for a week of bread and water with your budget like a saint doing devotions before the altar of his faith.

In welcoming La Guardia's decision not to leave the mayoralty, President Roosevelt did not rule out a role for him in preparing the nation for American participation in the war that they both knew was inevitable. FDR saw the best-known and most successful mayor in the nation as uniquely fitted to shape a civil defense program. La Guardia responded to the idea in his usual way, by telling the president what was and what was not needed. He handed FDR four pages of single-spaced do this's and don't do that's. The new civil defense agency, he said, must not be "just another Board, Bureau, Commission, Committee of Volunteer Firemen's Association."

Civilian defense was not "community singing, sweater knitting and basket weaving." He advised—demanded—a civil defense apparatus that would have sweeping authority over every governmental agency, federal, state, and local outside the military, including propaganda and domestic intelligence. (Because this would mean treading on the turf of the Federal Bureau of Investigation and its protective director, J. Edgar Hoover, the idea was dead on arrival.)

"If you approve the plan in general," Fiorello told Franklin, "I will be very glad to cooperate and help." He also let Roosevelt know indirectly that he would not insist on cabinet status, but that he felt the civil defense director should be equivalent in rank and welcome to sit in on cabinet meetings. If he took the job—unpaid—he assured the president he was perfectly capable of handling it and running New York City, assuming that he won reelection in 1941.

On May 17 he led a "preparedness" rally of nearly seven hundred thousand New Yorkers (almost equal to the population of the city of Munich, Germany, where Hitler went each year to mark the birth of the Nazi Party). It was held in Central Park's Sheep Meadow. The mayor spoke, bantered with pop-eyed comedian Eddie Cantor, and introduced famed soprano Marian Anderson and radio's popular Kate Smith. She rendered America's "second national anthem," Irving Berlin's "God Bless America." The former cornetist led a 250-piece Police Department and Fire Department combined band. He grinned with pleasure as his Great War buddy Albert Spalding played his fiddle.

The next day La Guardia boarded a plane at La Guardia Airport for Washington to accept the appointment as director of civil defense. The scope of the challenge he undertook at age sixty was pointed out by FDR's doubtful (and probably somewhat jealous) secretary of the interior, Harold L. Ickes. He conceded that no one was better qualified to head civil defense, but said, "Here are two very big jobs, each of which will take all the time and resources that any man possesses. Yet Fiorello is to run these two jobs, continue as mayor of New York, campaign for reelection, and at the same time oper-

If there was a fire of any significance in New York City, the mayor could be expected to show up and supervise. Accompanying him at this blaze was Fire Commissioner John McElligott.

ate as chairman of the Joint United States–Canadian Defense Board. It is absurd on the face of it. He has to eat and sleep like other human beings."

Why was La Guardia willing to do all this? Biographer Thomas Kessner saw him "still trying to prove himself." The post was also a relief from the "janitorial" work. And as head of the civil defense program he would remain in the national spotlight with dictatorial powers surpassing in scope those that had been a hallmark of his mayoralty.

In taking the position he saw a way to be closer to the president. By using that proximity he would become involved in policymaking and planning beyond civil defense. Evidently to tie himself even more to Roosevelt, he brought the president's wife, Eleanor, into the civil defense office as coequal with responsibilities in the area of public morale. It was a

As director of the
Office of Civil Defense,
La Guardia appointed
Mrs. Franklin D. Roose-
velt as his assistant,
then toured the country
to inspect preparedness.

mistake because they were dramatically different in personality, and second, because Mrs. Roosevelt was not at that time
the widely popular figure that she became after FDR's death.
His calculation that as Mrs. Roosevelt she would provide him
increased access to "the Chief" was based on the belief that
Franklin's relationship with Eleanor was as warm and as
close as Fiorello's to Marie. He did not know, as hardly anyone did at the time, that the president and the First Lady
were living as separate lives as occupying the White House
and being in politics permitted. Nor did he know that FDR
had given orders that Fiorello was not to enjoy an open door
to the president's office. In effect, Roosevelt had given him
the civil defense job, and let him continue to be mayor, to

keep La Guardia's hands out of White House business and the presidential hair.

The civil defense director quickly realized that Americans had believed FDR's pledge in the presidential campaign to keep America out of the war. Consequently, hardly anyone in the country saw a pressing need to prepare for conflict by getting ready to deal with air raids. The idea that Nazi planes could span the Atlantic Ocean and drop bombs on New York, Boston, and Philadelphia seemed silly. Most Americans saw La Guardia as Don Quixote tilting at nonexistent windmills.

⌁

Doffing his civil defense director's air raid warden's helmet in the summer of 1941, La Guardia put on his political war bonnet for a Republican primary skirmish with an isolationist, anti–New Deal, old-line Republican, John R. Davies. The mayor found an ally in a frequent foe, Robert Moses. The parks, bridges, and tunnels builder gave a genuine but backhanded endorsement from the point of view of Robert Moses. "I am for Mayor La Guardia," he said, "because in spite of his cussedness toward those whose support is indispensable in critical times, and in spite of excursions into the far capital [Washington, D.C.] where they give him nothing but husks and leavings, he has been the best mayor of New York in my lifetime."

Primary turnout was light. Only 4 percent of enrolled Republicans voted. The mayor won. "I feel free now to take up and lead the fight," he said to the Democrats as he looked to the fall campaign. "Don't count on laryngitis."

His opponent was William O'Dwyer, the district attorney in Brooklyn (Kings County). Like Thomas E. Dewey, he'd built a reputation as a crime-buster, primarily because his office had uncovered and smashed a mob murder-for-hire outfit (the brainchild of Arnold Rothstein) known as "Murder, Inc." The work had been done by a young O'Dwyer assistant D.A. in charge of homicide, Burton B. Turkus. By the time he was through, New Yorkers had met a menagerie of hoods and

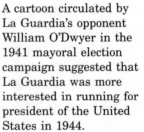

A cartoon circulated by La Guardia's opponent William O'Dwyer in the 1941 mayoral election campaign suggested that La Guardia was more interested in running for president of the United States in 1944.

killers with names that seemed made up by Damon Runyon or Chester Gould for his comic strip "Dick Tracy." Newspapers spoke of Buggsy Goldstein, Dukey Maffetore, Red Alpert, Pittsburgh Phil, Happy Maione, Joe the Baker, Blue Jaw Magoon, Dasher Abbadando, and a cold-blooded killer named Abe "Kid Twist" Reles.

The latter turned on the others by giving Turkus lurid details of more than two hundred unsolved murders, all contracted for with the Brooklyn boys by local gangsters and other mobs across the country. Unfortunately, before Reles could testify in court he was thrown through a window of a sixth-floor room where he'd been stashed by Turkus, under police guard, at the Half Moon Hotel in Coney Island. Reles's demise provided one of the most colorful quotations in the history of American crime: "The canary could sing, but he couldn't fly."

O'Dwyer's campaign against La Guardia was largely a re-hash of tired shibboleths. La Guardia was soft on Communists—witness his political protégé Vito "the Red" Marcantonio; real-estate taxes were too high; he was antilabor; too big for his britches; the Little Mussolini; he spent more time in Washington than in New York City.

A blow to the Democrats came from the number one Democrat in the nation. Although stating to a press conference that he was not taking sides in the mayoralty contest, FDR gave his opinion that Fiorello La Guardia had given New York City the most honest and most efficient municipal government "of any."

The mayor sent the president a one-word telegram: *"Merci."*

O'Dwyer got help from Governor Lehman. He denounced La Guardia for "abusing and vilifying" everyone who opposed him or criticized him. "New Yorkers," he said, "are sick and tired of Mr. La Guardia's unbridled tongue."

La Guardia appeared to validate the criticism of his shoot-from-the-lips habit one day as he walked past a vegetable stand. He stopped, picked up a cabbage, and said with a smile to the reporters with him, "My opponent's head."

The wisecrack caused a drop in his support. But on November 4, more than enough New York voters decided to keep him in City Hall. It was the closest mayoral election since 1904, but it was the first time in modern times that city voters gave a mayor a third term.

To the victor the result meant "four more years of hell."

A month and three days later, his job as civil defense director suddenly did not seem to be such a big laugh after all.

Part IV

Four More Years of Hell

There is not much glamor to it, but heartbreaking work—just hard labor.

—Mayor Fiorello La Guardia, 1942

25

On Sunday afternoon, December 7, 1941, Mayor La Guardia appeared in a studio of city-owned radio station WNYC in the Municipal Building opposite City Hall to participate with a group of civic leaders in the presentation of a plaque to the station for its public service work. As they waited to go on the air, the bell of a United Press teletype machine in the newsroom rang repeatedly. The FLASH bulletin reported that Japanese warplanes had attacked the U.S. naval base at Pearl Harbor and the U.S. Army's air base at Hickam Field, Honolulu, in the Hawaiian Islands.

La Guardia sprang into action. He issued orders "as mayor of New York and on my own responsibility" that all "Japanese subjects remain in their homes until their status is determined by our federal government." Officers of the Japanese consulate general in New York were put under the protection (and observation) of the Police Department. He also ordered "under my responsibility" the closing of a Japanese club. All this was pending action by the federal government, which eventually moved to incarcerate Japanese Americans everywhere.

The mayor then took to the air on WNYC, as both mayor and the national director of civil defense. In somber tone and unusually slow cadence he said, "I want to warn the people of this city that we are in an extreme crisis."

He stated that "anyone familiar with the world situation knows that the Nazi government is masterminding Japanese policy and the action taken by the Japanese government this

311

afternoon. It was carrying out the now known Nazi technique of murder by surprise, so there is no doubt that the thugs and gangsters now controlling the Nazi government are responsible and have guided the Japanese government in the attack on American territory and the attack on the Philippine Islands. Therefore, I want to warn the people of this city and on the Atlantic coast that we must not and cannot feel secure or assured because we are on the Atlantic coast, and the activities this afternoon have taken place in the Pacific. We must be prepared for anything at any time." After describing his orders concerning Japanese in the city, he appealed to New Yorkers to be calm. "There is no need of being excited or unduly alarmed," he said in a measured tone, "but we are not out of the danger zone by any means."

Anyone listening to a recording of the broadcast sixty years later might say La Guardia was overreacting and sounding alarmist, but in fact in the confusion and the shock felt by all Americans on that Sunday afternoon there was genuine cause for concern that more attacks were possible anywhere, and even likely. What is amazing about La Guardia's broadcast is that there was nothing of an "I told you so" nature in the remarks of a civil defense director whose earlier calls for preparedness had been greeted with scoffs and derision.

"My friends," said the mayor, "we must *toughen up*. We have our homes and our lands to defend! We must remain cool and yet determined. We are aware of the danger ahead, but unafraid. In the meantime, know that your city government is on the job and looking after your welfare and comfort and safety. Tomorrow in all likelihood we will know exactly where we stand when we hear from Washington."

On December 8, 1941, La Guardia and all Americans were by their radios to hear the address by President Roosevelt to a joint session of Congress. He labeled December 7, 1941, "a date that will live in infamy," and vowed that in the war into which the United States had been drawn "we will gain the inevitable triumph, so help us God."

With war declared against Japan, Germany, and their Axis allies, La Guardia at last lashed out at "all persons who have been sneering and jeering at defense activities, and even those who have been objecting to them and placing obstacles in their path." Assuring them that they would be protected, he made it clear that he expected their cooperation and that "there will be no fooling."

Leaving Newbold Morris in charge of the city, he dashed to Washington. After dictating a memo to FDR calling for seizure of enemy ships in U.S. harbors, he departed the capital with Mrs. Roosevelt for the West Coast for an inspection of civil defense preparedness. On their way they heard a report that San Francisco had been bombed. Assured that it was a rumor, they landed in Los Angeles and surveyed fire-fighting equipment and other preparations. Mrs. Roosevelt noted of her companion, "One could be exasperated with him at times, but one had to admire his real integrity and courage." She admitted, "I did not know and never have known how much all our plans, his and mine, really helped since so much of our equipment was lacking that they could not do things that were considered essential."

Almost immediately, New Yorkers expressed dismay that their mayor was not among them. Their concern was expressed in an editorial in the *New York World Telegram*. It said, "The situation does not call for a dizzy show off of one man juggling multiple jobs."

The *Herald Tribune* agreed, calling the mayor's dual role a "tragic absurdity."

The same sentiment found expression in Washington, D.C. Roosevelt's chief adviser, Harry Hopkins, whispered into FDR's ear that the office of civil defense would fare better if it were run by Wendell Willkie. The idea that the 1940 Republican presidential candidate be made part of the administration did not settle well with Mrs. Roosevelt. The president preferred James M. Landis of Harvard Law School. He informed La Guardia personally that he was being replaced by Landis.

Though disappointed, La Guardia masked his hurt with humor. At the end of January he told an audience at his alma mater NYU Law School, "Sin does not pay, I am about to give up the double life." He tendered his resignation officially on February 11, but by then Congress had voted to assign civil defense to the army.

On the day before La Guardia put away his air warden helmet, he found himself once again racing to the scene of a fire, but one that raised the specter that German saboteurs were at work on the New York City waterfront. At three in the afternoon on February 9, 1942, a thick plume of black smoke billowed across the busy lanes of the West Side Highway from the French ocean liner *Normandie.* Then flames were seen engulfing the ship's promenade deck. As this was happening, La Guardia was on the air on WNYC assuring New Yorkers that he would not permit an increase in the subway fare from a nickel to a dime. A note about the fire was slipped to him. He ended the broadcast abruptly and raced toward Pier 88. At the city's main hospital, Bellevue, a gong rang seven times, signaling the need to prepare to handle a catastrophe.

When La Guardia bounded from his car, wearing a corduroy-collared black raincoat and black homburg, he saw with horror that one of the grandest liners in the world was a mass of spiraling flames and roiling smoke.

In his mind, as in everyone else's who rushed to Pier 88, arose a suspicion that the fire had been set by Nazi agents.

In midtown souvenir shops and hotel gift shops visitors to New York could buy a postcard showing the three most beautiful ships in the world docked side by side at Hudson River piers: *Queen Mary, Queen Elizabeth,* and *Normandie.* Arguments could be had as to which was the grandest, swiftest, and most graceful. *Normandie* was 1,029 feet long, 10 more than *Queen Mary,* but two feet shorter than *Queen Elizabeth.* At 83,000 tons (2,000 more than *Mary,* 3,000 less than *Elizabeth*) *Normandie* was unique in design, with a rakish clipper bow and a rounded, overhanging stern. Her maiden voyage to

Never before and never again: five great ocean liners docked side by side on the Hudson River. Left to right: *Europa, Rex, Normandie, Georgic, Berengaria.*

New York had been a triumph. She'd glided across the Atlantic from Le Havre, France, at top speed of thirty knots and sailed past the Statue of Liberty on June 3, 1935, to a tumultuous welcome.

In 1939, after four years of service and 139 crossings carrying a total of 133,170 passengers, she had docked in New York on August 28, four days before Germany invaded Poland and triggered World War II. The ship was impounded by the U.S. government. After American entry into the conflict, she was seized by the U.S. Navy with the intention of converting her to a troop ship. Her smart black-and-white hull was painted a dull war gray. Her interior was stripped of its luxurious appointments, including 6 pianos and 18,000 bottles of wine. On February 14, 1942, she was scheduled to sail to Boston to begin wartime service.

The builder of *Normandie,* the Chantier de Penhoet shipyard, had been determined that she "should approach as nearly as possible to a 100 percent fireproof ship." Toward that goal all bulkheads were made with fire-resistant materials. Doors were designed to close electrically from a central control switch in case of fire. None of these precautions kept her from burning beside Pier 88 at Twelfth Avenue and Forty-eighth Street on February 9, 1942.

❧

Although there was no loss of life in the burning of *Normandie,* sixty years after Mayor La Guardia arrived at Pier 88 to find the great ship ablaze and listing slightly to port, the fire remained the most spectacular and widely witnessed disaster in the city's history until the attack on the World Trade Center on September 11, 2001. It was, in the words of a *Normandie* historian, "one vast, macabre carnival." For his definitive book on the pride of France and the French Line, author Harvey Ardman calculated that responding to the fire were thirty-five fire engines of all descriptions; dozens of police cars, vans, and horses; emergency squads; traffic control police; detectives; police mounted officers; FBI agents; men from the Manhattan district attorney's squad; dozens of ambulances with doctors and nurses; two hundred black soldiers in helmets for crowd control; air raid and fire wardens; an army of reporters and photographers; famed NBC radio broadcaster Graham McNamee and his technicians; volunteers from the Red Cross and the Salvation Army; Coast Guardsmen; sailors; employees of Robins Dry Dock Company; and more than ten thousand "patriots, fire buffs, and waterfront derelicts, all braving the cold and smoke."

The Red Cross and the Salvation Army would hand out ten thousand doughnuts and as many cups of coffee; eight thousand sandwiches; a thousand pairs of socks and a thousand sweaters; and innumerable packs of cigarettes. Also available were hot dogs and ice cream from vendors.

Farther removed were uncountable numbers of observers in office buildings and hotels in midtown and thousands of gawkers lining the Hudson shoreline in New Jersey. The smoke was visible miles distant in Brooklyn, Queens, Staten Island, and Nassau County. News of the fire went out over radio stations everywhere and, as noted, to listeners to the NBC network whose programming was suspended for McNamee's vivid descriptions, which usually had been heard in broadcasts of baseball games, horses races, and prizefights.

At about 3:40 P.M. La Guardia and two naval officers went on board to assess the progress in putting out the fire. As they went up a gangway, the ship lurched and almost sent them into the river. Fire Commissioner Patrick Walsh noted that the list was twelve degrees, which was not considered dangerous. The tilting of the ship was caused by the water being poured into her from fire hoses. Once the blaze was out, Walsh told the mayor, he would order the water turned off to prevent the ship from capsizing. When he was able to do so at 6:00 P.M., the order was not heard by fireboats. Noticing them continuing to work, La Guardia grabbed a radio-telephone. "This is the mayor," he said urgently. "Cease pumping as of this moment. I repeat: Cease pumping immediately."

The fireboats complied, but private firetugs were not tuned to his phone's frequency and went on pumping water for another half hour.

At 8:20 P.M. Admiral Adolphus Andrews declared *Normandie* saved, thanks to "the splendid and heroic efforts of the New York Fire Department."

They'd stopped the fire, but Andrews's assertion of salvation was premature. At 2:37 P.M. the next day the badly listing, waterlogged liner rolled over onto her port side. Looking like a beached whale, she would lie there for more than a year.

After pumping out the water that had capsized her, salvagers brought her upright at the end of October 1943. Towed to Brooklyn in June 1944 with hopes of rebuilding and a return to the high seas, she remained a derelict until declared "surplus property" on September 20, 1945, and later scrapped. Because the ship had been lost while in U.S. custody, the United States compensated the French with $13 million.

One of the many ironies in the burning of *Normandie* was that one of her designers was in New York during the fire,

When the French liner *Normandie* burned and capsized in February 1942 it was thought to be the work of German saboteurs, but the fire started accidentally as the ship was being converted to carry troops. La Guardia raced to the pier and boarded the burning ship to direct the fire fighting.

but he was unable to get through police lines. Had he gotten to the ship, he could have shown how to open devices that would let out the water and allow the *Normandie* to settle on her bottom, rather than tipping over.

The cause of the fire, it was decided, had not been German saboteurs. A worker had been careless with a welding torch and touched off a stack of government-issue mattresses.

One of Fiorello La Guardia's avowed goals as mayor was to make New York City the greatest shipping center in the world by revitalizing and expanding its waterfronts and docks.

Between 1934 and 1941 the Dock Department (renamed the Department of Marine and Aviation in 1942) had built fourteen new piers and erected superstructures on four others. One of the new wharves was No. 88, the pier where *Normandie* died. Along with piers 90 and 92, the cost of construction amounted to $11 million. Designed specifically for *Normandie* and the two great Queens, *Mary* and *Elizabeth,* the docks stretched eleven hundred feet into the Hudson and had three-story superstructures with every modern convenience to ease passenger arrivals and departures.

Along with encouraging ocean liner patronage of New York Harbor, La Guardia worked to have the port declared a "free port" in which foreign goods could be held for transshipment without payment of duties. As a result of his agitating, Congress passed the 1934 Foreign Trade Zones Act. Using WPA funds and workers, the Dock Department converted the Hylan piers at Stapleton on Staten Island into the nation's first free port.

To accommodate European travelers who preferred speed over the six-day crossings of the ocean liners, he insisted that his new airport be equipped with docks for Pan Am Clippers that had been using facilities at Port Washington, Long Island.

By opposing the bridge that Robert Moses wanted built between the southern tip of Manhattan and Brooklyn, the mayor inadvertently assured unimpeded access to the Brooklyn Navy Yard of warships needing repairs during the war, and unimpeded egress of the new destroyers, cruisers, and other navy ships built at the Navy Yard. A consequence of harbor improvements was that during the war New York City became a "navy town" filled with sailors on shore leave as their ships came and went. The harbor also became a major embarkation point, with thousands of soldiers sailing off to war aboard troop ships, including the refitted and camouflaged *Queen Elizabeth* and *Queen Mary.*

Because New York instantly became the major port for sending men and war matériel to Britain, resulting in German U-boats prowling the Atlantic within sight of the city, concerns were raised that the city itself was a beacon, providing guidance to the submarines. Lest a spy decide to use the top of the Woolworth Building, overlooking the harbor, as a place to spot ships, the observation roof was closed. Because the gold-leaf pyramidal top of the Federal Building at Foley Square still reflected sunlight at dusk, it was painted black. The torch in the hand of Lady Liberty was turned off. Lights of the Great White Way that cast a glow in the skies that could be seen by lurking Nazi subs were dimmed (the term was new: "brownout"). To make sure residents tuned off lights during blackouts, air raid wardens patrolled neighborhood streets. The penalty for noncompliance was a fine or imprisonment. Pedestrians were banned from East River bridges to forestall spies or a saboteur from dropping a bomb on a ship passing beneath.

The idea of Nazi agents operating in New York City appealed so much to the dramatic sense of film director Alfred Hitchcock that he made a movie on the subject. Starring Robert Cummings, 1942's *Saboteur* involved plans to blow up a defense plant. The climactic moment was played out as a struggle between Cummings and the German agent atop the Statue of Liberty in which the culprit plummeted to his death, accompanied by cheers and applause of patriotic movie audiences from coast to coast.

New Yorkers who thought spies were found only on movie screens learned that such people actually existed when the FBI rounded up a German espionage ring and fourteen of its members were convicted in Brooklyn federal court of being Nazi agents. A band of real-life saboteurs was nabbed with plans to blow up the Hell Gate Bridge over the East River. But the most spectacular episode, and a rather pathetic one, of German activity in New York involved the landing of four former members of the Bund who had returned to Germany and were trained as spies, then sent back to the United States on a U-boat. It dropped them off Amagansett Beach on Long Island on June 13, 1942. Arriving in Manhattan several hours later, they split up. But one of them, George Dasch, traveled on to Washington, D.C., and promptly gave himself up to the

FBI. The G-men quickly arrested the others, along with four agents who'd landed in Florida.

Neither the actions of spies nor the dimming of signs in Times Square kept New Yorkers from enjoying their city. If they were lucky as they went on with their lives as nearly normally as before the war they could catch a glimpse of their mayor tooling around town in his "wartime coupe." It was specially painted and equipped and immediately named the "Fiorellomobile." Four white enamel stars adorned the green hood. The headlights were as big as those on fire engines. Luminous paint was applied fore and aft, the better to be seen in a blackout. It had a police and fire radio. Tucked into the glove department was a pistol. With the touch of a switch a red roof light announced: MAYOR. Asked to pose at the steering wheel, Hizzoner the former airman confessed, "I don't drive." To sit behind the wheel, he said, would be faking it, and "I never faked anything in my life."

To boost city morale in June 1942 he allowed a huge patriotic parade. Two million New Yorkers turned out to watch tanks rolling up Fifth Avenue, hundreds of thousands of marchers, and fighters and bombers roaring overhead. The parade's fifth division consisted of air raid wardens and other groups associated with civil defense. It was led by the country's best-known advocate of preparedness, Fiorello H. La Guardia, grinning and waving, as "the people" made it unmistakable that they were glad that he'd left the office of civil defense so they could have him entirely to themselves.

ৎ৴৴

As La Guardia became a full-time mayor again, his home address was the one that had been his since his years in Congress, a tenement apartment at Fifth Avenue and 110th Street. On May 26, 1942, his address became simply "Gracie Mansion." The first official home for the mayor of New York, it was a large eighteenth-century house overlooking the East River with spacious grounds in a safer and decidedly more elegant neighborhood than East Harlem.

Built in 1799 by Alexander Gracie, the property on which it stood had been used in the Revolutionary War as a cannon emplacement ("Thompson's Battery") to protect Manhattan from the British. The house at that time was owned by Loyalist merchant Jacob Walton. It came under bombardment by the red coats in 1776.

The house that Gracie built was bought in 1819 by Rufus King. Father-in-law of Gracie's two daughters, he took over the property because Gracie lost his shipping business in an Anglo-French war. Four years later, King sold it to Joseph Foulke. When he died in 1857, his children inherited it. It went next to Noah Wheaton, a wallpaper merchant. By 1891 the place was in such disrepair it was condemned and the property turned into East River Park, which was subsequently named after civic reformer Carl Schurz. In 1922 it was the home of the Museum of the City of New York, but when few people came to see its exhibits, the museum decamped for Fifth Avenue. In 1941, as East River Park was being rehabilitated and renamed, the property was under the control of Robert Moses. Using WPA money and workers, he made the mansion a showplace fit for a mayor, then persuaded the City Council to designate it for that purpose.

Fiorello La Guardia, perhaps to needle Moses, told a friend that he was not interested in making it his home. "My family is not keen on it," he said, "and it has no personal advantages to me." He also disliked the name. Confessing he knew little about Alexander Gracie, he said, "I suppose he was a successful businessman, but nothing to get excited about."

Parks Commissioner Robert Moses, however, was very excited about the property, in part because he would in effect be the mayor's landlord, and because he felt that the mayoral home in the middle of a city park would provide security for the city's highest official and his family. The mansion also would be a showpiece for the city itself.

Evidently to elude the fuss and bother of shifting a household, Fiorello arranged to be in Canada on moving day, leaving it to Marie to supervise the five men with a van who showed up on Fifth Avenue on behalf of the Columbia Warehouse and Storage Company. They had to make four trips. Her husband's schedule had him coming back after everything was unpacked.

The *Times* opined that Gracie Mansion "is no unworthy companion of City Hall."

Two weeks after the move, the La Guardias hosted members of the Board of Estimate and their wives. After that, mayoral parties were few and far between. Although Fiorello may have felt uncomfortable surrounded by furnishings on loan from museums, the large lawns were places for occasional romps with Eric, and the big porch was nice for sitting and talking with daughter Jean; Marie; and his late brother Richard's son, William, who lived with them. There was also a live-in maid and occasional cook named Juanita.

The mansion also provided a private studio for Sunday afternoon broadcasts by the first government official to make regular use of radio as a means of reaching the people he had been elected to lead and inspire.

Beginning on January 18, 1942, New Yorkers were able to tune their sets to WNYC and hear "Talks to the People." In terms of the later era of TV and radio talk shows, the broadcasts by Mayor La Guardia were a mixture of the Saturday presidential radio chats begun by Ronald Reagan and continued by his successors, Robert Young on *Father Knows Best,* a Julia Child program on cooking, advice on "best buys" at the supermarket, a sermon, and Martha Stewart's discourses on domesticity.

Each 1:00 P.M. program began with the "Marine Hymn," followed by the squeaky-voiced, sometimes breathless mayor.

On many Sundays he spoke to two million people, outranking the top-rated entertainment and sports programs on the networks as measured by the Crosley survey of radio listeners.

The "talks" began with a review of the news and the mayor's opinions on the items. By one-ten he was in full flower, sometimes preachy, often angry, even threatening.

"I warn you chicken dealers," he said after finding prices had gone up in the market. "I'm not fooling. No more monkey business!"

Tirades against price gouging were combined with a vow that he would report violators to the office of price stabilization.

"Ladies" were encouraged not to go out in rain without rubbers, lest they "slip and fall."

"No-good thieving, chiseling tinhorns" were advised, "Cut it out right now!"

With an eye again on food market prices, he announced, "Fish! Take advantages of the low prices this week and buy fish."

In answer to a letter from a boy named George who said his father lost all his money by gambling at a certain store, the outraged mayor promised that Commissioner Valentine's cops would immediately "clean out" that store. George was told to "keep me informed." He then called on "other little boys" to follow George's example and report where the fathers gambled. "I won't tell anybody you told me," he whispered, "but I'll send the police."

Accused of soliciting children to inform on their parents, he denied it, pointing out that he was interested only in closing down gambling joints.

On another occasion he reminded a couple of million New Yorkers that in 1941 he had said he would not run for a third time, then said with a sigh, "Oh, I sometimes feel I should have stuck to that decision."

At Christmas and Easter he talked about the Bible and Christian ethics. On Easter 1943 he played recordings of parts of Wagner's *Parsifal* and the Hallelujah chorus from Handel's *Messiah,* followed by a discourse on "the great parade of mothers and wives, all moving toward God, all joining in the mighty chorus asking for the repose of sons or husbands, and the protection of loved ones, and constituting the great sisterhood of sorrow."

In August 1942 his subject was holding the subway fare at five cents. He went on the air to dispel fears prompted by a newspaper article that said that under state law the fare had to go up. He dispensed with the issue by pointing out that the statute cited in the article had been repealed. When gasoline rationing was imposed in December 1942 he warned,

"Owners of cars must not rush to gas stations to fill their tanks. Nothing could be more disastrous to the welfare, health, and safety of our city than that."

Learning that apartment owners were planning to raise rents, he produced statistics to show that they were raking in unprecedented profits. He warned that if rents went up he would go down to Washington and present his facts to the office of rent administration.

Restaurants that didn't go along with "meatless" days were told, "You're going to get what's coming to you. Get me?"

Barbers charging sailors $2.20 for a haircut were told, "Now, cut that out."

People who were throwing out day-old bread were reminded, "There is such a thing as bread pudding."

Concerned about the electricity supply in the city that never slept, he said, "Turn off unnecessary lights."

While New Yorkers eagerly turned their radio dials to WNYC at one o'clock on Sunday afternoons to hear what their unpredictable mayor had in store for them, they did not know that La Guardia also was being heard every week by the people of Italy. Via short wave he presented "Mayor La Guardia Calling Rome."

Speaking Italian, he began with, "This is your friend La Guardia speaking." He talked about the glorious history of Italy going back to the Roman Empire while exhorting listeners to oppose the "slavemaster Hitler," fight for their dignity, and free themselves of "this Fascist gang." He called on them to create trouble and "to riot."

On one broadcast he told King Victor Emmanuel III to "stand for peace and freedom as we did in 1918."

In October 1943, the U.S. Office of War Information noted that La Guardia's weekly talks were the most popular of all American programs broadcast to Italy. When the American Fifth Army liberated the town of Torre Annunziata, a resident told a correspondent of the *New York Times* that listening to La Guardia was "a great help to our morale," as he assured him and the townspeople that "Americans realized our plight."

By going on the radio directly to the people of New York, La Guardia also knew that he was being heard in city rooms of the daily newspapers, guaranteeing that those who missed him on the air on Sunday would find him quoted on Monday, usually on page one.

Of the meaning of these broadcasts to New Yorkers, biographer August Hecksher III wrote, "The garishly colored giants that peopled his imagination became alive as he excoriated gangsters, tinhorns and plain politicians. For a little while each week the people of the mundane city could believe that they dwelt within a brightly lit and comprehensible world, under the eyes of a wise parent who would reward the just and punish the wicked. In the darkest days of the war it was desperately needed reassurance."

26

If Fiorello La Guardia had been a little taller in the spring of 1898 he might have gone off to Cuba as a soldier to help kick Spain out of Cuba and perhaps found a life like his father's in the army. When President Woodrow Wilson reluctantly gave in to public opinion to take the United States to war in 1917, Congressman La Guardia had showed up at a recruiting station to volunteer his ability to fly airplanes in the cause of making the world safe for democracy. No form of address when he was mayor of New York satisfied him more than being called "Major." His heart and soul could be deeply touched and moved by music of the great classical composers and operatic arias, but nothing stirred him more than the blare of brass horns, the crashing of cymbals, and the beating of drums of a military band. Yet in the biggest war in the history of the world, he found himself in civilian clothes and in the third term of a job that no longer challenged and satisfied him.

"Why did I take it?" he asked his friend Charles Culp Burlingham. He answered the rhetorical query himself. "I *wanted* it the first and second time and you *asked* me the third time."

Twenty-six years earlier, as a congressman with a yearning to go to war, he'd arranged a leave of absence from the House of Representatives. As mayor of New York in 1943 he tried the same trick by quietly managing the introduction of a bill in the state legislature to empower the governor, in the event that a mayor went into military service, to name an acting mayor of the same political party. This meant that if La Guardia could get an army commission, Governor Dewey would appoint a Republican. Consequently, when the significance of the measure went unnoticed by Democrats and passed in the legislature, Dewey approved it. Now all La Guardia had to do was get his friend Franklin Roosevelt to grant him a commission.

The rank he wanted was brigadier general. In a chat with FDR on March 15, 1943, with the U.S. Army poised to invade Italy, he proposed that the ideal post for Brigadier General La Guardia would be "civil affairs director" after Italy was liberated. Roosevelt looked on the idea with favor. In a gleeful note to FDR's aide Harry Hopkins the mayor wrote, "I saw the Chief yesterday and I am so happy I can be of service to my country—besides cleaning the streets of New York City."

Roosevelt's press secretary, Stephen Early, announced, "All indications point to service in the army for the mayor."

La Guardia had himself fitted for a uniform and asked Albert Spalding to again be his top aide in Italy. The plan was for him to be commissioned after he completed work on the city's budget in April. On March 28 the *New York Herald Tribune* reported, "Clearly New York is about to lose a mayor and the army is about to gain an officer."

Then the rug beneath the exultant mayor's feet began slipping. As details of the new law that authorized the governor to appoint a substitute mayor became known, howls of protest and outrage arose in New York and in Washington. The *Times* pronounced it a "flimsy law." The *New York Post* found a sleazy deal with a strong odor of fascism about it.

Roosevelt floated the idea of Brigadier General La Guardia with the commander of the U.S. forces that would soon invade Italy. Dwight D. Eisenhower replied from his headquarters in Tunisia that he was hesitant to "complicate my staff problems" by bringing in La Guardia.

During a meeting of the Senate Committee to Investigate the National Defense Program, Missouri's Democratic senator Harry S. Truman volunteered that he was opposed to appointing "political generals." Democratic voices from New York rose in partisan chorus to denounce the law that would give Republican governor Dewey the right to appoint a mayor. With politics now in the equation, a cooling Roosevelt looked for the exit. With ice in his veins on April 6, 1943, he planted a "What about La Guardia?" question with a reporter. When it was asked at a press conference, FDR gave a familiar toss of head and blithely lied by denying that there had been any discussion of a plan to make the mayor of New York a brigadier general.

Crushed and embarrassed, La Guardia bit his lip and told reporters in Washington, "I'll carry on. I've got a uniform of my own up in New York, a street cleaner's uniform. That's my own little army."

Furious and feeling Franklin had betrayed him, Fiorello told friends, "I burned all my bridges ahead of me for *him!*"

Another man with the initial "F"—two F's, in fact—Felix Frankfurter, sent a sarcastic and smugly self-satisfied letter to Charles Culp Burlingham (CCB) speculating, "Wouldn't it be lovely for Fiorello to be prancing around somewhere in Africa?"

CCB forwarded the letter to La Guardia. He shot off a reply to Burlingham about "the dirty deal" he'd been given. "I have always been able to take care of myself," he said. "I do hope you will understand. I am very unhappy." Telling CCB, "Do not bother to reply and do not worry about it," and that he was sorry Burlingham had shown him the letter, he informed CCB that he would never speak to Felix Frankfurter again.

As if to rub salt in La Guardia's wound, Roosevelt approved a commission as brigadier general to a Democratic politician, William O'Dwyer. The post of civil administrator in Italy went to Charles Poletti, an aide to Governor Lehman whom La Guardia detested.

A week after FDR dashed the mayor's hopes of wearing an army uniform again, Fiorello attended a Good Friday performance of *Parsifal* at the Metropolitan Opera House. During an intermission he said to his friend Paul Windels, "Things are not going right for me."

By summer's end, events uptown would make the remark seem eerily prescient.

In 1940 the Harlem writer and poet Langston Hughes, in a book titled *The Big Sea,* said that the 1920s were years of Manhattan's Black Renaissance. "White people came to Harlem in droves," he wrote. "For several years they packed the expensive Cotton Club on Lenox Avenue. But I was never there, because the Cotton Club was a Jim Crow club for gangsters and monied whites. . . . Nor did ordinary Negroes like the growing influx of whites toward Harlem after sundown, flooding the little cabarets and bars where formerly only colored people laughed and sang, and where now strangers were given the best ringside tables to sit and stare at the Negro customers—like amusing animals in a zoo."

The situation continued into the thirties and beyond, so that a black jazz musician, bandleader, and composer named Duke Ellington in 1941 could write a popular song about going up to Harlem titled "Take the A Train." It had whites thinking that the people who lived there were as happy as anyone could be in a city with a mayor who was determined to improve the lot of everyone regardless of race.

Had not La Guardia appointed a committee to study and report on the conditions that had sparked the 1935 riot? Was he not sincere in working to alleviate them? Even before the report was finished, work had begun on building projects. The result four years later was the Harlem River Houses, the Central Harlem Center Building, the Women's Pavilion at Harlem Hospital, and two Harlem schools. The number of black nurses and attendants in the Hospital Department had doubled. The number of black doctors and medical board members tripled. Blacks were benefiting from better employment opportunities in civil service. In 1936 the mayor had appointed a black man, the Reverend John H. Johnson, to the Emergency Relief Board. Myles Page was the city's first black magistrate. Jane Bolin was the first black woman judge in the history of the country. Blacks were in the city marshal's office. In 1940 the first editorial in the new Harlem newspaper, the *Amsterdam News,* lauded La Guardia for appointing more Negroes to "big, responsible jobs" in the government "than all the other mayors of the city combined."

In 1940, officials of the Schomberg Collection of the New York Public Library and the Association for the Study of Negro Life had honored him for improving race relations. In the 1941 election campaign he'd drawn twenty thousand black supporters to a rally in Colonial Park. The black bandleader and popular singer Cab Calloway had greeted him, "Yeah, man! Hi, Butch! That's our mayor!"

As civil defense director La Guardia placed black volunteers in the air raid service and secured war matériel necessary to keep a plant operating that employed four hundred blacks. Looking beyond the war, he instructed the City Planning Commission to prepare a postwar program for completing housing projects in black areas that necessarily had to be suspended for the duration. He'd pressed Governor Dewey to permit the city to acquire land for postwar Abraham Lincoln and James Wheldon Johnson Houses in Harlem.

The mayor consulted regularly with black leaders A. Philip Randolph of the Brotherhood of Sleeping Car Porters and Lester B. Granger of the National Urban League.

When a "race riot" erupted in Detroit, Michigan, on June 21, 1943, resulting in thirty-four blacks being killed at the hands of riot police, and millions of dollars in property damage, La Guardia sent two ranking officials (black and white) of the New York Police Department to the "Motor City" to report on the apparent causes of the rioting. On June 28 he brought together an interracial group to study Detroit's mistakes so they would not be repeated in New York City. He then announced a "Unity Movement" to deal with "provocations" aimed at dividing and inflaming the races. In association with Commissioner Valentine he developed the ground rules for handling a riot if one should break out. The basis of the planning was "police restraint" to assure that there would not be a bloodbath like the one in Detroit. Deadly force was to be used only if a cop faced physical harm. Tear gas was the last resort. If trouble started, all bars, pawnshops, and gun dealers would be closed by the police.

Having taken these precautions and appealed to the better natures of all New Yorkers, the mayor crossed his fingers, prayed for a cool summer, and hoped for even cooler heads.

One of the causes of the Detroit riot and in similar disturbances in black communities in Los Angeles and other cities in the spring of 1943 was a deep-rooted resentment that America was in a war to assure the "four freedoms" named by President Roosevelt (freedom of speech and expression, freedom from want, freedom of the ability to worship God in one's own way, and freedom from fear), yet was unwilling to afford them to America's blacks.

Langston Hughes put the sentiment into verse:

> Freedom's not just
> To be won over there
> It means Freedom at home, too—
> Now—right here!

The first black member of the City Council, Adam Clayton Powell Jr. of Harlem, said, "You can't whip Hitler abroad without whipping Hitlerism at home."

He spoke on behalf of the Double V for blacks: victory abroad and in America, meaning victory in the black struggle for civil rights. Before the Pearl Harbor attack he had warned that "the hour of destiny" for blacks to protest for equality with whites existed only until the United States entered the war. After that, he said, strikes and picket lines would be "unpatriotic" and made illegal.

Thirty-five years of age, handsome, light-skinned, with hazel eyes and aquiline nose, with a Bachelor of Arts degree from Colgate University and a Master of Arts in religious education from Columbia, Powell was the son of the minister of

America's largest black congregation, the Abyssinian Baptist Church in Harlem. Succeeding his father in the pulpit in 1937, he saw the church as "a mighty weapon" in winning social justice. Practicing grassroots campaigning, he'd been elected to the City Council in 1941. In the following year he started a newspaper, *People's Voice,* that he said was "open to any organization engaged in the great fight for complete emancipation of all people."

Denying he was a Communist, he claimed to be "a radical and a fighter," but disavowal of communism did not keep him away from Communist Party rallies and lending support to the CPUSA's campaign to get its president, Earl Browder, out of federal prison.

In 1941 Powell led the Harlem Bus Strike Committee in obtaining an unprecedented pact with independent bus companies and the Transportation Workers' Union to employ blacks. He'd boasted that he brought ten thousand jobs and $10 million to Harlem, figures that were highly inflated. Exaggerated self-promotion did not matter to Harlem voters. What counted was that he was on the City Council with a vote that mattered as much as that of a white member.

Powell's relationship with Mayor La Guardia was initially cordial. By February 1942 they were often at odds, and members of the City Council viewed Powell as an opportunist seeking issues and scapegoats. La Guardia not only saw him that way, but practically said so explicitly in a note to Powell's newspaper on its first anniversary. He advised, "No greater mistake can be made than to seek to make an issue where an issue does not exist."

The tone reflected La Guardia's paternalistic attitude toward Powell. Three months later, the councilman from Harlem was accusing the mayor of indifference toward problems of blacks and saying La Guardia was "one of the most pathetic figures on the current American scene."

Following the Detroit riot, La Guardia suspected Powell of opportunism when Powell sent La Guardia a telegram stating that racial tensions required La Guardia to meet with him and a "Citizens' Emergency Committee" to discuss the crisis.

La Guardia declined the invitation by not acknowledging it. On June 24 Powell said that if riots occurred in New York City blood of innocent people would "rest upon the hands" of La Guardia and his police commissioner.

When Powell's Emergency Committee met in Powell's City Hall office, La Guardia had an informant attend. Powell was then put under police surveillance. The mutual suspicions of the two men were not alleviated when Powell said on July 3 that La Guardia was a "prima donna." He added, "Get rid of your inferiority complex and appoint an interracial committee . . . and we won't have a Detroit in New York."

Suspicions deepened and fears arose in the mayor's office that Powell's warnings about another Detroit were actually intended to foster trouble. This concern was reinforced by the inflammatory nature of the contents of Powell's *People's Voice*. In one issue an illustration had a Nazi chatting with an American policeman. In the background were ruins labeled "Poland" and "Detroit." The caption said "This Must Not Happen Here." A lengthy poem by Langston Hughes began:

Looky here, America
What you done done—
Let things drift
Until the riots come.

On Sunday, August 1, 1943, Mayor La Guardia offered sweltering New Yorkers one of his "Talks to the People" on WNYC, then spent the rest of the afternoon and early Sunday evening in the hope that a few cooling breezes would waft up from the East River. Uptown on West 126th Street in Harlem it had been a typical Sunday in summer. People escaping ovenlike rooms sat on fire escapes and front stoops or mingled on sun-baked sidewalks. Music came from radios perched on windowsills. Shirtless boys played in the streets. Girls defied the heat by skipping rope or playing hopscotch. And at seven o'clock Marjorie Polite sauntered into the Braddock Hotel and asked for a room.

Given the notorious reputation of the Braddock that had led police to declare it a "raided premises" and post an officer in the lobby, if Marjorie had been with a man, the cop on duty would have supposed that she was a prostitute. Marjorie registered, got a room key, and went into the elevator. The room proved unsatisfactory. Shown another, Marjorie shook her head. She wanted one with a shower-bath. Informed none was available, she checked out and asked for a refund. She also wanted back a dollar she said she'd tipped the elevator man. This assertion was hotly denied by the operator. With that, according to a subsequent account, Marjorie became "very boisterous, disorderly, and profane."

Police patrolman James Collins intervened and asked her to leave. Marjorie refused in a verbally abusive manner. Collins arrested her.

Witnessing this tableau were Mrs. Florine Roberts, a maid from Middletown, Connecticut, and her son Robert Bandy, whom she was visiting at the Braddock. Bandy was on leave from the Army's 703rd Military Police Battalion, stationed in Jersey City. Bandy expressed his opinion to Patrolman Collins that Collins should let Marjorie go.

Collins told Bandy to please mind his own damn business.

According to Collins's account of the unfolding drama, Bandy and his mother attacked him. During the fray, Bandy punched Collins and fled. Collins went after him and shouted to Bandy to halt. Bandy kept running. Collins drew his pistol and fired once. Bandy fell wounded.

The soldier's version differed in that he said Collins threw his nightstick at Bandy, and that when Bandy caught the baton and refused to return it, Collins shot him.

As this was going on, someone called for more police. When they arrived, Collins and Bandy were taken to Sydenham Hospital.

By the time they arrived, Harlem was alive with a story that a white cop had shot and killed a black soldier who had been protecting his mother. From all over West 126th Street and other blocks as the story rapidly spread between 110th and 145th Streets, and coursed up and down Seventh, Eighth, and Lenox Avenues, outraged citizens set out for the 28th Precinct police station house. The crowd soon reached three thousand, most of them shouting threats at the cop who'd gunned down an innocent black boy wearing the uniform of his country.

When the telephone rang at Gracie Mansion at about nine o'clock, Mayor Fiorello La Guardia's worst nightmare became real. Calls also were received at police and fire headquarters, then reported to Commissioners Valentine and Walsh. Both ordered all men who might be going off shift to be kept on duty. Valentine ordered headquarters to call for reinforcements and send them to Harlem. When the commissioners' home phones rang again it was the mayor. He told them to meet him at the 28th Precinct station house, "pronto!"

La Guardia sped uptown, but apparently not in the Fiorellomobile. Barging into the mob, he ordered everyone to go home. Inside the station house, he demanded a full report on the extent of the trouble while praying that Harlem was not on its way to becoming Detroit. When Lew Valentine arrived, mayor and police commissioner headed out to the streets to order everyone they encountered to go home. They were soon joined by three prominent black leaders.

As they toured the littered, trash-filled streets, five thousand police descended on the area. Worried and disgusted black men who volunteered to help were deputized and sent out to do all they could to persuade people to clear the streets.

No one knows when and who broke the first window of the first white-owned store on 125th Street, but by 10:30 P.M. the window-smashing and merchandise-grabbing were going on from 110th to 140th Streets and on the avenues. One observer thought the looters resembled "ants around spilled sugar." Another watched as "stuff" was carted off "in bundles and baskets and parcels" and several taxis. If protective metal gates stood between a looter and what he wanted, the gate was ripped open. Stolen items too big or unwieldy to be carried were destroyed.

Then the arson started.

The mayor confers with city leaders in makeshift headquarters at the West 123rd Street police station during the Harlem riot of August 2, 1943.

One gang running along Eighth Avenue was seen setting a fire a minute. If it could burn, it burned. Street-corner metal trash baskets became squat pyres billowing flames and smoke.

Pulled fire alarms were quickly answered by the ear-piercing sirens of fire engines that added to the noises of shattering glass, smashing beer bottles, shouts, screaming, and laughing—gales of excited laughter everywhere.

To calm the city, La Guardia went on the air. He broadcast five times throughout the most hideous night of his life. In the third appeal for calm and order he almost sobbed as he told whoever was listening, "Shame has come to our city and sorrow to the large number of our fellow citizens who live in Harlem."

Between broadcasts he issued orders. Seal off the area. Start planning to bring in food and medical supplies. A 10:30 P.M. curfew is imposed in the area until further notice. All bars must close at 2:00 A.M. Call in soldiers to guard the police stations. Open armories to handle the people who were arrested.

The mayor would not feel that he could leave City Hall and go home until 1:00 A.M Tuesday. At 9:55 P.M. on Monday he'd sat before a radio microphone to inform the city that the "disturbance" was under control. He chose not to call it a "riot." He knew that if he did, it would be given the adjective "race." Insisting that race had nothing to do with it, he blamed the riot on hoodlums, troublemakers, and vandals.

The cost was tallied: 6 dead, 185 wounded, hundreds of stores and shops wrecked and pillaged; property damage: $15 million.

For a few days Harlem was under virtual martial law. When night fell, streetlights stayed on despite the prevailing wartime dimout. It was not necessary. Harlem was again peaceful. On August 14, the police presence in Harlem was back to normal strength.

27

The people of New York and its newspapers judged their mayor favorably in handling the riot. Even Adam Clayton Powell Jr. felt that La Guardia had provided "wise and effective" leadership. Praise for the restraint and efficiency of the police noted that both were the result of La Guardia's planning, based on advice of the two police officers who had been sent to observe the riot in Detroit and consultations with Harlem community leaders. The after-riot consensus was that the NYPD had lived up to its motto "the Finest."

No one denied that what happened was a riot. But was it a *race* riot? Powell asserted that it could not "by any stretch of the imagination nor distortion of fact be called a race riot." La Guardia was no less emphatic in excluding race as a factor. He blamed "thoughtless hoodlums who had no one to fight with," so they attacked "their own people." Mayor and councilman for their own reasons were dancing around the truth. The riot was racial from the very beginning when accounts of the incident at the Braddock Hotel stressed that a *white* cop had killed a *black* soldier. Looting of stores was limited almost entirely to establishments owned by whites. Future national black leader Roy Wilkins said the riot was "the boiling over of pent-up resentment in the breasts of millions of American Negroes."

Explanations that the rioters were ignorant people at the bottom of the economic and social ladders, combined with uneducated black southern immigrants, also did not hold water.

An analysis of the participants showed that many were middle-class "solid citizens," including women, housewives, and children. Reports noted that some looters were gainfully employed and capable of buying the items they'd stolen. One police commander found the rioters to be of a "general type of person" from "varied occupations." Sociologist Harold Orlansky saw the Braddock Hotel incident and the false story that circulated as being "sufficiently close to the frustrations of all Negroes" that the result was a uniting of disparate groups, from hoodlums seeing an opportunity to make mischief to "respectable" people who ordinarily would never dream of breaking into stores and making off with goods, even if they nurtured resentment that a white man owned the store and that the owner did not employ blacks. The effect of the uniting of social strata that normally would have nothing to do with one another was termed "homogenization." It had happened in Harlem on that sultry Sunday evening in August 1943.

In the aftermath, the "respectable" people of Harlem felt ashamed. Whites expressed sympathy for the victims, the vast majority of whom were black. Many individuals of both races believed that the riot had been started and kept going by "agitators" who were more than likely Communists. A broad cross section of New Yorkers, and people in other cities that had experienced similar riots, called for action by the federal government. Appeals were made for President Roosevelt to get involved. But FDR believed that improving race relations was the responsibility of local governments.

Mayor La Guardia felt an obligation to deal with the underlying grievances of the city's blacks, but also to point out that despite appearances New York City was "a working model of democracy" in which people of all types had "learned to get along together." To spread this gospel he began a series of radio broadcasts he called "Unity at Home—Victory Abroad." Running five weeks, the programs featured himself, Mrs. Roosevelt, Senator Robert F. Wagner, author Pearl Buck, and other notables preaching tolerance and peace.

When public schools opened in September, they offered "intercultural relations" classes. They emphasized the contributions of blacks to American society and taught application of democratic principles in and out of school.

Intending to erase some of the causes for black alienation and resentment related to housing, La Guardia by executive order declared that discrimination in renting based on race was unlawful. His power to do so by fiat was questionable, but he did it. He also promised legal action against price-gouging merchants.

Joining in efforts to improve relations was a new "Emergency Conference for Interracial Unity." Chaired by Marian Anderson, it consisted of community leaders, clergy, educators, union officials (Mike Quill was a member), liberal politicians, and entertainers. Among a list of fourteen resolutions passed by the group was a call upon La Guardia to appoint a committee to identify opportunities for racial cooperation and identify causes of racial antagonisms.

Never an advocate of such extragovernmental bodies, and generally unsympathetic to outsiders advising him on how to do his job, he was cool and noncommittal. Instead, he set up the *Mayor's* Committee on Unity (emphasis added). Explaining it would be "something entirely different" from other blue-ribbon study groups, he said the fifteen members of his committee, supported by a staff of qualified experts, were to study "causes of discrimination, prejudice, and exploitation" with such thoroughness and scientific methods that its ultimate report would be "authoritative." It was sheer idealism that seemed to some doubters equal to coming up with a way to count the number of angels on the head of a pin. The committee was organized and at its tasks by the summer of 1944, a year after the riot. It helped arouse support for creation of the New York State Commission against Discrimination as well as the Fair Employment Practices Act. But, as history showed, it found no solution to racial antagonisms and no formula for preventing riots.

In the aftermath of the Harlem riot quite a different kind of committee convened in the Borough of Brooklyn to look into a crisis in public safety that appeared to be caused in part by racial discrimination and the city's indifference to it. It was a

Kings County grand jury looking into an increase in crimes in predominantly black neighborhoods. Because of the war there had been an increased need for workers in war-related factories. This resulted in an influx of black job-seekers from the South that strained the capacity of Brooklyn to house them. Hand in hand with the increase in population had come a rise in lawlessness by youths who were left unattended while their elders were at work. The sudden boost in the black population had caused white residents of the Bedford-Stuyvesant section of Brooklyn to move out.

In a scathing finding the grand jury blamed most of these problems on indifference by the mayor. It charged that because of his inattention "one of the finest residential sections of this borough" was dying. La Guardia's unfortunately phrased answer was that "when a neighborhood changes its complexion there is bound to be trouble."

The grand jury asserted, "No part of the City of New York should be regarded as dangerous and unsafe." The issue was not race, it was crime, it said, and offered the mayor a list of suggestions. They included requiring people to get a permit to carry a knife; to supervised after-school recreation programs; banning congregating in front of bars; tougher sentencing by judges in juvenile court; more police; use of the National Guard; and canceling the annual Mardi Gras celebration in the area, which often ended in disorderly conduct.

Envisioning himself being accused of dictatorship and Bedford-Stuyvesant being called an occupied territory if he did what the grand jury recommended, La Guardia dismissed them as "crackpots" and "publicity seekers."

The Brooklyn grand jury had made one point that Fiorello La Guardia could not brush aside. There was no denying that the city had become a magnet to migrants, but these were not the tired and poor "huddled masses" invited to America by the Statue of Liberty of earlier decades. The new arrivals were blacks from the American South. In addition to the availability of wartime jobs, they were drawn to New York because the city had become widely known for the generosity of its relief programs. So many arrived and promptly applied for relief that La Guardia urged a one-year residency requirement.

That the City of New York gained and continued to hold decades later the title "Welfare City" is one of the legacies of the La Guardia years. As blacks had flocked North in the wartime years, the allure of an economic and social safety net would result in "in-migration" of American citizens from Puerto Rico in the period after the war. Because many settled in La Guardia's old district of East Harlem, the area became known as "Spanish Harlem." They would provide a rich source of votes for La Guardia's political offspring Vito Marcantonio. Although he continued to deny he was a Communist, when President Harry S. Truman gave a historic speech outlining the Truman Doctrine for containing the spread of Soviet communism, the "only person in the hall who remained seated" during Congress's ovation, Truman noted, was Marcantonio.

While conceding that the war had wrought changes in the face of the city and imposed new strains on its resources, La Guardia remained committed to making New York City into a place where the people could turn to their government for help. In that city, La Guardia vowed, the people should not be denied the best possible health care. He wanted to make New York a showplace of decentralized health centers, outpatient services, and superb municipal hospitals, all of which would be affordable. A survey of economic conditions in 1944 showed that the most frequent cause of people going into debt was medical costs. His plan for a city-subsidized health care insurance program was revolutionary in concept and scope. When incorporation papers for the insurance plan (HIP) were filed in September 1944, he called it "historic," as indeed it was.

On March 27, 1944, he ruminated about New York in an interview that ran in the *Times*. "Taken in all it is a great city," he said, "a mighty city." As to himself, "One has to absorb a great deal of abuse, but it is worthwhile. Sometimes you get so discouraged at the end of the day, you say, 'Oh, what is the use?' But you look around and you see the playgrounds and the different parkways, you see these health centers and you see the happy children. Oh! I will tell you it is worthwhile, but it does require a great deal of patience and fortitude."

※

Looking around his city in the spring of 1943, the former cornetist had found it lacking in one important amenity. He saw no place where ordinary people of modest means could find and enjoy pleasures of the performing and musical arts that were available for the wealthy. What he wanted was a "people's" music hall that would be a "flame of art" and a place filled with "the beautiful, spiritual, and happy things in life."

If the federal government provided funds through the WPA for roads, bridges, tunnels, parks, playgrounds, swimming pools, and an airport, surely there must be money for New York to build a center for the performing arts. He envisioned it in the heart of Rockefeller Center, but Mr. Rockefeller had one of his own in mind (Center Theater, demolished in the 1960s). With funding secured, the site selected was the Mecca Temple on West Fifty-fifth Street. Given the name City Center, with La Guardia as president of the corporation and Newbold Morris as chairman of the board, the property was converted to a concert hall. In 1944 the celebrated Leopold Stokowski agreed to serve without pay as conductor of the City Center Symphony Orchestra (eighty members, men and women integrated racially). An opera company also was formed, then a theater company. Tickets ranged in price from a quarter to a dollar. The City Center was dedicated in December 1943 on the occasion of the mayor's sixty-first birthday. After he said a few words, the orchestra caught him by surprise by playing "Happy Birthday to You."

As La Guardia Airport had been his "baby" during its construction, City Center was like his personal plaything as he dropped in on rehearsals and expressed opinions on the programs. At a rehearsal for the play *Susan and God* he coached Broadway star Gertrude Lawrence on how to say her lines. When playwright and producer Marc Connelly played the role of the stage manager in Thornton Wilder's *Our Town,* he found himself getting directions during a rehearsal by Hizzoner the mayor. A proposal was made that City Center invite the Ballet Russe de Monte Carlo. The mayor was not keen on seeing "young men leaping around the stage in those white tights exhibiting their crotches." Misgivings notwithstanding, the ballet appeared in March 1944 with the mayor in attendance.

Concerned that the cheap seats and first-class bookings would hurt the regular theater business, the League of New York Theaters muttered such words as "unfair competition," but the City Center remained in operation. At the first meeting of the board of directors, the president of the organization perched his half-moon reading glasses on his nose and read the bottom line. The City Center's first season had earned a profit of $844.77. La Guardia gleefully noted that City Center was "no longer an experiment." It was "a success."

The fiscal situation for the city was not quite as rosy. Providing "welfare" in the form of relief payments had turned the bottom line of the city's ledger books red. City Council members proposed raising the subway fare. La Guardia countered with ideas for a "transportation tax" on rents and mortgages. He also advocated levying an income tax on out-of-city commuters. None of these proposals became a reality. Nor did a bill in the legislature to create a city transportation authority. The results on the issue of wiping out the red ink were stalemate and inaction. The city labored on in deficit.

Part of the reason for inaction was the fact that 1944 and 1945 were election years. That FDR would run again and be reelected was undisputed. Whether the mayor also would go for a fourth time was an answer only La Guardia could give, and he wasn't saying.

Also up in the air were La Guardia's intentions regarding the American Labor Party. In the years since its founding as an instrument of reform, the party had moved dramatically to the left to become, in the view of the editors of the liberal *New York Post,* a "blind" for Communists. The result was formation by labor leaders (and former ALP members) David Dubinsky and Alex Rose of a new vehicle for leftist, anti-

Communist politics: the Liberal Party. The ALP would disappear after 1948, following the defeat of FDR's former vice president Henry Wallace in an independent campaign that was taken over by Communists.

As the war in Europe and the Pacific headed for the "inevitable triumph" promised by FDR on December 8, 1941, Major La Guardia still hoped to get into action. In November he wrote to Roosevelt, "I am still out of service, but I haven't given up hope yet."

Hope is eternal, but time was running out, and La Guardia knew it.

Robert Moses said at this time that Fiorello was conflicted, "uncertain as to whether to be a national, an international, or a local character, whether to be a legislator whose every act is privileged or an executive who must be responsible tomorrow for everything he does today, whether to be a conservative or a radical, an artist or a tough boss, a broadminded cosmopolitan or an uncompromising reformer."

Of course, Fiorello H. La Guardia was at once all of them. He always had been a man with many hats and several parts. If everyone else was confused, so be it.

Often frustrated, frequently feeling abused by the press, and increasingly irascible, he told former friends in the House of Representatives, "I'd rather be a third-rate congressman from a third-rate district than a first-rate mayor of a first-rate city."

As to being mayor of New York he complained, "There is not much glamor to it, but heartbreaking work—just hard labor."

Was he signaling, everyone wondered at the end of 1944, that his third term was his last?

28

"New Yorkers, reinforced by out-of-towners, gave 1945 a tumultuous welcome," the Associated Press reported concerning the traditional New Year's Eve celebration in Times Square. The crowd was estimated at 750,000. "Easy-spending pleasure seekers filled nightclubs, cafés, and theaters, yet the police said the holiday celebration was the most orderly and sober New Year's Eve on record. None of the rendezvous spots lacked patronage, though tariffs ranged as high as $36.30, without drinks. Everybody, everywhere seemed pretty glad to see the end of 1944, in the arena of which had been packed monumental events."

On June 5, 1944, the U.S. Army had liberated Rome, where, if things had gone Mayor La Guardia's way, Brigadier General Fiorello H. La Guardia might have established an office to oversee a transition to peace and democracy. The next day would be forever known as "D-Day," and in a decade-later book by Cornelius Ryan, *The Longest Day,* as thousands of American soldiers, along with British, Canadian, and Free French troops breached Adolf Hitler's vaunted "Western Wall" in the beginning of the end of the Third Reich. In the Pacific, victory also was seen in the near future as the U.S. Army, Navy, and Marines island-hopped on their way to Japan.

Fiorello also had noted that on Christmas Day the Soviet Red Army encircled Budapest, Hungary, where his sister Gemma lived.

In Washington two days before Christmas the government had increased the draft rate for January and February 1945 from sixty thousand to eighty thousand; raised its sights on war production on the basis of a theory that the fighting in Europe would continue for a year; froze production of civilian goods at current levels indefinitely; and sharply reduced the allotment of tires for civilians. Gasoline was scarce, but cigarettes were even scarcer. After looking into the shortages, Senate investigators were convinced that the only way to end them was by winning the war.

Looking ahead to inauguration day, January 20, when he would become vice president of the United States, Missouri senator Harry S. Truman said that he would not take on any auxiliary jobs, as Vice President Henry Wallace had done. Truman would devote his time to being the liaison man between the White House and the Senate.

People were singing or whistling sentimental popular songs of loneliness and hoped-for future homecomings: "I'll Be Seeing You," "I'll Walk Alone," and "Long Ago and Far Away"; and the novelty ditties "Mairzy Doats," "Is You Is or Is You Ain't My Baby?," and "Milkman, Keep Those Bottles Quiet."

Three days after Christmas a show had opened at the Adelphi Theater that suddenly had New Yorkers and people who had never set foot on Manhattan Island singing "New York, New York, it's a wonderful town." With music by Leonard Bernstein and lyrics by Betty Comden and Adolph Green, choreography by Jerome Robbins, and directed by George Abbott, *On the Town* was about three young sailors on shore leave who had twenty-four hours to take in sights of a city where people rode in a hole in the ground, the Bronx was "up" and the Battery "down."

It was a theatrical production glorifying the city in which it was set and therefore met with the mayor's approval. The same could not be said of a play titled *Trio*. The drama involved the struggle of a girl in choosing between affections of a young man and those of an older woman. The reviews of the drama were not enthusiastic, but their accounts of the implied lesbianism proved too much for La Guardia. He ordered the commissioner of licenses, Paul Moss, to close the show by revoking the license of the theater where it was playing.

The curtain came down on *Trio,* but another went up on a performance on the stage of public opinion in which the mayor was cast as the villain. The theatrical union Actors' Equity's reaction to the order to shutter the offending theater provided a name for the unfolding drama, "Outrageous Action." The Authors' League demanded that La Guardia fire Moss, evidently not knowing that Moss had carried out the mayor's edict. Rebellion spread to the board of directors of City Center when playwright Elmer Rice and noted actor-director Margaret Webster resigned in protest against City Hall censorship. Representatives of the theater business (one of the cash cows of the city's economy) and the Civil Liberties Union demanded a meeting with La Guardia. He consented, reluctantly, and came out after the conference to declare, "We had a more or less harmonious meeting." Translation: UNharmonious. "Everyone," he stated, "has retained the same views he held before the conference."

In fact, he had been forced to relent. He agreed to let the play reopen "for a test."

The curtain went up again, then quickly came down because, in fact, the critics had been right. *Trio* was a bad play. Ironically, if La Guardia had restrained his prudery and had kept his mouth shut, it would have quickly closed because of poor reviews.

Perhaps because La Guardia wanted to demonstrate that he was not a "bluenose" and a "stick-in-the-mud" about people having a little fun, he found himself in another contretemps on the issue of an order from the head of the office of war mobilization, James Byrnes. Apparently in the hope that savings could be attained in the use of gasoline by civilians, Byrnes had issued a request in February 1945 that a midnight curfew be imposed on restaurants, cafés, and bars. The closing times for New York bars was 4:00 A.M. except Sundays, when it was an hour sooner. La Guardia at first went along with Byrnes's request, but on March 18 he used his radio program to announce that New York watering holes could stay open an extra hour, to one in the morning.

Instead of being hailed, as La Guardia had expected, he found himself being called unpatriotic and accused of "indefensible lawlessness." A Queens City Councilman went so far as to recommend that he be stood "against the wall" and shot. The *Times* said he had put himself on "a very high horse" by treating with "contempt a wartime request of the United States government" and giving the city "a black eye."

La Guardia retorted, "I am running the city." He then tossed a grenade at Washington. "I tried to run the army," he said, "but they wouldn't let me."

Caught between the mayor and an order from the War Department to GIs to obey the midnight curfew, restaurants, cafés, and bars closed at twelve.

City Hall analysts of La Guardia's behavior thought that the mayor's fight was not with Byrnes, but FDR. The president had been making noises about backing a Democrat for mayor in 1945 even if La Guardia's hat was in the ring for a fourth term. Defying the midnight curfew, the boys in Room 9 surmised, was La Guardia firing a shot across FDR's bow.

But on April 12, 1945, political squabbling suddenly became meaningless with the news bulletin from FDR's getaway home in Warm Springs, Georgia, that the president was dead of a stroke. The shocking news caught New Yorkers on their way home from work. La Guardia got the word at City Hall. Less than an hour later he was at a WNYC microphone. Sounding shaken and grim, he said (in part):

> My fellow New Yorkers, the one dominant fact in our minds is that shared by one hundred and thirty million Americans in our country and hundreds of millions of men and women throughout the world. The greatest casualty of the entire world is now suffered by all the people of the world. The shock is so great that under ordinary conditions it would be exceedingly difficult to absorb. But we must carry on because of him whose death the entire world mourns.

This is the most difficult task I have ever had. It means so much to you and to me. It means so much to people that you and I will never hear from, will never know, people who have been suffering for years, for generations, who'd looked forward to this man as their hope. Not hope for them, because they have lost everything, perhaps not hope for any of their own, of their age, but hope for their children and their grandchildren. But we must buck up.

Our leader has died, but he lives on. His inspiration is with us. His leadership is with us. An additional duty and responsibility has now been thrust upon every American, no matter how humble; a responsibility and duty to carry on, to carry on as he would have us carry on. To insist that his ideals may be translated into reality, into everyday life. A better world for all. Economic security for the impoverished people of impoverished countries of this world. For a permanent peace. Franklin D. Roosevelt is not dead. His ideals live.

As La Guardia spoke, tanks of the American Ninth Army were smashing across the Elbe River into Germany, while the First and Third Armies (under General George S. Patton) thundered at the gates of Weimar, birthplace of the German Republic of 1919. In Berlin, Gestapo chief Heinrich Himmler declared that every German town and every house must be defended to the last man, and threatened death to anyone disobeying the order. Hitler himself greeted Roosevelt's death as an omen that Germany would win the war.

The next day, Patton's tanks and infantry, in a dazzling thirty-two mile eastward thrust, cut all direct roads and railways between southern Germany and Berlin. After a week's siege, the Red Army captured Vienna.

On April 14, as FDR's body was borne by train for burial at Hyde Park, the Americans in Germany were within eighty-five miles of Russian lines. In the Pacific war four hundred B-29s rained thousands of tons of incendiary bombs on the Japanese capital of Tokyo. In Italy the Fifth Army was ready for a final push to defeat die-hard German forces in Italy.

By April 22 the Russians held twenty-one districts of Berlin. On the twenty-third the blackouts that had kept nighttime

London in the dark since 1940 were ended. Two days later, in San Francisco, America's new president, Harry S. Truman, opened the first meeting of the U.N. organization that had been envisioned in 1940 by Roosevelt and Winston Churchill. On the twenty-sixth Americans and Russians "linked up" at the town of Torgau on the Elbe. The twenty-ninth saw the body of Benito Mussolini hanging from its heels, along with his mistress and sixteen Fascist leaders, as a crowd cheered in Milan.

On that day at the Brooklyn Navy Yard the mayor of New York participated in a colorful but somber ceremony to christen a forty-five-thousand-ton supercarrier the USS *Franklin D. Roosevelt.*

May 1 brought an announcement by Hamburg Radio that Adolf Hitler had died "at his command post at Berlin," and had been succeeded by Admiral Karl Doenitz. In Milan, Mussolini was secretly buried in an unmarked grave in a potter's field. In Red Square in Moscow, Premier Josef Stalin stood atop Lenin's Tomb and watched the greatest May Day parade in the twenty-seven-year history of the Soviet regime.

Berlin fell to the Red Army the next day. Russian soldiers found the burned remains of Hitler in the bomb-blasted garden of the Chancellory Building. They noted a bullet hole in its head and small shards of glass in his mouth, the result of biting into a capsule of cyanide. Also found were the corpses of Hitler's new bride, Eva Braun, the family of the propaganda minister Josef Goebbels, including his six children, and Hitler's dog, killed in a test of the efficiency of the cyanide capsules that had been provided to Hitler and the others.

On May 4, 1945, troops of the U.S. Seventh Army took over Hitler's aerie getaway atop a Bavarian-Austrian mountain named Berchtesgaden.

On Sunday, May 5, with Marie, Jean, and Eric, as well as friends and city officials seated in the Blue Room, Fiorello La Guardia announced on his radio program that he would not seek a fourth term. But not without looking back. Men who stayed in office too long, he noted, became "bossy." He added with a feigned tone of surprise, "They tell me I am sort of inclined that way at times." He again spoke with pride of driving out "the political riffraff, the chiselers, the racketeers, the tinhorns." In his administration, he boasted, there had been found "not a single boss, not a single clubhouse loafer." He also rattled a sword. If the next government in City Hall were to develop corruption and inefficiency, he would be back. New York, he said affectionately, was a "city of spaces that are too small" but full of "millions of people that are really big."

On May 8, 1945—V-E Day—the people of La Guardia's city flowed into Times Square to celebrate the surrender of Germany. As the announcement flashed on the news zipper there were a few hundred people on the streets to see it. An hour later, there were twenty thousand; at 11:00 A.M. the crowd was between thirty thousand and thirty-five thousand celebrants and three hundred extra police, ordered into place by Commissioner Valentine.

The Associated Press reported:

> Paper and prayers, laughter and tears, jubilance and sobriety marked the city's emotional expression. Thousands went to church for thanksgiving. Special services were held throughout the day and far into the night, Other thousands, excited by the news, deluged the city with paper and ticker tape. Work went on as usual in most places, but not until after office girls and factory workers, in some instances, had temporarily quit their stations. In one factory thirty girls fainted at the news. Bars and grills were filled, and most restaurants ran out of food, so heavy was the patronage.
>
> Wall Street seethed with hatless and coatless stenographers and clerks who started to jam the narrow streets in the financial section within an hour after the word came. At the peak, the crowd jammed Wall Street for five blocks up to the entrance of Trinity Church on Broadway.

Six long years before V-E Day, Mayor La Guardia had ridden up Broadway in an open car seated next to Howard Hughes in the biggest ticker tape parade in the city's history, then in a salute to Wrong Way Corrigan. Both receptions along the Canyon of Heroes seemed minor to the welcome afforded on June 19, 1945, to General Dwight D. Eisenhower as he rode with the mayor down Fifth Avenue. At a City Hall ceremony La Guardia said of the man who had not wanted his job complicated by the arrival in Tunisia in 1943 of a brigadier general named La Guardia, "History is yet to record the achievements of a great commander of a mighty army equal in gallantry, courage, brilliance."

Ike spoke of his gratitude for the city's wild reception and charmed New Yorkers with the admonition "You can't do this to a simple country boy from Kansas."

A sound meter set up by General Electric to measure the noise of Ike's reception went off the scale. The ovation was later described as the equivalent of three thousand peals of thunder at the same time.

Other official greetings were given to General Jonathan Wainwright, the hero of Bataan, Corregidor, and Japanese prison camps; Admiral Chester Nimitz, whose ships and planes had fought on and above the Pacific Ocean; and General Claire Chennault, dashing leader of the famed "Flying Tigers" in U.S. actions in Burma and China.

All of these Americans were taller than La Guardia. But when France's war hero General Charles De Gaulle got a City Hall reception, he towered so much over his tiny host that he had to almost double over to give the mayor France's Grand Cross of the Legion of Honor. The little Napoleon called De Gaulle "my illustrious friend." New York and Paris, he said, were "two great cities of art and beauty and happiness."

There were in that glorious, victorious summer in La Guardia's city four morning and five afternoon daily general-circulation newspapers. Their photographers had gleefully snapped picture after picture of the stately French general and the dumpy-looking mayor who might have been a general, and had in his closet an appropriate uniform, but still cherished the title "Major."

Suddenly, on June 30, New York became a city with no newspapers.

The men who drove the trucks that delivered them went on strike. Left stranded were people who enjoyed reading their favorite paper at breakfast or when they got home from work, straphangers who folded them tightly for perusal on the way to work in subways, housewives who scanned them for department store sales, moviegoers who relied on them to list the current pictures, Broadway theatergoers, sports fans, and children who looked forward to the adventures of heroic figures and the comic antics of others in "the funnies."

Deciding that kids "should not be deprived of them due to a squabble among the adults," La Guardia picked up a phone and called the program director of WNYC. He said, "I want a program so long as the papers are not being delivered, of the funnies for the children."

Of all the things he'd done in three terms as mayor, this decision was unquestionably the one that transformed Fiorello H. La Guardia from "a municipal official," or "politician," if that was what some people considered him, into an American folk hero. However, if he had been satisfied with confining himself to the radio airwaves, he might not have been remembered for that act beyond those who had heard him. His "immortality" as the mayor who'd read "Dick Tracy" over the radio was ensured after the first of the broadcasts by the arrival of five men with movie cameras. They recorded his performance for newsreels that were shown in theaters across the country, and then preserved in film archives for use by generations of documentarians.

The footage shows La Guardia at a desk, a WNYC microphone looming before him, a Sunday newspaper's funny pages opened to one of the most popular "comic strips" as he says:

> Now children, I know you're all disappointed today that you didn't get the funnies, so gather around. Ah, here's Dick Tracy! Let's see what Dick Tracy is doing. Now, get this picture! Here is "Wetwash." The doors of the laundry wagon are open. He's leaning with his back toward the wagon, and he's counting his money. Two, three, four thousand. Now he's getting into the hundreds. Six hundred, seven hundred,

"Here's Dick Tracy!" La Guardia reads the "funnies" over the radio to children during a strike by newspaper delivery truck drivers in July 1945. Ironically, he is remembered by more Americans for that than for any of the historic reforms and changes that he fought for and instituted in the city during twelve years as mayor.

eight hundred. And the picture shows, a *hand* of "Breathless." She's got hold of that iron pot. Remember the iron pot she took from the "Van Hoosens." And CRASH. She crashes it on his head. Knocked out. The next picture we see Dick Tracy. You know the fine type of Dick Tracy? He's been a detective so long, and he still has that slender form.

Lew Valentine! Why do our detectives get fat I wonder?

And say, children, what does it all mean? It means that *dirty money never brings any luck.*

The delivery truckers' strike lasted until July 17. Newsstands were quickly filled, and just as quickly sold out. In the meantime, said the Associated Press, "Housewives had missed bargains, nightclub attendance dropped, mail and phone orders fell off at department stores, jobs and even apartments went begging."

With presses and trucks rolling again, the papers brought out extra editions with all the comic strips that had been missed, along with columns and other features that had been denied to the adults.

During the newspaper drought, La Guardia found himself disappointed and insulted by the successor to FDR. The mayor of New York had been invited by De Gaulle on behalf of the French government to represent the United States at the first Bastille Day observation in Paris since before the war. La Guardia had accepted.

Truman said that he could go in a "personal capacity."

The displeased mayor retorted, "This private person that they're talking about in Washington—I don't know him."

When Truman announced that he was going to Potsdam, Germany, for a conference with British prime minister Churchill and Josef Stalin, the still-stung La Guardia sniped that he hoped the president was not going in a personal capacity.

Two weeks after Parisians had their celebration under sparkling skies, the weather in New York City on Saturday, July 28, 1945, was a dismal mix of fog, alternating rain, and drizzle. Low slate-gray clouds nipped off the tops of Manhattan's tallest buildings. But far to the north at Bedford Field, near Boston, conditions were fine for flying. Army air force lieutenant colonel William Smith had orders to wing to Newark, New Jersey, to pick up his commanding officer. Smith was a highly decorated pilot who'd flown five hundred hours of combat in the skies over Europe. His plane was a Mitchell B-25. With twin engines and dual rudders, it stood parallel to the tarmac on three wheels. Sixteen planes just like it had flown from the carrier *Hornet* to strike the first blow against Japanese cities by attacking Tokyo under command of Lieutenant Colonel James H. Doolittle on April 18, 1942, just four months and eleven days after the attack on Pearl Harbor. The raid scored little damage, but the boost to home front morale had been incalculable.

After a smooth flight from Bedford Field, Smith's B-25 approached La Guardia Airport. Observing the cloud ceiling over New York City, Smith radioed for a report from the La Guardia tower on the weather at Newark. Concerned that it might be socked in, he requested clearance to put down at La Guardia. He was told that he would fare better by continuing across Manhattan to Newark as long as he found three miles forward visibility.

A few minutes later, Smith radioed La Guardia tower, "From where I'm sitting, I can't see the Empire State Building."

He should have been flying at two thousand feet, well above the Empire State. No one knows why he was lower, but he barely missed the office tower above Grand Central Terminal. A man on the ground figured the plane was no higher than its twenty-second floor. Moments later, at 9:25 A.M., the B-25 smashed the Empire State Building at two hundred miles an hour on the northern side, at the seventy-ninth floor.

People on Thirty-fourth Street heard an explosion, looked up, and saw a ball of flame followed by a shower of metal, concrete, and glass. What they could not see were wings being sheared off the bomber and one engine plowing through the building and crashing through the southern facade. The second engine and part of a landing gear plummeted down an elevator shaft to the basement.

Eight hundred gallons of burning gasoline flooded stairways and halls down to the seventy-fifth floor. The mangled fuselage protruded from an eighteen-by-twenty-foot hole in the northern side.

If the plane had hit on a workday, hundreds, perhaps thousands, of people would have been killed. Most of the people working in the Empire State's offices that morning were in the seventy-ninth floor space occupied by Catholic War Relief Services. One of the workers was Catherine O'Connor. She reported, "The plane exploded within the building. I was tottering on my feet trying to keep my balance—and three-quarters of the office was instantaneously consumed in this sheet of flame."

She saw ten coworkers incinerated, along with the three-man crew of the B-25. With a few other survivors, she made it down to the street. Twenty-year-old elevator operator Betty Lou Oliver found her elevator in a free fall from the seventy-ninth floor. Rescuers discovered her alive in a tangle of cables in the basement.

While Betty Lou was experiencing the wildest ride of her life and the firemen on the scene sounded a fourth alarm, the mayor's car was arriving at City Hall. As the radio crackled the fourth alarm and gave the address, Thirty-fourth Street and Fifth Avenue, La Guardia exclaimed to his driver, "This could be very bad. Go!"

Almost immediately after he arrived, he was in an elevator to the sixtieth floor. Drenched with cascading water, he slogged up nineteen flights of stairs and remained on the crash floor until the fire was out.

The death toll was fourteen, including Lieutenent Colonel Smith and two crewmen. Twenty-six were injured.

~

Seventeen days after the B-25 hit the Empire State Building, on August 14, 1945, after Japan had felt the blast of two atomic bombs, the Japanese government announced its unconditional surrender, ending World War II. Thousands of New Yorkers thronged Times Square to celebrate. To guarantee the public safety and a modicum of order, Commissioner Lew Valentine mobilized all fourteen thousand members of the police force. When the official news of the surrender was flashed, the mayor again heard it over his car radio.

Getting into the mood of his city, he promised himself "a couple of hours of relaxation and celebration."

But only after he was certain that the big party was not getting out of hand, and a passing regret that his friend Franklin had not allowed Fiorello to join the fray in army uniform.

29

In September 1945, while preparations for trials of Nazi war criminals were being made in Nuremberg, Germany, the last word in Fiorello La Guardia's dramatic campaign against Nazism in New York City was spoken in Washington, D.C., by Attorney General Tom C. Clark. On the sixth of the month he ordered ex-Bund leader and ex-convict Fritz Kuhn deported to his fatherland.

On the same day, President Truman sent Congress a twenty-one-point program intended to smooth the way for the greatest era of "high prosperity" in American history. The sixteen-thousand-word plan was read by a clerk of the House of Representatives. A congressional historian noted for the record that the document was the thickest since a twenty-thousand-word message sent to Capitol Hill in 1901 from the desk of President Theodore Roosevelt.

Republicans gasped at the breadth of Truman's vision, then denounced it as "the same old New Deal dressed up in new clothing." Among the provisions was a "full employment" bill to prevent future economic depressions. Truman also had a warning for both capital and labor. "This is not the time for shortsighted management to seize upon a chance to reduce wages and try to injure labor unions," he said. "Equally, it is not the time for labor leaders to shirk their responsibility and permit widespread industrial strife."

He had good reason to be concerned. By September's end nearly two million workers were idle, some four hundred thousand of them on strike and the rest with no jobs to go to in

120 factories that closed because of the strikes' ripple effect. The issues were more pay and fewer working hours. The strike with the greatest effect on all Americans was a walkout by the soft coal miners of John L. Lewis's United Mine Workers. Then the CIO's Oil and Refinery Union closed refineries. Determined to keep petroleum flowing, Truman seized twenty-six of them on the basis of supplying the "needs of the armed forces." Workers agreed to do their jobs "for the U.S. government," but made it clear they were "still on strike against the companies." Their official employer became the U.S. Navy. The seizure was the first by a president in peacetime.

Of considerably more bother to New Yorkers was a strike in the city by building workers who opened apartment house doors, carried out the trash, and ran the elevators. When they went on strike on September 23, chaos ensued. Many employees of firms on upper floors did not go to work. Some anticipated the strike by arranging to sleep in their offices and have food hauled up to them in baskets tethered to ropes. Two radio technicians who serviced the transmission units at the top of the Empire State Building carried up cots and three days' worth of victuals. It ran out long before the strike was ended six days later. An executive order from Governor Dewey imposed binding arbitration. In the meantime, hundreds of thousands of New Yorkers had been discomfited and city businesses had lost millions of dollars.

The strike also required overtime pay for the Police Department in making sure that when tempers flared, no one got hurt. Quick intervention by Lew Valentine's cops also was needed after a downtown store advertised that it had ten thousand pairs of nylon stockings for sale. Twenty of the Finest and three patrol cars were dispatched to keep thousands of women from rioting to get their hands on a luxury most had not seen since before the war.

Extra officers were needed on October 27 when President Truman came to town to take part in Navy Day ceremonies and a parade of seven warships, veterans of the battles of Midway, Guadalcanal, Saipan, Leyte Gulf, and Okinawa. Truman said it was the happiest day of his life. Before the naval review, he dropped in at City Hall—the first time a sitting president had done so. It was a perfect, sparkling, blue-sky, warm New York autumn day, but the atmosphere in City Hall between mayor and president was frosty.

The man who could gush over FDR said to his successor, "It's nice to have you here."

Truman answered, "It's nice to be here."

They were a pair of prickly personalities who'd clashed once in the matter of La Guardia going to Paris for Bastille Day. In retrospect several months later, the flap would be viewed as the opening round in a contest of wills in a wrestling match over the role of the United States in the postwar world.

What Truman believed America's foreign policy should be was outlined that day in a speech setting out twelve points, from "a free exchange of fundamental scientific information" related to the atomic bomb to "a world in which Nazism, fascism, and military aggression cannot exist," freedom of the seas, "access on equal terms to the trade and the raw materials of the world," Roosevelt's "Four Freedoms," and a United Nations "composed of all the peace-loving nations of the world who are willing jointly to use force if necessary to ensure peace."

La Guardia found nothing in the speech with which he disagreed. Only when Truman in 1947 declared "the Truman Doctrine" of "containment" of communism, thereby accepting the unofficial declaration by Winston Churchill of a "Cold War" and his recognition that the Soviet Union had built "an Iron Curtain" across Europe, did Fiorello La Guardia, as shall be seen, break with Truman's postwar policy.

If New Yorkers, political foes, and the City Council thought Fiorello La Guardia would be a lame duck mayor following his announcement that he would not go for a fourth term, they did not savor the picture long. He was in his last year as president of the Conference of Mayors and as such presided at its annual meeting, held in Madison Square Garden. It was a sentimental farewell at the end of which La Guardia led a combined services band. When he left the conductor's podium, a reporter asked, "Is this your swan song?"

"I'll be writing my swan song," said La Guardia, "when I lose interest in my city." After a long, thoughtful pause, he added, "Chopin wrote my swan song long ago."

Now the reporter thought. He asked, "You mean the funeral march, Mr. Mayor?"

"That's right. That's right."

He wasn't dead yet, physically or politically. Absent from the ballot for mayor for the first time in twelve years, he could not stay out of the fray. The Republicans had chosen as their candidate a judge of the Court of General Sessions, John J. Goldstein, who was, of all things, a lifelong Tammany Democrat. The venerable Judge Samuel Seabury denounced the choice as a "sham Fusion ticket."

Democrats nominated William O'Dwyer.

The political waters were muddied by the birth of the "No Deal" party. It had Fiorello La Guardia's backing. The mayoral candidate was Newbold Morris. Why the mayor encouraged the creation of the third party puzzled everyone. Detractors found it a ploy to retain control over City Hall. Others discerned a familiar "divide and conquer" tactic in which La Guardia somehow would benefit by an O'Dwyer victory, perhaps in the form of Democrats backing him for the U.S. Senate in 1946. The nonpartisan Citizens' Union condemned La Guardia for "an irrational and solitary caprice."

To those who saw devious maneuvering for his own political gain, La Guardia snapped, "When I run for office, I'll come and ask the people for the nomination."

In November the people went for O'Dwyer, but they did so in an election with fewer registered voters than in any since the days of Jimmy Walker. When the last ballot was tallied, O'Dwyer had a seven hundred thousand plurality, the biggest victory margin to that time.

La Guardia was faulted for not having built a lasting "machine" to oppose the enemies of reform. Bristling at the idea that he could be a "machine boss," he answered, "In a democracy a public official cannot designate his crown prince."

The La Guardia years had been, in the analysis of biographer Thomas Kessner, "a great flashing star that tore across the firmament for its moment. It shone so because the sky was so dark, and because it had an enormous energy and a huge tail of followers, but it was a product of time and place."

But what a time! What a place! In 1934 La Guardia did not find New York City a place of brick and leave one of marble, the *New York Times* would say, but long, long after Fiorello La Guardia left City Hall his fingerprints were everywhere. One of his last ceremonies marking a new city was held in October 1945. With the ugly el a thing of the past, Sixth Avenue became "The Avenue of the Americas." The mayor welcomed the name change as a symbol that New York had become the great international city of his vision. However, New Yorkers found it hard to accept the new designation and went on calling the avenue between Fifth and Seventh by its old numerical designation. So persistent has "Sixth Avenue" been that street signs for "Avenue of the Americas" still bear the subscript "Sixth Avenue."

In keeping with the La Guardia vision of New York City as the focus of international commerce, he announced plans for a "world trade center" where buyers and sellers from all over the globe would do business. The realization of his concept would take two decades. It rose as the "twin towers" of the World Trade Center, with the adjoining World Financial Center.

Fifty-six years later when terrorists destroyed the World Trade Center by crashing two airliners into the towers, Mayor Rudolph Giuliani emerged to take bold control of the disaster in a way that forcefully reminded New Yorkers of La Guardia's taking command on the day that the B-25 bomber hit the Empire State Building in 1945. Reflecting on Giuliani's reaction to the crisis, *New York Times* columnist John Tierney properly found another comparison between the two mayors. Noting that La Guardia had exhibited the same "flaws" of confidence, authority, and intransigence that marked the Giuliani years, and that "a control freak can seem essential when things are out of control, but can get irritating when life returns to normal," Tierney wrote, "Mr. Giuliani's model, Fiorello La Guardia, was also convinced that he could run anything better than anyone else, and his arrogance became more destructive the longer he was in office. [La Guardia] was hailed as the city's savior during an economic crisis, and then he became more willful and blind to his own mistakes. There were no term limits in his days, enabling him to serve three terms, and the last one gets the lowest marks from historians."

In December 1945, with power slipping away, he fought against a City Council cut in funds for the building of hangars for another of his dreams, an international airport in a Queens area called Idlewild. He said that the council's act to lop off funding "smashes to smithereens" ten years of hard labor at the airport. Behind the action, he believed, stood Robert Moses with a scheme to grab control of the airport for a Moses-controlled Port of New York Authority. He was right. Idlewild (later JFK) and Newark's airport eventually became part of the Port Authority, as did the World Trade Center, much to the frequent consternation of subsequent mayors.

The Christmas season began with the traditional Thanksgiving Day parade down Broadway to Macy's department store at Herald Square, culminated by the arrival of Santa Claus. At Rockefeller Center a fifty-five-foot Christmas tree went up. The Associated Press, with offices in the next block, reported that it "glowed with ultraviolet rays, and at night beams of mercury light transformed seven hundred ten-inch balls treated with fluorescent paint into glowing spheres of red, green, yellow, blue, white, and orange."

On the mayor's Sunday broadcast before Christmas he said invitingly, "Come, children, we'll celebrate Christmas together! Christmas is for children, and I'll tell you what happens when you sleep." Sleigh bells were heard in the background as he read Clement Clarke Moore's "A Visit from Saint Nicholas," also known as "'Twas the Night before Christmas."

The program was his next-to-the-last from City Hall, but New Yorkers would not be left without his familiar voice coming at them out of their radios. He'd signed a contract for more than $50,000 a year to continue the Sunday chats on another station. He also made a deal with the American

Broadcasting Company for a weekly commentary program that would be carried by two hundred stations coast to coast. The sponsor was *Liberty* magazine. La Guardia opinions also would be available in the afternoon newspaper *PM* in a column. The requirement in all of these ventures was that the people who paid him would have no control over what he said. Help in turning out scripts and manuscripts would come from a staff of six, ensconced in an office at 30 Rockefeller Center (the RCA Building), where ABC had its studios. Formerly known as the "Blue" network and owned by NBC, which also had the "Red" network (nothing to do with the Communists), ABC was born after NBC sold the Blue Network to settle a federal antitrust suit.

The La Guardia letterhead chosen for use in his office bore a little flower.

Looking forward to a post–City Hall period of "thinking, writing and talking," he also contracted with J. B. Lippincott Company, publishers in Philadelphia, to write his autobiography, in collaboration with a professional writer and editor, M. R. Werner. The deal anticipated a multivolume work. The first would end at 1919 and be titled *The Making of an Insurgent*.

His dozen years as mayor were summed up in his last Sunday broadcast. "The City government," he said, "has acquired a soul."

Then he had a final admonition for family men who gambled: "Put two dollars on the wife, two dollars on the oldest boy, and two dollars on the little girl. I guarantee you will win."

As always, he signed off with "Patience and fortitude."

On Monday, December 31, 1945, he greeted his successor at City Hall. Immediately after William O'Dwyer was elected, he'd sent him a "Dear Bill" letter promising his full cooperation. "At best the job is tough," he'd said. "There can be but one mayor of the city and I hope you will be it. The hardest part of the job is to say no, and to say it quickly, definitely, and emphatically."

Posing for a crowd of press photographers with O'Dwyer, La Guardia wisecracked, "They're all waiting for me to sock you."

La Guardia's Desk Cleared For O'Dwyer

City's 87th Mayor Will Take the Oath Tonight, Start Work Tomorrow

La Guardia in Last Talk Over WNYC

In Mellow Mood, He Sounds a Farewell and Reviews His Prospects

Mayor F. H. La Guardia, the son of an Italian immigrant, was finishing up yesterday the job of administering the nation's biggest and the world's most expensive city, and Mayor-elect William O'Dwyer, an immigrant from Ireland, was preparing to begin it.

At City Hall, Mr. La·Guardia made his last Sunday broadcast as Mayor in a thirty-one-minute session of benign chatting during which he kept the claws of his voice sheathed, even when he assailed horse-race betting and newspapers.

At the Metropolitan Club, Fifth Avenue and Sixtieth Street, Mr. O'Dwyer delivered a fight talk to thirty-two of his highest key appointees, and told them that they had three months to produce or get off the team.

Mr. La Guardia, who loses his title and office at midnight tonight, was relaxed and good-humored as he said "patience and fortitude" for the last time officially, and made himself ready to enter a private life of "thinking, writing, talking."

After Final Broadcast as City's Head

Herald Tribune—Rosenberg
Mayor F. H. La Guardia at the end of his talk over WNYC yesterday

New York Herald Tribune front-page story on La Guardia's last day as mayor, December 31, 1945. The headline infers he was the eighty-sixth mayor, but later and current official city directories cite him as the ninety-ninth mayor, which is the designation used in this book.

On the way out of City Hall he said to onlookers, "I'll be around."

The headline on the front page of the *Herald Tribune* that day was:

La Guardia's
Desk Cleared
For O'Dwyer

An accompanying photo was La Guardia hunched before a WNYC microphone, taken the day before. His left hand is raised as if to prop up his head. The right holds his glasses. The story reported, "Mayor F. H. La Guardia, the son of an Italian immigrant, was finishing up yesterday the job of administering the nation's biggest and the world's most expensive city, and Mayor-elect William O'Dwyer, an immigrant from Ireland, was preparing to begin it."

On page 11 of the paper, John G. Rogers offered a review of "12 Color-Packed years." It began, "The longest run in town finally comes to a close today after 4,383 days of a performance that for color and sparkle is not likely to be equaled by a successor in a long time. The La Guardia production was always a good show. It was lively, erratic, provocative, irritating or funny. It was always dominated by its star who brooked no understudies, no competition, under the main spotlight."

The mayor's last official act was the release of a 393-page "final report," which he called "New York Advancing: The Victory Edition." In a chatty twenty-page introduction he listed the "outstanding accomplishments" of his regime: improvement of the city's physical plants; administration and research of Health and Hospitals Departments ("models for the entire world"); conversion of the Sanitation Department from a "disorganized, graft-ridden, forsaken outfit" to "an efficient, well knit organization"; consolidation of all city buying; elimination of graft in city markets, public housing, and welfare; and a $1.25 billion public works fund, half of it to be financed with federal funds. He begged, "Don't mess it up."

Proud of his friendship with Franklin D. Roosevelt, and delighting in having made "the politicians mad" because of the relationship, he wrote, "Oh what trouble the poor President had with his own politicians whining: 'Don't let La Guardia do it.' Let us do it."

The *Herald Tribune* story concluded by pondering what might be next:

> Mr. La Guardia, the fighting Little Flower, had made a good many enemies in his long political life. He wouldn't be La Guardia if he hadn't done that. And, as he leaves City Hall, a good many of those enemies are wondering about his political plans, if any.
>
> A seat in the United States Senate is generally believed to be one of his ambitions. Only he knows whether he is likely ever to try for it. If he does try, a lot of fur will fly before he wins or loses.

Fiorello H. La Guardia, with wife, Marie, saying good-bye to City Hall on January 1, 1946, after watching his successor, William O'Dwyer, take office.

Meanwhile, New York loses a colorful, capable and valiant Mayor—a man who never ducked a fight and who never asked quarter in the midst of one. Perhaps the best summing-up of his complicated character can still be done in the words of one who watched him in action more than twenty years ago: "He cares enough to get angry."

During one of his Sunday afternoon radio programs in the summer of 1945, La Guardia joked about his impending joblessness. Noting that he would soon have to move out of Gracie Mansion, he asked his "good friends" in the real-estate business (a joking reference to having raised property taxes) for help in finding a house in the Riverdale section of the Bronx. The one he and Marie found in August cost $40,000. It was a four-story Tudor-style house near a good school for Eric.

On January 1, 1946, Fiorello and Marie got into their Ford sedan to go to City Hall for the official oath-taking by William O'Dwyer. The route took them over the Henry Hudson

Bridge. When they stopped at a toll booth, neither had a dime. "I built the damn thing," said La Guardia. "Now I have to pay for it."

The amused toll-taker waved them through.

After the power of the mayoralty passed into O'Dwyer's hands, the ex-cornet player, ex-consular official, ex-congressman, ex-bomber pilot, ex-aldermanic president, and ex-mayor posed for one more news photo.

In front of City Hall, he raised an arm, grinned, and waved his hat.

30

Shortly after leaving his beloved city in others' hands, La Guardia was asked by President Truman to go to Brazil as a special emissary. He received a warm welcome and went on to amuse, charm, and assure Brazilians that the United States was a friend and a partner, not the ogre of the North that many of them supposed Uncle Sam to be. When President Roosevelt had talked about a "good neighbor policy" and Pan American friendship, he said, he'd meant it. Had not the City of New York named one of its grandest avenues "Avenue of the Americas"? Brazilians loved his earthiness, his sincerity, and his big hats.

Three months later, Truman offered him the director generalship of the U.N. Relief and Rehabilitation Administration (UNRRA). He replaced former governor Lehman. The job paid $15,000 a year, but La Guardia turned down a salary. The work required fifteen-hour days as he traveled through most of the war-devastated countries of the world. What he found left him appalled. "I thought I had seen some pretty hard and difficult situations," he said, "but there is nothing I have been through where so many people were facing death by starvation."

His journeys took him from Europe to Korea. When confronted with the fact of more than eight hundred thousand Jewish refugees, he said they represented "the most pathetic and difficult problem facing the world today." They were not the only "displaced persons," known everywhere as DPs. He urged the United States to immediately take 150,000 of them.

Declaring, "I am not a diplomat, so from this point on protocol is off," he assailed the system of international free enterprise as outdated and ineffective. The more he traveled and the more he saw of suffering, he saw the answer in a kind of global WPA. Hearing fears expressed that the Soviet Union posed a threat to the West, he retorted, "Let us stop talking cynically about the next war and think sincerely about future peace."

Hardly anyone in Washington cared to listen to him. Those who did said that he was naive and blind to the designs of Stalin to spread Soviet communism throughout the world.

As the Truman administration shaped a policy of containment, La Guardia argued for "one world." Rather than preparing for a confrontation between East and West, he pleaded, the United States ought to adopt a foreign policy of understanding and cooperation. The way to "lick communism" was by "making democracy work, by proving to the world that people can live properly and decently."

Quixote was again tilting with windmills, but on a grander scale. He was hearing hymns of heavenly possibilities in which swords were beaten into plowshares, while the president of the United States was listening to advisers who counseled toughness in facing down the Soviets. In the hard reality of an emerging Cold War there was no room for a man who counseled patience and fortitude, not with the Red Army massed behind the Iron Curtain stretching, in the chilling words of Churchill in a speech at Westminster College in Missouri in March 1946, "from Stettin in the Baltic to Trieste in the Adriatic."

Yet, in all those in the Truman inner circle who advised "standing up" to a dictator in the Kremlin, whom Truman bitterly called "Uncle Joe," none was as personally familiar with the conditions of ordinary people behind the Iron Curtain as Fiorello La Guardia. Among the DPs was his sister Gemma.

On the day after the Allied landings on the Normandy beaches, June 7, 1944, she and her Jewish husband, Herman Gluck, had been seized by the Germans and taken to the Mauthausen concentration camp. Soon set free, but separated from Herman, Gemma had spent the next eleven months fearing for herself and her daughter, Yolanda, and Yolanda's young son, Richard. Not until April 1945 did she find out that Herman was dead and Yolanda was in Ravensbruck, waiting to be taken to Berlin to be exchanged for prisoners. Gemma went to Berlin and found herself imprisoned again and made to suffer throughout the Red Army's battle to capture the Nazi capital.

Informed by the Red Cross of Gemma's whereabouts at war's end and that Gemma had been freed by the Soviets, Fiorello was able to talk with her by phone. Gemma had pleaded for his help in getting to the United States. In periodic letters she told him, "We are beggars." She wrote of "the soul of suffering." The Soviets were "beasts."

Her brother coldly said that her case was "the same as that of hundreds of thousands of displaced people." But he did everything he could to rescue her, while sending her $150 per month. He urged her not to reveal who she was. Eventually she and her grandson Richard got to the United States (in May 1947). Fiorello arranged a modest home for them and provided for the boy's education.

Gemma was left feeling that her brother had treated her shabbily, that he had been more concerned about avoiding publicity than in helping her. She spoke of him having been "unsentimental, brisk, and businesslike." In his defense it's fair to note that he correctly feared that if Gemma's relationship to a prominent American political figure became known, his efforts to aid her might have become even more difficult, if not impossible. But the details of the episode lend credence to Gemma's complaint that her brother appeared to be more concerned about masses of the displaced and the tormented than in one person who happened to be his sister.

Observing the development of the Marshall Plan to rebuild Western Europe, not for humanitarian purposes but to ensure a bulwark against the Red Army, La Guardia railed against "bread diplomacy." He declared, "You can't go to them with a piece of bread in one hand and a ballot in the other."

When the time came for the U.S. government to decide whether to renew its support for UNRRA by paying 72 percent of its budget, with the bulk of the funds going to Soviet "satellites" behind the Iron Curtain, the verdict was "No."

Almost to the time of his death from cancer, after leaving office La Guardia remained a political force in the city and nation with weekly and coast-to-coast radio broadcasts from his home in the Riverdale section of the Bronx.

La Guardia called it "wrong, morally wrong; it is wicked."

Discouraged and disheartened, he went home to Marie, Jean, and Eric. He was tired and looked it. He was also complaining about abdominal pains. Dr. Baehr examined him and said that he'd found a stone blocking his pancreas. It was a deliberate lie. The blockage was a tumor, it was cancerous, and it had spread.

Fiorello labored on, working on his autobiography, writing, broadcasting, and shouting in alarm that good government was going to the dogs. "There is a deliberate and determined effort to revert back," he complained. "The struggle is on."

When Robert Moses dropped in at the Riverdale house, he was shocked by the change he found in his old nemesis. He recalled, "He was in bed so shrunken, so chapfallen, and yet so spunky. I felt like crying. It was a battle not even the most courageous fighter could win."

On September 16, 1947, La Guardia fell into a coma.

Four days later, at 7:22 A.M., he died.

Marie got a telegram from Truman: "He was as incorruptible as the sun."

On September 21, a line of forty thousand mourners who wanted a last look at the Little Flower made its way past his open coffin in the Cathedral of St. John the Divine.

The funeral service was the next day. Burial was in Woodlawn Cemetery in Queens.

Ten years later, in a slender commemorative book, *La Guardia: A Salute and Memoir,* Robert Moses wrote:

"He was much more than a colorful personality. We doff our hats to a record of extraordinary accomplishment in almost every field of municipal works, in plan and performance, in health and hospitals, in schools, housing and recreation, in the arts and sciences, in protection, in personnel. Countless evidences are still about us. Only those who recall the cynicism of the late Twenties and early Thirties and remember how low the City's credit and civic morale had fallen can properly gauge what this man did to lift us up and to attract to New York the lost respect of the nation. He lifted dispirited public morale and raised public enterprise to a permanently higher level. There are no gaps in this record, no chinks in the armor of righteousness."

Chronology

The first forty years in office are the hardest.

—La Guardia, 1945

December 11, 1882	Born in Greenwich Village, New York City.
1891–1898	Raised at Whipple Barracks, Prescott, Arizona.
Spring 1898	Correspondent for *St. Louis Post-Dispatch,* with U.S. Army troops at Tampa, Florida.
1898–1901	Lives in Foggia, Italy, with parents, sister, and brother.
1901–1907	Serves in U.S. Consular Service in Budapest, Hungary, and Fiume, Italy (then part of Austria).
1907–1910	Interpreter, Ellis Island, New York; studies law at night.
1910–1915	Practices law; affiliates with Republican Party.
1915–1917	Deputy attorney general of New York State.
1917–1918	Member of Congress, Fourteenth District, New York City.
1918	Captain, then major, Army Air Service; pilots bomber on the Italian-Austrian front (on leave of absence from Congress).

March 1919	Marries Thea Almerigotti; Thea and daughter die in 1921.
1919–1920	Resumes seat in House of Representatives.
1920–1921	President, New York City Board of Aldermen.
1923–1932	Member of Congress, Twentieth District, New York City.
February 1929	Marries his longtime secretary, Marie Fisher. Later adopted two children, Jean and Eric.
November 1929	Defeated for mayor of New York by James J. Walker.
1934–1945	Mayor of New York City. Beginning in 1941 also serves as U.S. director of civil defense.
1939–1940	New York World's Fair; opening of New York City Municipal Airport, later renamed La Guardia Airport.
March–December 1946	Director general, U.N. Relief and Rehabilitation Administration (UNRRA).
1946–1947	Radio commentator, newspaper columnist; writes first part of his autobiography (published posthumously).
September 20, 1947	Dies of pancreatic cancer; buried, Woodlawn Cemetery, Queens.

Author's Note and Sources

I think the reporter should get his facts straight before he distorts them.

—La Guardia, 1939

My personal preparation for writing about Fiorello La Guardia began one dazzling night in Times Square. I can't recall the date, except that I was probably about six years old. I was in New York with my parents, brother, and three sisters for a visit to my uncle Walter Tinney, to whom this book is dedicated. Awed, I was awash in the spectacular lights of the big signs, the crowded sidewalks, traffic-jammed streets, blaring car horns, and all the other sounds of that amazing place in the year before Fiorello La Guardia ordered the lights dimmed for the duration of World War II. Of course, I had no inkling that one day I would write a La Guardia biography, or the life story of anyone else. At the time I had not a clue as to what I wanted to do when I grew up, except that sooner or later I was going to go to New York City and stay there.

The permanent arrival did not occur until twenty-four years later. I hit town at the time of the opening of the 1964 World's Fair, still holding it against my parents because they had gone to the 1939 World's Fair and left five-year-old me at home in Phoenixville, Pennsylvania, in the keeping of my sisters, Doris, Jean, and Arlene, and brother, Jack. However, Mom and Dad did bring me a souvenir: a miniature Trylon and Perisphere.

My first memory of seeing Mayor La Guardia was by way of a movie screen as a newsreel showed him reading the funnies on the

378

radio in 1945. In 1959 I saw the pre-mayoral *Fiorello!* portrayed by petite and pudgy actor Tom Bosley in the Broadway musical of that name. By then I was a broadcast newsman looking for a way to get to New York. When the chance came in the spring of 1964, I plunged into Manhattan living and into the lore and legends of the most exciting city in the world.

Getting to know New York led me inexorably to getting to know its hands-down, let-there-be-no-argument-about-it, greatest mayor, before his time and after.

Simply because I was interested in the history of New York in general and the city of the La Guardia years of the 1930s and early 1940s particularly, I began accumulating books on both subjects. I bought them to read, not because I had plans to write a book on the subject. I didn't. Although I'd always wanted to be an author, I had little expectation of realizing that goal. But to use La Guardia's favorite motto, with "patience and fortitude" and a good deal of luck I found myself living my six-year-old's dream of residing in New York, and my later ambition to earn a living by writing. One book led to another and so on and so on until my editor for several of my nonfiction works and biographies, Hana Umlauf Lane, posed the thrilling question "Would you be interested in doing a biography of La Guardia?"

Would I! The very next day I was off and running, beginning with rereading books on my subject, many of which through wonderful serendipity over a period of more than thirty years were already on my shelves. Without having to tap the fabled resources of the New York Public Library (whose twin lions flanking the front steps are named "Patience" and "Fortitude"), I had at hand the midstream, first-term biography by Lowell Limpus and Burr Leyson, as well as Limpus's book on Police Commissioner Lew Valentine. Both books provided portraits of them while in office, along with the results of interviews conducted with La Guardia at City Hall and Valentine at police headquarters. Also picked up in passing as I'd browsed used-book stores was a slender, scholarly, analytical 1937 La Guardia biography by Jay Franklin. These and several latter-day biographies, combined with Fiorello's autobiography up to 1919, provided road maps through the La Guardia years from birth to burial.

Details of events of his public years, 1914–1945, were abundantly available in thousands of newspaper stories and magazine articles. On one of my excursions into stores selling used books and phonograph records I'd discovered an LP from 1969 ("The Little Flower:

Fiorello La Guardia") with recordings, excerpts, and six of his radio broadcasts: reading "Dick Tracy," Pearl Harbor, gas rationing, the possibility of a subway fare increase, an endorsement of Senator Robert F. Wagner for reelection in 1944, and his moving tribute to FDR on the evening of Roosevelt's death. Reading La Guardia was one thing, *hearing* him was quite another.

Because I was writing for a general audience, I wanted to bring to life on the page as well as I could the man more than the office; the personality as much as the policies; his style; and his methods in going after his goals, rather than the minutiae of meetings and "my eyes glaze over" nitpickings in dense treatises intended for political science courses and policy wonks. This was an approach that sometimes required momentary deviations from chronology into themes and an occasional leap ahead or back in time, while still keeping a linear account of his life and times.

Outstanding detailed treatments of the political and governmental milieu in which he rose to prominence and then dominated New York City politics for twelve years were found in three volumes by Arthur Mann (*La Guardia: A Fighter against His Times, 1882–1933; La Guardia Comes to Power: 1933,* and *The Progressive Era: Liberal Renaissance or Liberal Failure?*), and Charles Garrett's *The La Guardia Years: Machine and Reform Politics in New York City.* All of these afforded me a context and background as I researched and wrote. For a magnificent overview of the extraordinary life and achievements of Robert Moses, Fiorello's constant battler in shaping New York's future, I referred to Robert Caro's massive biography *The Power Broker: Robert Moses and the Fall of New York.*

Primary sources for part I, "A Little Flower Blooms," were La Guardia's autobiography, Lowell Limpus and Burr Leyson's biography, and Arthur Mann's two volumes covering La Guardia's life to his election as mayor in 1933. Valuable information was found in numerous newspaper stories and magazine articles.

Material relating to events of 1898 and conditions at the U.S. Army camps at Tampa was found in Theodore Roosevelt's autobiography and his book on the Rough Riders. Enlightening information on La Guardia's escapades with the Army Air Service during World War I was found in Albert Spalding's memoir *Rise to Follow,* and in reports in New York newspapers.

Events following La Guardia's return from the war, resumption of his seat in the House, and his first bid for mayor, in 1929, were covered extensively by the New York press, Limpus and Leyson, Mann, Franklin, and other biographers and writers on events and politics of the period, including several biographies of Jimmy Walker. The La Guardia demonstration of how to make a potent alcoholic drink by mixing malt extract and near beer received extensive coverage in the press.

The Seabury investigations are detailed in several sources. Of great value were Herbert Mitgang's history *The Man Who Rode the Tiger,* and William B. and John B. Northrup's *The Insolence of Office,* as well as extensive reportage by the New York newspapers.

La Guardia's campaign and victory in 1933 are detailed in Limpus and Leyson, Franklin, Mann, and numerous other accounts in books on La Guardia, Walker, Seabury, and the general topic of "reform" and "progressive" political movements of the period, along with La Guardia's support in Congress of President Roosevelt's New Deal programs. The newspapers provided day-by-day coverage of the campaign, election day, and counting returns on election night.

Significant sources for La Guardia's first term, as described in part II, "Animal Crackers," were the contemporary Franklin biography and Limpus and Leyson's book on La Guardia and Limpus's book on Valentine. Robert Caro's biography of Commissioner Robert Moses afforded insights into the La Guardia–Moses generally contentious relationship.

Of value, too, was George Martin's biography of Frances Perkins, *Madam Secretary,* on the subject of Moses and, earlier, concerning the Triangle Shirt Waist factory disaster.

Newspaper and magazine coverage of the new La Guardia administration and the La Guardia-Valentine attack on tinhorns, chiselers, slot machines, and crime in general was plentiful, colorful, and instructive. Commissioner Valentine's disputes with the press were found in Lowell Limpus's Valentine biography and the newspapers.

Information regarding Thomas E. Dewey was abundantly available in the press. Of great value was Dewey's autobiography, dealing extensively with his war on gangsters, and a contemporary biography by Rupert Hughes. The Dewey sources also provided details of the prosecution of German American Bund leader Fritz Kuhn and the trial and retrial of James J. Hines.

For a penetrating analysis of machine politics in New York City in the La Guardia era I am grateful for the work of Charles Garrett in *The La Guardia Years.*

Most of the above sources contributed enormously to the writing of part III, "Patience and Fortitude," and part IV, "Four More Years of Hell." Fiorello's activities related to the 1939–1940 World's Fair and La Guardia Airport, his vociferous scorning of Hitler, and his dictatorial use of the powers of the mayor were found in countless sources. Especially useful in appreciating the scope of changes in New York City in the 1930s was *The WPA Guide to New York City*, along with other books on the state of the city at that time. Numerous volumes deal with the World's Fair.

La Guardia's fervent campaign for preparedness as director of civil defense was vividly reported in the press and La Guardia biographies. His relationship with Roosevelt and attempts to obtain a commission as brigadier general in the army were related in the New York City and Washington, D.C., press and many articles in local and national magazines, as were his activities with UNRRA and his break with President Truman on postwar recovery projects and foreign policy.

The *Normandie* fire was a major news story. The definitive book *Normadie*, by Harvey Ardman, added importantly to my understanding of the disaster.

Photographs in this book are from New York City Municipal Archives and the author's collection, including pictures of the *Normandie* afire and capsized.

While it would be clever to conclude this book on Fiorello H. La Guardia by claiming that the writing required patience and fortitude, in fact it was too much fun to be called work.

Selected Bibliography

It is usually a mistake for a prominent man to write his own biography.

—Robert Moses in his tribute to La Guardia, 1957

Adler, Polly. *A House Is Not a Home.* New York: Rinehart, 1950.

Allen, Frederick Lewis. *Since Yesterday: The 1930s in America, September 3, 1929–September 3, 1939.* New York: Harper & Brothers, 1939.

Ardman, Harvey. *Normandie: Her Life and Times.* New York: Franklin Watts, 1985.

Capeci, Dominc J. Jr. *The Harlem Riot of 1943.* Philadelphia: Temple University Press, 1977.

Caro, Robert. *The Power Broker: Robert Moses and the Fall of New York.* New York: Alfred A. Knopf, 1974.

Cuneo, Ernest. *Life with Fiorello.* New York: Macmillan, 1955.

Curran, Henry. *Pillar to Post.* New York: Scribner's, 1941.

Dewey, Thomas E. *Twenty against the Underworld.* Garden City, N.Y.: Doubleday, 1974.

Ellis, Edward Robb. *Epic of New York City.* New York: Coward-McCann, 1966.

Federal Writers' Project. *The WPA Guide to New York City.* Washington, D.C.: Works Projects Administration, 1939.

Fischler, Stan. *Uptown Downtown: A Trip through Time of New York's Subways.* New York: Hawthorn, 1976.

Footner, Hulbert. *New York: City of Cities.* Philadelphia: J. B. Lippincott, 1937.

Fowler, Gene. *Beau James: Life and Times of Jimmy Walker.* New York: Viking, 1949.

———. *The Great Mouthpiece: A Life Story of William J. Fallon.* New York: Blue Ribbon Books, 1931.

Franklin, Jay. *La Guardia.* New York: Modern Age Books, 1937.

Garrett, Charles. *The La Guardia Years: Machine and Reform Politics in New York City.* New Brunswick, N.J.: Rutgers University Press, 1961.

Gluck, Gemma [La Guardia]. *My Story.* New York: David McKay, 1961.

Hecksher, August III, with Phyllis Robinson. *When La Guardia Was Mayor: New York's Legendary Years.* New York: W. W. Norton, 1978.

Hughes, Rupert. *The Story of Thomas E. Dewey: Attorney for the People.* New York: Grosset & Dunlap, 1944.

Kessner, Thomas. *Fiorello La Guardia and the Making of Modern New York.* New York: McGraw-Hill, 1989.

La Guardia, Fiorello H. *The Making of an Insurgent: An Autobiography.* Philadelphia: J. P. Lippincott, 1948.

Limpus, Lowell M. *Honest Cop: The Dramatic Life Story of Lewis J. Valentine.* New York: E. P. Dutton, 1939.

———— and Burr Leyson. *This Man La Guardia.* New York: E. P. Dutton, 1938.

Mann, Arthur. *La Guardia Comes to Power: 1933.* Philadelphia: J. P. Lippincott, 1965.

————. *La Guardia: A Fighter against His Times, 1882–1933.* Philadelphia: J. B. Lippincott, 1959.

Manners, William. *Patience and Fortitude: Fiorello La Guardia.* New York: Harcourt Brace Jovanovich, 1976.

Martin, George. *Madam Secretary, Frances Perkins.* Boston: Houghton Mifflin, 1976.

Miller, Nathan. *F.D.R.: An Intimate History.* Garden City, N.Y.: Doubleday, 1983.

Mitgang, Herbert. *The Man Who Rode the Tiger: The Life of Judge Samuel Seabury and the Story of the Greatest Investigation of City Corruption in This Century.* New York: W. W. Norton, 1963.

Morris, Newbold, and Dana Lee Thomas. *Let the Chips Fall.* New York: Appleton-Century-Crofts, 1955.

Moses, Robert. *La Guardia: A Salute and Memoir.* New York: Simon & Schuster, 1957.

Northrup, William B., and John B. Northrup. *The Insolence of Office: The Story of the Seabury Investigations.* New York: G. P. Putnam's Sons, 1932.

Page, Thomas Nelson. *Italy and the World War.* New York: Charles Scribner's Sons, 1920.

Rodman, Bella. *Fiorello La Guardia.* New York: Hill & Wang, 1962.

Spalding, Albert. *Rise to Follow.* New York: Holt, 1943.

Tugwell, Rexford G. *The Art of Politics.* Garden City, N.Y.: Doubleday, 1958.

Turkus, Burton B, and Sid Feder. *Murder, Inc.: The Story of "the Syndicate."* New York: Farrar, Straus, & Young, 1951.

Valentine, Lewis J. *Night Stick.* New York: Dial, 1947.

Walsh, George. *Gentleman Jimmy Walker: Mayor of the Jazz Age.* New York: Praeger, 1974.

Zinn, Howard. *La Guardia in Congress.* Ithaca, N.Y.: Cornell University Press, 1959.

Index